Culture in Translation

The anthropological legacy of R. H. Mathews

Culture in Translation

The anthropological legacy of R. H. Mathews

Edited by Martin Thomas

Translations from the French by Mathilde de Hauteclocque
and from the German by Christine Winter

ANU
THE AUSTRALIAN NATIONAL UNIVERSITY

E PRESS

ANU

E PRESS

Published by ANU E Press and Aboriginal History Incorporated
Aboriginal History Monograph 15

National Library of Australia
Cataloguing-in-Publication entry

Mathews, R. H. (Robert Hamilton), 1841-1918.
Culture in translation : the anthropological legacy of R. H. Mathews.

Bibliography.
ISBN 9781921313240 (pbk.)
ISBN 9781921313257 (online)

1. Mathews, R. H. (Robert Hamilton), 1841-1918. 2.
Aboriginal Australians - Social life and customs. 3.
Aboriginal Australians - Languages. 4. Ethnology -
Australia. I. Thomas, Martin Edward. II. Title. (Series :
Aboriginal history monograph ; no.15).

305.800994

Contacting Aboriginal History
All correspondence should be addressed to Aboriginal History,
Box 2837 GPO Canberra, 2601, Australia.
Sales and orders for journals and monographs, and journal subscriptions:
T Boekel, email: sales@aboriginalhistory.org, tel or fax: +61 2 6230 7054
www.aboriginalhistory.org

ANU E Press
All correspondence should be addressed to:
ANU E Press, The Australian National University, Canberra ACT 0200, Australia
Email: anuepress@anu.edu.au, http://epress.anu.edu.au

Aboriginal History Inc. is a part of the Australian Centre for Indigenous History, Research School
of Social Sciences, The Australian National University and gratefully acknowledges the support of
the History Program, RSSS and the National Centre for Indigenous Studies, The Australian National
University.

Cover design by ANU E Press

WARNING: Readers are notified that this publication may contain names or images of deceased
persons.

Contents

Part 4: Language

Part 5: Ceremony

Part 6: Correspondence

RHM Bibliography

Acknowledgements

The work for this book commenced during an Australian Postdoctoral Fellowship at the University of Technology, Sydney, funded by the Australian Research Council (ARC). It continued when I was granted a Sesqui Postdoctoral Fellowship at the University of Sydney. I thank both universities and the ARC for their generous support of the project. In 2002 I was supported by the National Library of Australia (NLA) in Canberra, home of the R. H. Mathews Papers, which granted me an honorary Harold White Fellowship in 2002. I acknowledge the collective support of the NLA staff and offer particular thanks to Margy Burn, Sylvia Carr, Mary Gosling, Graeme Powell and Susan O'Neill. Many of the graphics reproduced in the book come courtesy of the NLA.

From the outset, Aboriginal History Inc. showed tremendous enthusiasm for the project. I thank all members of the editorial board and offer special thanks to Peter Read and Ingereth Macfarlane for keeping it moving, to Luise Hercus and Harold Koch for their attention to linguistic detail, and to Isabel McBryde who gave so generously in a multitude of ways. Isabel's entry on Mathews in the *Australian Dictionary of Biography* was a starting point for me, as it has been for so many others. Her constant affirmation of Mathews' importance was one of the factors that kept me going.

The book could not have happened without the support at home of Naomi Parry and our son Aaron. I thank you both. Friends and colleagues helped in a multitude of ways. Special thanks to Val Attenbrow, Badger Bates, Richard Barwick, Tamsin Donaldson, David Kaus, Ian Keen, Anna Kenny, John Mulvaney, Brad Steadman and John Strehlow. I owe a unique debt to the descendants of R. H. Mathews—to Susan Upton, her husband Ron, and to Jane Mathews. Their support and friendship have been some of the many privileges of carrying out this work.

Among other institutions, I thank Llyfrgell Genedlaethol Cymru, Aberystwyth (the National Library of Wales), for allowing me to reproduce letters from R. H. Mathews to E. S. Hartland. The Strehlow Research Centre, Alice Springs allowed publication of the letters from Moritz von Leonhardi. For access to manuscript resources, thanks to the Australian Institute of Aboriginal and Torres Strait Islander Studies, Canberra; the American Philosophical Society, Philadelphia; the Mitchell Library, Sydney; the National Anthropological Archives of the Smithsonian Institution, Washington; the Pitt Rivers Museum, Oxford; the Royal Anthropological Society, London; the Royal Society of New South Wales, Sydney; and the State Library of Victoria, Melbourne.

My greatest debt is to Mathilde de Hauteclocque and Christine Winter for their wonderful translations, and for making the hard work enjoyable. Our efforts have been enhanced by the keen eye of Kitty Eggerking who was up and running as soon as she arrived as an editor for Aboriginal History. I am grateful for the attentiveness, good humour and professionalism with which she steered the book through the production process. Thanks also to the team at ANU E Press.

Finally, I acknowledge the 'founders of the feast', though they are not here to share it. Still, it is only appropriate to recognise the energy and enterprise of R. H. Mathews and the many Aboriginal people with whom he worked. I hope that this volume is an apposite tribute to their collaboration.

M. T.

Preface

Almost 90 years on from his death, this is the first book-length collection of the writings of Robert Hamilton Mathews. It has been a long wait for the Australian-born surveyor who began his career as an anthropologist at the age of 52 with the 1893 publication of a brief paper on New South Wales rock art.[1] Apart from a few short booklets, Mathews' book of 1905, *Ethnological Notes on the Aboriginal Tribes of New South Wales and Victoria*, was his only work of anthropology to be published as a freestanding volume.[2] A reprint of a long article published the previous year,[3] it was a modest tome in that age of doorstopper monographs—'little more than a pamphlet' according to Mathews' friend, the British folklorist E. S. Hartland.[4] There was certainly an expectation that a writer so prolific as Mathews would disseminate his work in a substantial book. As Arnold van Gennep, the Parisian anthropologist, pointed out to him, 'your publications are for the most part overlooked ... because they are scattered amongst a mass of periodicals and it is a very difficult matter to have them all at one time in hand'. Van Gennep recommended that Mathews immediately arrange for their 'publication in 2 or 3 volumes'[5]—advice endorsed by Hartland who was enlisted to work with Mathews' ornithologist son Gregory, then living in England, to place a manuscript with a London publisher (see 'Correspondence', this volume). But these efforts were unsuccessful and R. H. Mathews died in 1918 without ever publishing his magnum opus.

His formidable success as an author of journal articles, and his failure as an author of books, is one of the many paradoxes surrounding this quixotic and extremely private man. The publications reproduced in this volume are evidence that he enjoyed quite a measure of international success. In total, his 171 works of anthropology run to more than 2,200 published pages. Even this output, substantial as it is, does not convey the full scale of Mathews' ethnographic labour. As scholars of his work have come to realise, further invaluable material survives in the collection of R. H. Mathews Papers, held by the National Library of Australia.

This book was unwittingly conceived in 2002 when I was studying the Mathews Papers during a Harold White Fellowship at the National Library in Canberra. That Mathews published in French and German, as well as English, was fairly well known. But the extent of his linguistic ability remained unclear. I began to investigate, and quickly established that translators played a role in preparing for publication *all* of Mathews' foreign-language articles. From that point, other questions emerged. Were they original writings or did they replicate material published elsewhere in English? Initially, I suspected the latter, partly because I knew that in the early days of his anthropological research, Mathews was criticised for duplicating his findings in different journals.[6] The texts reveal, however, that Mathews had learnt his lesson from the duplication controversy. The majority of his 18 works in French and German are unique. As such, they have been largely inaccessible to the Anglophone world, especially to the Aboriginal communities whose culture and heritage they discuss.

A desire to make the foreign language material readily available was the initial motivation for this book. In so doing, it gives, for the first time in a single volume, a survey of Mathews' ethnographic publications. Not accidentally, he ensured that his readers in continental Europe were exposed to almost the full range of his inquiries. There are works of linguistic documentation; descriptions of art and material culture; studies of kinship and marriage rules; and more general discussion of his theories about the Aboriginal settlement of Australia. The longest paper and the first in this volume, 'Contributions to the Ethnography of the Australians' (1907), contains detailed description of leisure activities, cookery, tool-making, body ornamentation and many other aspects of daily life. To ensure that all Mathews' major interests are represented in this book, I have also included examples of how he documented Aboriginal myth. My introductory essay provides the context for Mathews' bitter relations with his contemporaries in Australia. It also gives biographical background to his anthropological practice, and makes some suggestions about how his cross-cultural project informs the history of colonisation and modernity.

I have long believed that the sum of Mathews' anthropological inquiry is greater than its individual parts. His network of international associates (formed through correspondence rather than personal association) saw him published in both specialist anthropological journals and more general scientific periodicals. This strategy evolved because Mathews, who in his most prolific period pumped out more than a dozen articles a year, wrote more than he could ever hope to place in the handful of Australian learned journals. Soon he was savouring the prestige of overseas recognition. Perennially on the hunt for new venues, he developed an internationally dispersed mode of publishing that gained him exposure, but which had the unfortunate effect of diluting his impact since it created for the reader the very problem identified by van Gennep. As the latter realised, the meaning of a short article on kinship or a description of a particular ceremony is transformed by the knowledge that each is just a fragment of a broad inquiry that spans hundreds of pages. The large number of often short papers tends to exaggerate the antiquarian quality of Mathews' reportage. Writing under headings such as 'folklore', 'ceremony' or 'rock art', he appears to compartmentalise aspects of culture that are necessarily connected. These limitations are partially circumvented when Mathews' reports are read in the context of each other. The impact is cumulative and the work acquires a critical mass.

Inevitably, my editorial bias has shaped this collection. On one hand, I hope that a selection of his writings will allow Mathews to be better understood as a writer and researcher; on the other, I have tried to explain why a scholar so serious and prolific in the documentation of Aboriginal culture is not better known. As I argue in the introduction, Mathews' reputation was severely diminished by the campaign of his Melbourne-based adversary W. Baldwin Spencer, aided and abetted by Spencer's close friend, A. W. Howitt. Spencer's opinion of Mathews was, by his own admission, 'too libellous' to publish, but this did not prevent him from sharing it liberally in private communications, particularly with anthropologists in Britain. Howitt chose to ignore Mathews, despite the fact that he was amassing a substantial portfolio of work on southeast Australia—his own area of specialisation. Howitt went for a decade without ever quoting Mathews or otherwise acknowledging his existence. Only in 1907, when Mathews accused Howitt of both plagiarising and ignoring him in the letters pages of *Nature*, did the two rivals debate each other. Further insights into these murky interpersonal politics, and their personal effect upon Mathews, can be derived from his correspondence with E. S. Hartland and Moritz von Leonhardi's letters to him, reproduced in the final section of the book. In this way I have tried to represent various faces of Mathews. We meet him as an ethnological reporter and a correspondent.

Many collections could be made from so prolific a scholar. While I hope that more will follow, I suspect that none could claim to be truly representative. His opus is simply too vast. As the title suggests, *translation* emerged as the overarching theme of this book. It developed during dialogue with Mathilde de Hauteclocque and Christine Winter, who displayed such generosity and humour as they re-translated Mathews from the French and German. Presented with the reality that a retranslation could never entirely restore the 'original' text, we began to think about the degree to which *all* anthropological labour involves translation. The message is both cautionary and illuminating. Mathews is now read for his localised accounts of Aboriginal knowledge. Yet his arrangement and interpretation of that knowledge—and even the fact that he recorded it at all—was contingent on him having an international audience, most of whom had little sense of the people with whom he worked.

Finally, an explanation of the terminology I use for non-Aboriginal people in my introductory text. When referring to 'white people' and 'whitefellows' I am not suggesting that the non-Indigenous population of Australia is, or ever has been, racially homogenous. Rather, I take guidance from the contemporary anthropologist Ghassan Hage who argues that deliberate and critical use of the term 'white' is a way of acknowledging that people who are part of this large, powerful and diverse social group have their own collective values and mores; their own language and forms of kinship. That is to say, *they are an ethnic group*.[7] In R. H. Mathews' period, settler-society saw itself as predominantly white and made considerable efforts to maintain the racial uniformity of its members. Inevitably, Mathews' ethnographic inquiries were informed by this social and political situation. When I use the descriptor 'white', I acknowledge this history without wishing to endorse it.

M. T.

ENDNOTES

[1] R. H. Mathews (henceforth RHM) 1893, 'Rock Paintings by the Aborigines in Caves on Bulgar Creek, near Singleton', *Journal and Proceedings of the Royal Society of New South Wales*, vol. 27.

[2] RHM 1905, *Ethnological Notes on the Aboriginal Tribes of New South Wales and Victoria*, F. W. White General Printer, Sydney.

[3] RHM 1904, 'Ethnological Notes on the Aboriginal Tribes of New South Wales and Victoria', *Journal and Proceedings of the Royal Society of New South Wales*, vol. 38.

[4] Hartland, E. Sidney 1906, 'Review of *Ethnological Notes on the Aboriginal Tribes of New South Wales and Victoria*', *MAN*, vol. 9, no. 99, p. 153.

[5] Van Gennep to Mathews, 1 July 1907, R. H. Mathews Papers, National Library of Australia (henceforth NLA) MS 8006/2/13.

[6] Thomas, Martin 2004, 'R. H. Mathews and anthropological warfare: On writing the biography of a "self-contained man"', *Aboriginal History*, vol. 28.

[7] Hage, Ghassan 1998, *White Nation: Fantasies of white supremacy in a multicultural society*, Pluto Press and Comerford & Miller, Annandale, NSW. A fuller response to Hage is contained in Thomas, Martin 2001, *A Multicultural Landscape: National Parks and the Macedonian Experience*, NSW National Parks & Wildlife Service and Pluto Press, Annandale, NSW.

Note on Text

Most of the writings in this book were first published in French or German. The task of translating them back into their original language posed several problems. Were we trying to give a warts-and-all impression of how Mathews was read by his European audience or were we endeavouring to restore the 'original' Mathews as he is known through his English publications? Generally, the approach taken is biased towards the latter. Stylistically, we have tried to be faithful to Mathews' diction, and where his translators obviously blundered, we have weeded out the errors. Where the meaning or intention seems uncertain, this is indicated in a footnote.

Another factor influencing the translating process was the fact that drafts of some German articles were found in the R. H. Mathews Papers, National Library of Australia. One of these, the manuscript of 'Bemerkungen über die Eingebornen Australiens' (1906) (published as 'Remarks on the Natives of Australia'), is particularly revealing. It bears annotations that seem to have been made by the translator (see NLA MS 8006/5/8). This suggests that *Mitteilungen der Anthropologischen Gesellschaft*, Mathews' Viennese publisher, returned the manuscripts at the end, or perhaps during, the translation process. These manuscripts were consulted by Christine Winter while translating the German. Unfortunately for Mathilde de Hauteclocque, our French translator, the Parisian journals did not return authors' manuscripts.

Mathews' original footnotes have been translated, but where possible the full reference is given in lieu of his own abbreviated and often cryptic notation. In some of the German publications, explanatory footnotes were added by the original translator. These have been retained and are indicated by the words 'Note—German translator'. The original footnotes are designated by Arabic numerals, and appear as endnotes in this volume. Explanatory notes inserted by us are also denoted by numerals and are distinguished from the original notes by [Editor's note]. The exception to this way of organising the explanatory notes is Part 6, Correspondence: all the notes here are mine and they are denoted by Arabic numerals and appear as endnotes. A full bibliography of Mathews' anthropological publications appears at the end of the book. The introductory texts contain frequent references to the R. H. Mathews Papers in the National Library of Australia (NLA MS 8006). These citations contain page numbers in those cases where notebooks are paginated. However, much of the manuscript material is loose and unpaginated.

Mathews was often inconsistent in his spelling of Aboriginal words, including names of language groups and communities. Even today, there is little unanimity about the spelling of these terms. This explains the inconsistency within Mathews' body of work and the variant spellings used by other authors cited in the book. In the translations and in all quotations, the spellings as originally published have been retained. Since many are antiquated, and thus unlikely to be recognised by contemporary readers, standard contemporary spellings, recommended by the Australian Institute of Aboriginal and Torres Strait Islander Studies (AIATSIS) through its AUSTLANG database, are used in the introductory text.[1] To reconcile the various spellings, see the following Table of Aboriginal Groups and Languages. It gives the contemporary names recommended by AIATSIS, followed by the variant spellings that appear in the book and a rough guide to locality.

On occasions Mathews made use of diacritics to convey the phonetic values of Aboriginal languages. Sometimes *n* was marked with a tilde to make *ñ*. This denotes the *ny* sound, common as a word-ending in Australian languages. The placement of a macron above a vowel denotes a 'long' sound, so that *ū* is pronounced as in 'b*oo*t'. A breve above the vowel, normally a *ŭ*, indicates a 'short' sound, as in 'p*u*t'. The use of diacritics varies considerably from publication to publication. These variations have been preserved in the translations, except where Mathews refers to his own articles. In such cases the spelling (including diacritics) as it appeared on the title page of the original publication has been used.

M. T.
M. de H.
C. W.

ENDNOTES

[1] AUSTLANG was still under development at the time of publication. It will become available in late 2007 or early 2008: http://austlang.aiatsis.gov.au. The South Australian Museum provides a valuable on-line tool for locating Aboriginal communities and reconciling antiquated spellings, based on the work of N. B. Tindale. http://www.samuseum.sa.gov.au/orig/tindale/HDMS/tindaletribes/a.htm

Names of Aboriginal Groups and Languages

AIATSIS Spelling(s)*	Spelling(s) used by Mathews and others in the text	General Location†
Arrernte / Aranda	Arranda / Arran'da / Arrente	Central Australia, Northern Territory
Bidawal	Birdhawal	Eastern Victoria
Bigumbil	Pikumbil	Weir and Moonie rivers, southern Queensland
Binbinga	Binbingha	McArthur and Glyde rivers, Northern Territory
Bundjalung	Bunjellung	North Coast of New South Wales
Buyibara	Kaiabara	Southern Queensland
Darkinung	Darkiñung / Darkinyung	Ranges north of Sydney, New South Wales
Dharawal	Thurrawal	Botany Bay and South Coast of New South Wales
Dhurga	Thoorga	New South Wales South Coast
Diyari	Dieri	Cooper Creek and adjacent areas in the Northern Territory
Djadjala	Tyatyalla	Lakes Werringen and Albacutya, Victoria
Djirringany	Jirringañ	Southern New South Wales
Dulua / Duluwa	Dippil	Southern Queensland
Dyadyawurung	Tyeddyuwurru	Lodden, Avoca, Wimmera and Richardson rivers in Victoria
Gubbi Gubbi	Gubbi Gubbi	Southern Queensland
Gumbaynggir	Kumbainggeri	Ranges and coast of northern New South Wales
Gundungurra	Gundungurra	Blue Mountains and Southern Highlands, New South Wales
Indjilandji	Inchalanchu	Barkly Tablelands and adjacent areas, in Northern Territory and western Queensland

Jingulu	Chingalee	Newcastle Waters, Ashburton Range and adjacent areas, Northern Territory
Kamilaroi	Kamilaroi	Northern parts of central New South Wales
Kurnai	Kurnai	Eastern Victoria
Kurnu	Kurnu / Kurnū / Kūrnū / Gunu	Darling River, western New South Wales
Luritja	Loritja	Central Australia, Northern Territory
Marawara	Maraura	Western New South Wales
Mayi-Yapi	Miappe	Cloncurry River and adjacent areas, Queensland
Milpulo	Mailpurlgu	Far west of New South Wales
Muruwari	Murawarri	Culgoa River, northwest New South Wales and southern Queensland
Nawalgu	Ngunnhalgu	Darling River, western New South Wales
Ngemba / Ngiyampaa	Ngeumba / Ngiyampaa	Northwest New South Wales
Nggerigudi	Ngerikudi	Batavia River, North Queensland
Ngunawal	Ngunnawal	Highlands west of Shoalhaven River in New South Wales and Australian Capital Territory
None	Gamete	Batavia River, North Queensland
Paakantyi	Barkunjee / Bāgandji / Bagandji	Darling River, western New South Wales
Tainikuit	Tanegute	Batavia River, North Queensland
Tjungundji	Chūnkūnji	Batavia River, North Queensland
Wailwan	Wailwan	Western New South Wales
Wambaya	Wombaia / Wombya	Barkly Tablelands and adjacent areas, Northern Territory
Wangaaybuwan	Wongaibon	Western New South Wales

Wiradjuri	Wirraidyuri / Wirradyuri / Wirradthuri	Central and southern New South Wales
Yangman	Yungmunni	Northern Territory between Roper and Victoria river systems
Yawarawarka	Yowerawarrika	Cooper Creek, Northern Territory
Yugambal	Yukimbil	Glen Innes and Tenterfield areas, New South Wales
Yuwaalaraay	Yualeai	Northwest New South Wales

* Spellings used on AUSTLANG Database — http://austlang.aiatsis.gov.au
† Locations given as a general indication only. They are not intended to express the specific geographic boundaries of groups or languages.

Darwin
Northern Australia
Western Australia
South Australia
Queensland
New South Wales
Victoria
Tasmania
Cape York
Alice Springs
Hermannsberg
Broome
Roebuck Bay
Beagle Bay
Carnarvon
Geraldton
Perth
Port Lincoln
Adelaide
Kingston
Mt Gambier
Melbourne
Canberra
Sydney
Newcastle
Brisbane
Cairns
Townsville
Rockhampton
Gladstone
Port Curtis
Maryborough
Gympie
Goondiwindi
Mungindi
Hobart
Bass Strait
Torowie
Cooper Creek
Murray R
Lachlan R
Darling R
Barwon R
Culgoa R
Finke R
Alberga R
Roper R
Daly
Victoria R
Fitzroy R
Drysdale R
Kimberley Ranges
De Grey R
Fortescue R
Ashburton R
Murchison R
Mapoon
Jardine R
Mitchell R
Gilbert R
Norman R
Flinders R
Georgina R
Diamantina R
Thomson R
Barcoo R
Belyando R
Dawson R
Burnett R
Albert R
Fraser Id
Warrego R
Halifax Bay
0 500 1000 1500 Kilometres
© 2007 Richard Barwick

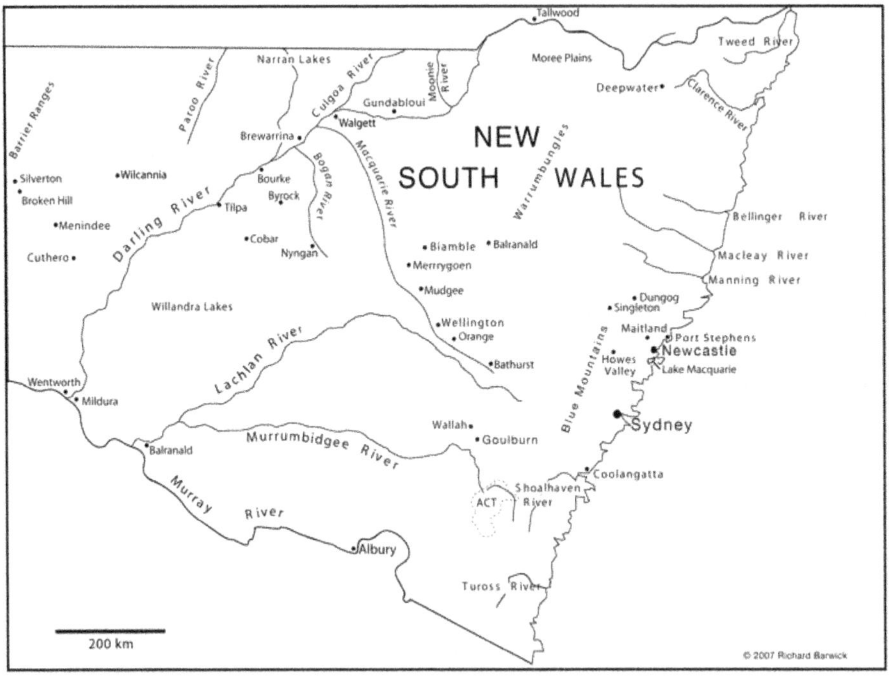
NEW SOUTH WALES
Tallwood
Tweed River
Moree Plains
Deepwater
Clarence River
Narran Lakes
Culgoa River
Moonie River
Gundabloui
Walgett
Brewarrina
Paroo River
Barrier Ranges
Silverton
Broken Hill
Wilcannia
Bourke
Byrock
Bogan River
Macquarie River
Warrumbungles
Tilpa
Darling River
Menindee
Cuthero
Cobar
Nyngan
Biamble
Balranald
Merrygoen
Mudgee
Bellinger River
Macleay River
Manning River
Dungog
Singleton
Maitland
Port Stephens
Newcastle
Howes Valley
Lake Macquarie
Blue Mountains
Willandra Lakes
Wellington
Orange
Bathurst
Lachlan River
Wentworth
Mildura
Wallah
Goulburn
Sydney
Murrumbidgee River
Balranald
Coolangatta
Shoalhaven River
ACT
Murray River
Albury
Tuross River
200 km
© 2007 Richard Barwick

Mildura

NEW SOUTH WALES

Swan Hill

Murray River

Albury
Wodonga
Mitta Mitta River
Wangaratta

Lake Hindmarsh

VICTORIA

Wimmera River

Bendigo

Goulburn River

Ovens River

Stawell

Pyalong

Yarra Valley

Mount Ararat

Gippsland

Maroona

Ballarat

Yarra River

Port
Philip

Melbourne

Tower Hill

Geelong

BASS STRAIT

200 km

© 2007 Richard Barwick

Cox's River

Hawkesbury
River

Bobbin Head

Katoomba Creek

Cowan
Creek

Parramata

Turramurra

Port Jackson

Jenolan Caves

Narellan

Sydney

Picton

La Perouse
Botany Bay

Port Hackiing

Lake Burragorang

Wombeyan Caves

Guineacor
River

Taralga

Berrima

Wollondilly River

Wincaribee River

50 km

© 2007 Richard Barwick

Abbreviations

AIATSIS – Australian Institute of Aboriginal and Torres Strait Islander Studies, Canberra

ML – Mitchell Library, State Library of New South Wales, Sydney

NLA – National Library of Australia, Canberra

PRM – Pitt Rivers Museum, Oxford

RHM – R. H. Mathews

SLV – State Library of Victoria, Melbourne

USyd Archives – University of Sydney Archives, Sydney

SRC – Strehlow Research Centre, Alice Springs

Mr. R. H. MATHEWS, L.S., Assoc. Anthrop. Soc., Paris, Parramatta.

R. H. Mathews had himself photographed in this throne-like chair for a portrait published in his booklet *Some Peculiar Burial Customs of the Australian Aborigines* (1909). By permission of the National Library of Australia.

Introducing R. H. Mathews

'Birrarak is the name given to me by the natives'

Ethnological Notes on R. H. Mathews

Martin Thomas

In 1872, while surveying at Narran Lakes in New South Wales, R. H. Mathews wrote a letter to Mary Bartlett, who would soon become his wife. 'I was talking to a blackfellow,' he wrote, 'who can speak English, and he told me a lot of their words and expressions which I made a note of in my book'.[1] He then complained: 'I can't find letters in our language to express the proper sounds.' From the outset, Mathews was involved in a labour of translation.

While evident in all his writings, the limits of translatability are most conspicuous in his descriptions of Aboriginal language where, beneath the subheading 'Orthography', you always find a stream of directives on how to sound the words transcribed.

> *G* is always hard. *R* has a rough trilled sound, as in the English word *hurrah! W* always commences a word or syllable. *Y* at the beginning of a word or syllable has its ordinary consonant value. The sound of the Spanish *ñ* often occurs.[2]

When Mathews tried to re-create the Aboriginal words, his English notation showed signs of stress. Diacritic symbols caution us against habitual pronunciation; analogies are drawn from other European languages, perhaps recalling the eight months of his life spent outside Australia. It was unusual then (as now) for someone of British background to be interested in the non-English aspect of Australia's linguistic heritage. Whether he attained fluency in an Aboriginal tongue is doubtful, but even the smattering of words and phrases that he documented, and must at times have used, would have won him favour in the communities where he worked.

Always secretive, Mathews recorded little about these interactions with his Aboriginal teachers. But a few memories became part of the family lore. William Mathews, second-youngest son of R. H., recalled his father's sessions with Emma Timbery, a senior Dharawal woman of Botany Bay. Her name appears often in his notebooks, so presumably she was one of the people with whom Mathews discussed the three large rock engravings, described in his paper 'Rock Carvings and Paintings by the Australian Aborigines' (1898) (this volume). William and his father took the suburban tram to La Perouse. The boy played with the local children while his father worked. He remembered peering into Mrs Timbery's humpy where she and Mathews smoked pipes as they sat on boxes. Mathews with his small notebook and pencil was 'writing very hard' and young William was waved away.[3] We can think of them there, working within and across their respective languages, engaged in a process of translation that will never entirely stop so long as there are readers of Mathews' work.

He studied with people such as Mrs Timbery and returned to his home in the western suburbs of Sydney. He wrote up articles which he posted to journals. Months or even years later when the journal article was published, he received a package of 25 or 50 offprints—the 'pamphlets' or 'separates' as he called them. They were the only payment he received for his labour, and he liked them to circulate. He posted them to colleagues and to settlers out bush in the often forlorn hope that they might gather information from the Aboriginal people they knew, following his example. The process was circulatory and hopefully generative. Sometimes, as happened with much of the work in this collection, the information gathered by Mathews was marked by a further transformation. Journals in France and Austria commissioned French and German translations from his English manuscripts. The haphazardness of this process was brought home to me, comically at times, when, in the preparation of this book, I regularly conferred with Mathilde de Hautecloque and Christine Winter who translated the French and German texts back into English. The curious process of *retranslation* rekindled some of the bewilderment that Mathews' European translators might have felt when they came across his references to stringybark and grey box trees, or tried to follow his detailed description of making a stone axe. Their errors are sometimes deliciously preposterous. For the French reader a human torso becomes a tree trunk (*tronc d'abour*) in a description of a ritual, and the sandstone of the Sydney basin is mysteriously metamorphosed from sandstone to limestone (*calcaire*). Needless to say, we eliminated these errors from the retranslations. But in their quirky way they were instructive. If such discrepancies are possible in the shuffle between European languages, how much more was lost or transformed when Mathews used the language of anthropology (still an inchoate discipline) to describe ceremony, art, kinship and other aspects of Aboriginal life? Here we are reminded of both the necessity and the impossibility of translation. When putting a concept into another language we inevitably transform it. That is a danger. But if we refuse to take this risk, we pursue the even more dangerous course of barricading our world against outside influence. In so doing we refuse the possibility of hearing ourselves through the ears of an other.

In excavating and interpreting Mathews' legacy, I frequently wonder whether I am narrating or translating. Perhaps it is a combination of the two. Working from fragments of evidence (and Mathews left little more concerning his own life story), I will try to chart the context for his remarkable and too often neglected work. There is an occupational tendency among historians to try to render the past as a seamless narrative. Yet to do so belies the randomness of working with evidence; the chaos of flashes and fragments that occurs daily. Take for example the experience of searching a microfilmed newspaper. Reports of the Great War, now in its final catastrophic year, are whizzing past—a typographic blur—as I look for, and eventually find, an obituary, telling how Mathews died aged 77 at his home in Sydney. The funeral occurred at the Presbyterian cemetery, Parramatta, and was reportedly well-attended. The newspaper noted that he had been engaged in 'many years of survey work in the northern and north-western districts of New South Wales'. He was survived by his wife, four sons and a daughter; his anthropological work gained him honours, including the Prix Godard from the Anthropological Society of Paris. 'His investigations,' we are told, 'were, with very few exceptions, carried out by personal interviews with the natives themselves, and he spared no labour to make his information absolutely reliable before embodying it in his writings.'[4]

*

Little more was said publicly about Mathews' legacy. None of the journals to which he contributed published an obituary or even a notice of his passing. Perhaps the oversight is understandable in a world ravaged by war. Or perhaps his international mode of publishing, which straddled both sides of the Rhine, smacked of the old order. Then, three years after his death, Mathews' old foe, W. Baldwin Spencer, made a brief and unfavourable mention of his work in an Australian journal.

Born in Manchester, Spencer arrived in Australia in 1887 to take up the first Chair of Biology at the University of Melbourne. He was 26 years old. Spencer's impact on his adopted city was profound. He made a major contribution to Australian zoology, collected the work of the Heidelberg school artists, served as museum and gallery director, and was for a time president of the Victorian Football League. He was also a magnificent photographer. As a student at Oxford he was introduced to anthropology by E. B. Tylor, a founding father of the discipline, whose lectures he attended. He satisfied both his photographic and ethnographic curiosity during a series of missions to Central Australia, beginning with the Horn Expedition in 1894. There he met the Alice Springs postmaster F. J. Gillen with whom he wrote *The Native Tribes of Central Australia* (1899) and other weighty tomes. From that date Spencer became internationally recognised as one the brightest stars in the anthropological firmament.

Anthropologists F. J. Gillen (front left) and W. Baldwin Spencer (front right) at Alice Springs, Northern Territory, in 1901. The men in the back row are (left to right) Erlikiliakira, Mounted Trooper Chance and Purula. Spencer's opinion of R. H. Mathews is expressed in his remark: "I only wish I dare say in print what years ago I said to him in private but it was just a bit too libellous." By permission of Museum Victoria.

When Spencer attacked the late R. H. Mathews in 1921, he expressed particular objection to study he had done with Ngemba people who resided near the Barwon River at Brewarrina in northwest New South Wales. Spencer never worked in this part of the country, nor even visited it so far as I am aware. Mathews had first seen the waters of the Barwon at the age of 19 while working for a drover. Then, after qualifying as a surveyor, he worked there on occasions in the 1870s. After he began to publish in anthropology in 1893, he went to Brewarrina for the express purpose of meeting with Ngemba people. He published articles about their burial customs[5] and the ancient maze of drystone walls, built into the bed of the Barwon—the fish traps of Brewarrina.[6] He spoke to them about material culture and trade, as seen in 'Contributions to the Ethnography of the Australians' (1907) (this volume). He also explored marriage and kinship rules, a subject that interested him greatly. As Mathews described

Ngemba kinship, the community was bilaterally divided into moieties (which he usually referred to by the Greek term *phratry*). Each moiety was itself divided into another two groups (which Mathew referred to as *sections*). In addition to the moieties and sections, the community was also grouped according to totem.

This in itself was not news to any student of Australian kinship. Comparable forms of social organisation had already been documented across much of the continent. Some communities had the two moieties only. Others divided each moiety into two or four groups. Designated groups (sections or sub-sections) of opposite moieties were expected to marry each other. (The principle of marrying outside one's classificatory group made it an *exogamous* system, a key term in the anthropological argot.) But according to Mathews—and it was this that Spencer found problematic—the kinship system of the Ngemba had further attributes.

> Beside the phratries, sections and totemic groups … the whole community is further divided into what may, for convenience of reference, be called 'castes'. These castes regulate the camping or resting places of the people under the shades of large trees in the vicinity of water or elsewhere. The shadow thrown by the butt and lower portion of a tree is called 'nhurrai'; that cast by the middle portion of the tree is 'wau-guē'; whilst the shade of the top of the tree, or outer margin of the shadow is 'winggu'.[7]

Mathews later reported the Kurnu people to the west, the Kamilaroi to the east and other neighbours of the Ngemba also had bloods and shades.[8]

Mathews claimed that these 'castes', like the moieties, sections and totems, were taken into consideration when marriages were being arranged. But that was not the extent of their influence. The very basics of social responsibility and interpersonal association were affected by the bloods and shades.

> Again, the men, women and children, whose prescribed sitting places are in the butt and the middle shades of the trees are called 'guai'mundhan', or sluggish blood, while those who sit in the top or outside shade are designated 'gai'gulir', or active blood. This further bisection of the community into Guaimundhu and Guaigulir, which may be referred to as 'blood' divisions, has happened so long ago that the natives have no explanation regarding it. The Guaingulir people—those who occupy the 'winggu' or outer margin of the shade—are supposed to keep a strict watch for any game which may appear in sight, the approach of friends or enemies, or anything which may require vigilance in a native camp.[9]

In describing these beliefs, Mathews was steering kinship study away from the laboured taxonomy of marriage rules which had preoccupied so many anthropologists of the Victorian era (including himself). He later declared that his approach would 'revolutionise all the old-school notions respecting the organisation of Australian tribes'—a view that proved overly optimistic.[10] Mathews' legacy was already fading by the time Spencer took the trouble to criticise his findings on the blood and shade 'castes', disparaging them as 'very vague, and somewhat difficult to understand'. He also argued that Mathews 'was dealing with very decadent tribes, who had, for nearly half a century, been in contact with white men, and whose numbers also were so depleted that, of necessity, old marriage customs had become profoundly modified, whilst more important still the beliefs of their forefathers were to them, for the most part, only a matter of past history in which they took practically no interest'.[11] In this way, Spencer stigmatised the long-settled communities of eastern Australia—the areas where Mathews worked in person—as anthropologically clapped out. In the years following Mathews' death, when anthropology became more professional and academic, this odour of redundancy began to hang not only around Mathews' informants, but around the anthropology of his generation. The First World War marked the terminus of so many things raised in the hothouse of the nineteenth century, including the ethos of 'enlightened amateurism' that had permitted Mathews, a country surveyor who never went to university, to make a voluminous contribution to the scientific culture.

To me there is nothing vague or confusing about Mathews' description of Ngemba kinship. And while Spencer's assertion that European occupation brought cultural transformation is necessarily correct, it by no means confirms his view that Mathews' Aboriginal informants were indifferent to their cultural heritage. If that is the case why, over a period of more than 20 years, did they take such trouble in explaining it to him? From a contemporary vantage point, Mathews' comments about spatial organisation in the Ngemba community are not so much strange as tantalising. If there is a problem with them it is that don't go far enough. Even in truncated form, however, these observations provide a welcome antidote to the preoccupation with marriage rules which is in part a polite way of talking about the regulation of sexual intercourse—an anthropological fixation that probably says as much about Victorian and Edwardian mores than it does about the people being studied. This was a time when Aboriginal kinship was typically presented as an almost endless series of tables, accompanied by algebraic formulations showing who can marry whom. It now seems terribly restricted. After decades of tuition from Aboriginal teachers, westerners have come to understand that the moiety, sectional and totemic groupings influence far more than one's choice of spouse. Mathews himself hinted at this. 'The human subject, animals, plants, inanimate objects, the elements, the heavenly bodies—everything on the earth or above it,' he wrote, belong to a moiety and a section.[12] This means that the affiliations and responsibilities of every person—to the land and to each other—are shaped by relations of kinship.

*

Although preoccupied with kinship, the anthropologists of Mathews' day were inexpert in displaying it amongst themselves. One gets the impression that Spencer might have intended his dismissal of Mathews' work on bloods and shades as a final nail in his coffin, for in making it he was breaking a 17-year silence during which time he had never acknowledged his rival's existence—in public at least.[13] The rift between them was no secret in Australia or even in Britain. Spencer dispatched numerous epistles damning Mathews; the latter sent pleas for recognition, often to the same people. We see this in a letter from the Scottish man of letters Andrew Lang to the English folklorist E. S. Hartland, the recipient of several letters from Mathews (reproduced in this volume). Lang wrote:

> If Mr Mathews has written to you in the same way he did to me, you will understand why I tried to prove to him that there was no conspiracy against him. His letters did not increase my opinion of his evidence, while Spencer's about *him*![14]

I have not been able to locate the correspondence mentioned between Lang and Spencer. But an impressive example of the latter's vitriol is revealed in a letter to his great friend A. W. Howitt, also an anthropologist from Victoria, and the other key participant in the feud with Mathews. Spencer wrote to him in 1907:

> As to that miscreant Mathew [sic] … I don't know whether to admire most his impudence his boldness or his mendacity—they are all of a very high order and seldom combined to so high a degree in one mortal man.[15]

As the Lang letter indicates, Mathews was well aware that Spencer was working against him. This was in contrast to the early days of their acquaintance when the relationship was at least civil.[16] In 1896 Spencer had viewed Mathews with sufficient favour to present two of his papers at meetings of the Royal Society of Victoria.[17] This was also a time when Mathews could describe Howitt as a 'friend and co-worker'.[18] For reasons that were never fully articulated by any party, the relationship between Mathews and the Victorians had completely fallen apart two years later. A letter to Hartland conveys Mathews' perspective. 'Ever since 1898 the fact has been thrust upon me that Spencer and Howitt looked upon me as "the opposition candidate" and never lost a chance of doing me an injury.'[19] The problem, Mathews said, was his research on the Northern Territory (carried out not from personal interview, but with the assistance of outback correspondents). This part of Australia, Mathews believed, had been singled out by Spencer for Gillen and himself.[20] In addition to Spencer's territorialism towards the Territory, which also put Carl Strehlow and others on the outer, kinship study played a part in aggravating the differences between Mathews and the Victorians. Both evolutionists, Spencer and particularly Howitt were influenced by the American scholar Lewis Henry Morgan who believed that power and property in the most primitive societies were vested with women. The transition to patriarchal power marked a 'higher' level of development.[21] This theoretical model influenced the questions that were asked of a moiety-based social system (the likes of which existed in Australia and elsewhere). Since a spouse must come from the opposite moiety, does a child belong to the moiety of the maternal or the paternal line? Exhibiting an understanding of gender that was itself fairly primitive, the evolutionists regarded the answer to this question as a key indicator of whether a society was patriarchal or matriarchal.

Being more an on-the-ground reporter than a theorist, Mathews did not subscribe to evolutionism or any other 'ism'. So possibly he did not realise the theoretical import of his intervention when, in 1898, he politely argued against Howitt's report that the kinship system of the people living around Maryborough in Queensland descended through the father.

> There is, however, no question that he is in error … and has evidently been misinformed. I have drawn attention to the matter now, because on a former occasion I was misled by Mr. Howitt's conclusions respecting the line of descent of the Kaiabara tribe. I have since, however, from personal inquiry, reported that descent is through the mother.[22]

One might have thought that such dialogue would be permissible—even desirable—in a community of scholars. But these findings were highly inconvenient to Howitt, who was developing the theory, fully elaborated in his major book of 1904, that various phases of social evolution were represented in Australia. Unlike Mathews, Howitt categorised the marriage rules of different tribes as a hierarchical order, with the most 'primitive' inhabiting the centre of the continent.

> I shall give instances, commencing with the Dieri, which is one of the socially backward standing tribes; going through the tribes in a socially progressive series, until the end is reached, with tribes of which the Kurnai are an example. In this way I hope to be able to show the actual advances made in the local and social organisations, but also the character of these important changes.[23]

Since Mathews' claims about the Kaiabara challenged this lofty (if specious) paradigm, Howitt pretended they had never been made. (Interestingly, on the point in question, Mathews was almost certainly correct. His view was endorsed by John Mathew, the Melbourne clergyman and anthropologist, who had lived in that part of Queensland for five years, during which time he had constant dealings with Aboriginal people and learnt Kabi Kabi, the local language.[24] Mathew shared Mathews' view that Howitt was 'altogether wrong' in discerning patrilineal descent.)[25]

It is also likely that Howitt was annoyed or embarrassed that Mathews had directly approached Harry Aldridge who was the source of his information. Aldridge, who came from a family of Queensland pioneers, had married into the Aboriginal community where he is still fondly remembered.[26] This won him a certain notoriety, and he was approached by a number of researchers. He admitted in a letter to Mathews that to some of these investigators he had told 'tall tales' on occasions.[27] Such were the hazards of working with correspondents, but all the anthropologists of the period relied on them to varying degrees.[28] Settlers prepared to forgo what leisure time they had to do unpaid research for anthropologists were always in short supply. Mathews' correspondence files contain many letters expressing incredulity at his pleas for assistance. As a consequence, the anthropologists were possessive towards their correspondents, and often implored them not to assist their rivals.

There was no department of anthropology at an Australian university until 1925 when A. R. Radcliffe-Brown was appointed to the first professorship at Sydney. Until that time, the highly competitive research environment was largely unregulated by academic protocols. This helps explain the rift between Mathews and the Victorians which assumed grotesque proportions after that first polite criticism of Howitt in 1898. So passionately did Spencer dislike Mathews, according to the psychologist E. Morris Miller, that when he saw the article 'Social Organisation of some Australian Tribes' (1906) (reproduced this volume), Spencer 'convulsed at Mr Mathews' audacity'.[29] There was at least one occasion when Mathews and Spencer met in person, perhaps in an effort to settle their differences. The extent of their failure is revealed in Spencer's remark to Howitt: 'I only wish I dare say in print what years ago I said to him in private but it was just a little bit too libellous.'[30]

As the policy of ignoring him persisted, as months became years, Mathews became increasingly strident. He hurled insults, declaring on one occasion that if Howitt and his collaborator Lorimer Fison 'had never been born, it could not have made an atom of difference to my work'.[31] Perhaps he resorted to these measures in the hope of provoking a response. If so, he finally enjoyed some success. In 1907 he took Spencer and Howitt to task in the letters page of *Nature*.[32] He pointedly complained about the extent to which Howitt had ignored his work, and the latter judged it too prominent a forum to ignore. Howitt's response is highly revealing. He claimed to have

> learnt from Mr. Mathews's letter that he has sent 'more than one hundred contributions to various scientific societies'. I have only met with two of them, neither of which recommended itself to me by its accuracy. It is therefore difficult to understand how I can have 'ignored' statements of which I am ignorant.[33]

As Mathews pointed out in a forceful rejoinder, this was a bare-faced lie. Howitt had been receiving the *Proceedings of the Royal Society of Victoria* and the *Journal of the Anthropological Institute* through all the years of Mathews' anthropological research. In these journals alone he had published 16 articles. After the contretemps in *Nature*, Mathews and Howitt finally did what years earlier they could have done productively: debated each other. The forum was the journal *American Antiquarian*, and in this exchange the differences between them are most clearly articulated.[34] The debate centred on whether the Aboriginal traditions of southeast Australia were more or less dead, as Howitt claimed, or whether, as Mathews believed, they had survived into the twentieth century. So intense was the hostility that even on his deathbed, Howitt (who died in 1908), was busily fulminating against Mathews. He condemned him in a text titled 'A Message to Anthropologists' which was posted to a who's who list of anthropological luminaries and published in the Parisian journal *Revue des Études Ethnographiques et Sociologiques*.[35]

Mathews acquitted himself well in *American Antiquarian*, but it was arguably too late for his reputation. Howitt's magnum opus, *The Native Tribes of South-East Australia*, had been published in London in 1904 and it contained what can only be described as a travesty of omission. Mathews had received not so much as a footnote in the 819 pages of Howitt's book.

The personal effect of this treatment is best measured in the 'Correspondence' section of this volume. Squirming at the way they silenced him, Mathews took pot-shots at his opponents, and sometimes it was he, not they, who looked absurd. Howitt and Spencer's achievements were considerable, but this he refused to acknowledge. It is significant to an understanding of Mathews' character that he rarely expressed his feelings about this or other matters of a personal nature. A substantial collection of his notebooks, correspondence and other manuscripts survives in the National Library of Australia. But even so dramatic an event as the meeting with Spencer could slip by without so much as a note in his diary. Getting a sense of Mathews the person is made more difficult by his failure to keep copies of the thousands of letters he wrote. Communications from his correspondents were carefully filed, but his own voice is missing from the dialogue. Fortuitously, there is one major exception to this rule. From 1905 to 1907 Mathews corresponded with Daisy Bates, and since they both kept each other's letters, an exchange could, in this one case, be reconstructed. However, this is not to understate the extraordinary value of the Mathews manuscripts. His notebooks, drafts and annotated offprints of articles reveal much data that he never published, including the particulars of communities visited and the names of many informants. Mathews' personal papers are an outstanding record of intercultural history in the turn-of-the-century period. But so little do they illuminate his inner life that to the biographer they seem a carapace. They evoke not Mathews, but a space where Mathews has been.[36]

The image of a private and isolated individual is confirmed in a short memoir, apparently written by his son William Mathews.

> Owing doubtless to the fact that he was what usually is known as a self-contained man, RHM felt little or no desire to seek the society of his fellows, but rather was disposed to avoid them as much as he reasonably could … For, to be quite candid, RHM was inclined—frequently, it must be admitted with good reason—to look upon the majority of people with considerable disdain, if not with something very akin to contempt.[37]

R. H. was not so misanthropic in the recollection of Frank Mathews, his grandson. Perhaps, as often happens, he was less remote as a grandfather than a father. Frank Mathews noted his shyness, although he said that this trait lessened in old age. He remembered his 'Irish sense of humour' and that he had 'an amusing way of quizzing people and drawing them out'.[38] Mathews' tendency to shield himself was probably accentuated by a lifetime of exerting authority over others. Or else his innate sense of isolation drew him towards such roles. A copy of a letter to his wife Mary, written from the field, reveals that he was routinely addressed as 'sir' by members of his survey team. When, from the age of 40, he wound back his surveying practice and regularly served on the bench as a magistrate and coroner in local courts, he was required to sit in judgement of his fellow citizens—a role that required aloofness from those around him. That Mathews had difficulty in dropping the mask of authority is suggested in letters he wrote to Carl Strehlow. The latter was a man of the cloth, a fellow professional, and also a scholar of anthropology. Yet at times Mathews seemed to treat him as more of a subordinate than a colleague, as when he asked him to do research on the pronouns of the area.

> You will be able to get all the information about these 'inclusive' and 'exclusive' forms in a few hours from any native.

> Please also enquire how far north the language extends. For example, would your blacks understand a blackfellow from Barrow's Creek Telegraph Station? I presume your blacks speak substantially the same language as at Charlotte Waters …

> Please answer this letter by the return mail.[39]

Mathews' diary lists many overseas luminaries to whom he wrote.[40] In that class-ridden age, a degree of humility would have been expected from a colonial surveyor writing uninvited. Yet seldom was it forthcoming. The mighty J. G. Frazer of Trinity College, Cambridge, author of *The Golden Bough*, had been forewarned by Spencer that Mathews was of nuisance value, so his prospects in that quarter were never promising.[41] Even so, it is interesting that Frazer complained that Mathews wrote 'in a tone which showed the character of the man. I did not answer his letters and shall hold no communication with him'.[42] Andrew Lang was no friend of Frazer's, but he too was uncomfortable with Mathews' tone, even though he had a high opinion of his work, having praised him as the most lucid and 'well informed writer on the various divisions which regulate the marriages of the Australian tribes'.[43] In a letter to Hartland he expressed reservation about Mathews' manners and his failure to reciprocate in the exchange of publications.[44]

There were other irritations for contemporaries, not all of Mathews' doing. But their frequency suggests, at best, a tendency to mismanage his interactions. The Queensland anthropologist, W. E. Roth, claimed (incorrectly) that Mathews had published 'as his own' the grammatical findings of Mary Everitt, a Sydney researcher linked with the Gundungurra community of the Blue Mountains.[45] This misunderstanding led Roth to denounce Mathews as a 'common or garden blackguard' and 'a *true* parasite—no "mutualism" or "commensalism" about him'.[46] Early in his anthropological career Mathews had lost favour with learned societies in Melbourne, Sydney and London by publishing the same or similar findings in multiple journals.[47] He also had a habit of imposing his grievances with Howitt and Spencer upon uninterested parties. He once offered a paper to the Anthropological Institute, London, on condition 'that it should not be referred to any Australian Ethnologist'. This did not endear him to the executive of the Institute, and the paper went unread until he withdrew the condition.[48]

Lest this sound like a life of unmitigated faux pas, I should emphasise that Mathews *did* have friends and confidants. He once declared that he practised anthropology 'in the fervent hope of exciting the interest and encouraging the investigation of younger students'.[49] That he enjoyed some success in this regard is shown in his mentorship of W. J. Enright, a Hunter Valley solicitor, whose memories of Mathews were recorded by A. P. Elkin in his important trilogy of articles, 'R. H. Mathews: His Contribution to Aboriginal Studies'.[50] Another, younger man whom Mathews inspired was J. A. (later Sir John) Ferguson, who wrote to Mathews in 1918 seeking 'a complete set of your many monographs'.[51] After Mathews died later that year, Ferguson wrote a highly complimentary obituary of him.[52] An eventual supreme court judge and a noted bibliophile, Ferguson's Australiana collection, containing many offprints of Mathews articles, is now a cornerstone of the National Library of Australia.

Mathews also enjoyed friendship with some of the more prominent anthropological figures of the period. In addition to the correspondence with Hartland (this volume), with whom he found a rapport, he became allied with a number of his Australian contemporaries. 'Your letter is like a good cup of tea to me,' wrote Daisy Bates, 'which is my most stimulating beverage, & I cannot give it higher praise.'[53] For a period Bates and Mathews entertained the idea of working collaboratively in Western Australia where Mathews had never been, but he was only prepared to do so if the government met his expenses.[54] Such largesse was not forthcoming, and Bates herself struggled to get reimbursement of modest expenditure from the Western Australian Registrar General, for whom she worked. Mathews' correspondence with John Mathew was extensive and mostly warm, lasting from 1895 until 1909.[55] To some extent, Mathews, Mathew and Bates, who all wrote to each other, were thrown into alliance by the exclusionary behaviour of Spencer. He cared little for Bates[56] and is alleged to have staged a coup de grâce against John Mathew by orchestrating the rejection of his doctoral thesis by the University of Melbourne.[57] So Mathews was by no means a lone soldier in these 'anthropology wars'. Aboriginal studies in this formative period is a tale of attack and subterfuge. The pool of researchers was small but fractious, with the central players competing on an array of fronts: for correspondents, for international patronage, and for access to Aboriginal people themselves. The urgency with which Mathews and his coevals went about their work is evident in their prolific output. They assumed, like most white Australians at the time, that the Aboriginal race was hovering at the edge of extinction. Rhetoric to this effect helped justify the value of their work to editors, publishers and perhaps even to themselves. Among the many effects of the dying race fallacy was its exclusion of any possibility that a future generation might regard the knowledge they were studying as *their* cultural property. In this regard, early anthropology can be regarded as a shadow of the imperial expansion that made it possible. Knowledge and tradition, like the land itself, became territory that could be claimed and divided.

*

This is the competitive terrain that Mathews entered when he became interested in anthropology in the 1890s. In trying to get a sense of him, we depend—too heavily perhaps—on the letters he wrote and the way people perceived him, frequently from their reading of these very letters. That is to say, we know Mathews from the persona he presented as a correspondent or as an author of learned papers. Perhaps it was his manner as a correspondent, more than anything he did, that put him on the wrong side of Howitt and Spencer. In thinking about this persona, we must acknowledge how it affected others, influencing the terms in which they wrote to him and about him. We must also recognise that this persona might have borne only a slight relation to the man himself. Perhaps he was accomplished at some transactions and poor at others. Claude Lévi-Strauss once observed that a calling to anthropology allows an individual in 'an initial state of detachment' to find advantage when approaching different societies 'since he is already halfway towards them'.[58] In his own society Mathews was long inured to personal and intellectual isolation. But as he sometimes communicated in his published writings, his affinity with Aboriginal people allowed a form of kinship to develop between him and them—a kinship that grew from his interest in their kinship structures and other aspects of cultural life. This affection is sometimes revealed in his writings. We see it, for example, in a paper dated 1896 when he described his reunion with a group of Kamilaroi people whom he knew from his surveying years:

> I entered into conversation with the head men ... I had been kind to them in those days, while listening to their legends and their songs, and studying their wonderful class [i.e. kinship] system; and when I met them now I found their friendship of the greatest value to me.[59]

Illuminations such as this are fairly rare in Mathews' opus, but his familiarity with the social fabric of Aboriginal communities is nonetheless evident. His remarkable 1907 paper 'Contributions to the Ethnography of the Australians' (this volume) is his most detailed evocation of everyday camp life. The narrative is notable for the comfort, indeed the fondness, he feels for Aboriginal communities. He describes ball games, wrestling, story-telling, spear practice, technology, trade. He tried, not always successfully, to write in a dispassionate and scientific manner. Sometimes this makes him seem remote from his subjects, but it also brings a remarkable lack of judgement. While Mathews shared the prevailing view of his epoch that Aboriginal culture was less developed than his own, he seldom complained about its simplicity. Assumptions to this effect were difficult to sustain when dealing with the complexity of grammatical construction or piecing together the puzzle of kinship. Even in Europe the vanguard anthropologists were beginning to acknowledge this, as is evident in criticism of Durkheim by Arnold van Gennep, a supporter of Mathews. As van Gennep's biographer paraphrases his argument: 'so-called primitive societies are not simple societies; they are just as complex as "civilized" societies from the point of view of their internal mechanism and the interweaving of their functions; they are never uniform nor homogenous.'[60] In Mathews' writings, we can often sense his admiration for practices or traditions, sometimes because they *are* simple, though beautifully efficacious. When Mathews describes a bird or small animal baked in clay, he evokes the very texture of the food. 'When they were taken out, the skin or feathers stuck to the hard clay crust while the animal remained clean and juicy.'[61]

This photograph of an Aboriginal camp at Tabulam, northern New South Wales, was taken by commercial photographer Charles Kerry, circa 1895. It is a part of a set of Aboriginal portraits and scenes commissioned by the NSW government. R. H. Mathews visited many such camps from the 1890s. By permission of the National Library of Australia. [NLA.pic-an3298931].

Mathews was attentive to protocol even before he entered a camp where he might have partaken of such a meal. As his friend Enright explained to Elkin, Mathews 'observed Aboriginal courtesies of approach and the patterns of behaviour that he had learnt from childhood onwards'. The two men visited a number of communities in northern New South Wales in the 1890s, and 'when RHM got near a camp, he usually lit a small fire and sat at it until invited to join the group'.[62] The etiquette of approaching strangers was apparently so habitual for Mathews that he never thought to mention it in his diaries or letters. Hence the value of Enright's recollection which explains a great deal about his success as a fieldworker. Although he never wrote directly about how his Aboriginal collaborators were affected by the invasion of their country, a sense of devastation must have been commonplace. There are hints of this in a letter to Daisy Bates where Mathews responded to her failure to find totems in the area where she was working.

I feel *certain* that there are totems. The blacks of now-a-days don't like to admit that they are rats, chicks, grubs &c for fear of the white larrikin's derision, and need to be approached cautiously and kindly on the subject.[63]

Here he reveals a compassionate awareness of the loss of self-esteem, the often daily sense of humiliation, that so many people endured. If we are to explain the troubling issue of why the old languages and kinship affiliations of eastern Australia did not survive the twentieth century, much of it is to do with the sense of shame that Aboriginal people were made to feel about themselves and their traditional way of life. This lack of self-worth was instrumental in discouraging parents from teaching languages and traditions to their children. Loss of language can be partially attributed to feelings of shame.[64] In many cases, including the descriptions of the Wailwan and Kurnu dialects in this volume, Mathews' work is among the few surviving fragments of these now unspoken tongues.

I get a sense of him as a cabalistic person. His extensive documentation of ceremonial life is an indication of how he was drawn towards matters of secrecy. A cryptic reference in his diary, 'Went to Lodge' at an address in Sydney, suggests he may have been involved in a Masonic order.[65] Although I can find no further evidence concerning this, it is worth mentioning that Mathews' eldest son Hamilton attained seniority as a freemason and that Masonic connections frequently pass from father to son.[66] That Aboriginal people were aware of—and interested in—the secret societies of whitefellows is occasionally revealed in anthropological records. Evidence can be found in the work of Janet Mathews, the wife of R. H.'s grandson Frank, who extended the family tradition of cross-cultural research when she became a sound recordist for the Australian Institute of Aboriginal Studies in the 1960s.[67] Janet was told by Howard Timbery, a descendant of Emma Timbery who tutored Mathews in Dharawal, that the anthropologist had been initiated.[68] Herbert Chapman, a Dharawal man, confirmed this story. He explicitly compared the initiatory Bunan ceremony of his culture with the Masonic rituals of white men.[69] The perceived correlation between Masonic and Aboriginal secrecy is seldom acknowledged, but it is interesting to note that as early as 1936 Elkin received a letter from a Melbourne freemason inquiring about the advisability of admitting 'a full-blooded aboriginal' who had applied to join the organisation.[70] Interestingly, Elkin recommended his acceptance: 'let us remember that no one can keep a secret or guard his membership of a secret society better than an Aborigine.'[71]

Mathews was certainly treated as an initiate. Enright once accompanied him on a visit to an Aboriginal camp near Port Stephens, north of Sydney. Whereas Mathews was 'at once received by them as one of the initiated,' Enright 'remained in the camp "with the women and children," as they jocularly expressed it '.[72] Mathews possessed his own bullroarers, perhaps the most secret and sacred ceremonial objects in eastern Australia.[73] He took one with him when documenting ceremonies, secretly showing it to the senior men, who 'treated me as one who had been initiated, and gave me all the further information I wished to obtain'.[74] The wording of this statement, dated 1896, implies that he had not at that time been initiated himself. Perhaps it happened at a later date, or maybe he was given the status of an initiated man because he was recognised as a lawman and a figure of authority in his own society. The fact that he never wrote about his own initiation—if it occurred—could reflect his willingness to keep the secrets that were confided.

One of the most interesting hints of how he was regarded by Aboriginal people can be found in Mathews' own copy of A. W. Howitt's *The Native Tribes of South-East Australia*, the book that snubbed him so comprehensively. Hamilton Mathews lent this and other items from his father's library to Elkin who never returned them. They can now be found in the Elkin Collection of rare books at the University of Sydney's Fisher Library. In the margins of Howitt's book Mathews made pencilled comments: 'No, no!', 'Bunkum', 'Rot', 'Nonsense', 'Bosh', 'Not so!' and, *very* occasionally, 'Correct'.[75] As a point of principle, it seems, Mathews' spelling of Aboriginal words differed from Howitt's. But he could have only been referring to the same thing when he annotated a page on which Howitt described those persons who were known by the Kurnai of Gippsland as the *Birraark*. A pencilled note states: 'Birrarak is the name given to me by the natives.'[76]

The lack of self-reflection in Mathews' records is such that I am reliant on his arch-enemy's description to convey an understanding of what this name might have meant to the people who bestowed it. Howitt claimed that the Birraark

> combined the functions of the seer, the spirit-medium, and the bard, for he foretold future events, he brought the ghosts to the camp of his people at night, and he composed the songs and dances which enlivened their social meetings. He was a harmless being, who devoted himself to performances which very strikingly resembled those of the civilised 'mediums.' A man was supposed to become a *Birraark* by being initiated by *Mrarts* or ghosts, when they met him hunting in the bush; but, that they might have power over him, he must at the time be wearing a *Gumbart*, that is, one of those bone pegs which the Australian aborigine wears thrust through the septum of his nose. By this they held him and conveyed him through the clouds.[77]

From Howitt's description it is clear that Birraarks were highly esteemed and widely known. He names eight who were living in Gippsland when whites arrived in 1842, although none had survived by the time he started his ethnographic research in the 1870s. Several individual Birraarks were remembered by Howitt's informants who related numerous observations, all of which enliven an understanding of how Mathews' documentary project might have been construed in eastern Victoria and the culturally connected communities of southern New South Wales. As a medium between the living and the dead, a Birraark could travel from one realm to the other at will. He conveyed messages and information about the movements of friends or enemies who had died and he could also bring material benefits, the makings of a feast, as happened, for example, when 'the *Mrarts* informed them of a whale stranded on the shore'. Not only was the Birraark a leader of ceremonial activities during large inter-communal gatherings, but through his mediation with ghosts he brought songs and dances into the world of the living.[78] Here is rare and compelling evidence of how Mathews was regarded in an Aboriginal community. As a person who *moved between worlds* he could facilitate the transmission of understandings. In that intermediary capacity he evidently encouraged a two-way traffic in ways of speaking, singing and moving.

*

So how did a Parramatta-based surveyor come to acquire the sobriquet Birrarak in Aboriginal communities? Here we must consider the subject that Mathews was least prolific in documenting: himself. In trying to get a sense of him, I have drawn from his own writings and papers, and also from the biographical manuscript, already cited. This invaluable document is in the handwriting of R. H.'s son William Mathews (1883-1967), a keen genealogist and to some extent the keeper of the family lore. Frequent references to 'we' and 'our father' suggest that some of his siblings could also have contributed to this account which was based on discussions with R. H. in his later years. The National Library of Australia acquired this document from Mathews' descendants in 2003.[79]

Robert Hamilton Mathews was born in 1841 at Narellan, now a south-western suburb of Sydney. The previous year his protestant parents had arrived from Ulster. Most of his childhood was spent on a pastoral property at Breadalbane near the town of Goulburn in New South Wales. Mathews had no formal schooling; his education, and that of his siblings, was entrusted to a private tutor, a so-called 'remittance man' and an alcoholic, who regularly absconded when payments arrived from England. As William Mathews' memoir quaintly puts it, the children's father 'came to the conclusion that the harm likely to be done by the tutor's unworthy example outweighed the value of his teaching, and so he reluctantly felt obliged to dispense with his services'. From that time Mathews senior (also a William), oversaw their education.[80] He had attended Foyle College, a well known school in Derry, and was 'a sound classical scholar'.[81] Signs of classical learning are evident in Mathews' manuscripts and publications. He knew the basics of Latin, as would be expected at the time, and seems to have modelled his descriptions of Aboriginal grammar on the primers used by him or his children.[82] For most of his life Mathews was a regular churchgoer, attending Presbyterian and sometimes other services. He knew his Bible, regarding it, in the words of his son, as 'a collection of the folk tales of an eastern people'. He saw clear analogies between this folklore and the Aboriginal mythology he later documented.[83]

That he was Australian-born is fundamental to understanding Mathews. In this respect he differed from Spencer, Howitt, Fison, Mathew, Bates and Roth—in fact all his anthropological contemporaries. Aboriginal people were not exotic to Mathews in the way they were to more recent immigrants. He once stated that 'black children were among my earliest playmates,' revealing that Aboriginal people lived near, or were employed on, the property at Breadalbane.[84] According to his own documentation of tribal boundaries, this would make them Gundungurra or perhaps Ngunawal people, unless (as sometimes happened) they had shifted from more distant territory. In 1854, then 13 years old, Mathews was greatly intrigued by the activities of John F. Mann, a surveyor then working on the Great Southern Road which passed near the family homestead. Mathews spent time in the surveyor's camp, and Mann explained his work in detail. Captivated, the boy made his own mock instruments and with a surveyor's chain made of bark he played at measuring the country with an Aboriginal friend.[85]

As a young man R. H. Mathews was involved in various pastoral activities. In 1860 he joined a droving party taking sheep from New England to the Moonie River in Queensland where he remained until 1862. The Moonie is an upper branch of the Barwon River, a locale often mentioned in the later anthropological writings. On returning, he worked on his father's property and selected land nearby. But his childhood interest in surveying never diminished. He eventually received on-the-job training with a railway surveyor named Kennedy, passing his final exams in 1870. Then followed 10 hard years doing government and private surveys. He married Mary Bartlett of Wallah in 1872. He had met her while surveying in the Maitland district. Of their seven children, the ornithologist Gregory M. Mathews (1876-1949) is the best known. An autodidact like his father, he wrote and published the 7,000-page *Birds of Australia* (1910-27), a work intended to outdo Gould. Hamilton B. Mathews (1873-1959) (the freemason) was also distinguished. He joined his father's profession and attained high office, serving as surveyor-general of New South Wales.

The experience of working on the land and dealing with the everyday detail of topography was clearly fundamental to Mathews becoming an anthropologist. He and his team travelled with bullocks and wagons, living out bush for weeks at a time. Inevitably, they encountered signs of Aboriginal occupation, sometimes occupying the ancient camping grounds. Meetings with Aboriginal people would have been unavoidable and he once stated that some found employment in his surveying business.[86] Although, by this time, the Aboriginal people of southeast Australia were dispossessed of their territory, many maintained connections with country by working for settlers or living as 'fringe dwellers' on tribal grounds.

The great bulk of Mathews' survey work occurred in central and northern New South Wales. He was first stationed at Deepwater in New England from 1872. Two years later he moved to Goondiwindi on the Queensland border. Then in 1876 he moved to Biamble near the small town of Merrygoen on the upper Castlereagh River where he bought land. A notebook in Mathews' hand, recently found among family papers, gives a job-by-job inventory of his work for the decade from 1874. It shows that during the Merrygoen period he worked extensively on the Moree Plains in areas around Warrumbungle and Wellington, ancestral territory of the Kamilaroi people, who are discussed extensively in his anthropological writings. The notebook indicates that many leading pastoralists were among Mathews' clients, including the Rouse, White and Cox families.[87] In 1880 the Mathews family moved again, this time to the town of Singleton in the Hunter Valley, 190 km north of Sydney. Gregory Mathews remembered the move.

> It was a long overland journey and, young as I was, I can remember the gaping crowds that stared at our cavalcade as we passed through the various settlements along the road—my father driving the big buggy with four horses, and all the other vehicles following. Except for an occasional bush inn, we camped out in the open at night ...[88]

His experience as a surveyor familiarised Mathews with the land and its inhabitants—and made him wealthy. Both were integral to his anthropological labour. As Gregory described it, his father had, by the age of 40, amassed 'a competence and could call himself an independent gentleman'.[89] How he achieved this within the period of just 10 years was explained by William Mathews:

> Perceiving that a considerable income could be earned by an energetic man who arranged his work in such a way as to avoid any serious loss of time while moving from place to place, Robert decided to apply for a district where he would not only be given all the Government work but would have the right to engage in private practice.[90]

In his business activities, Mathews displayed the same industriousness that he later applied to anthropology. In one month in 1873 he submitted to the surveyor-general plans for 591 portions of land, a departmental record.[91] The notebook held by the family indicates the vast range of work performed: selecting properties; laying out schoolyards, churches and cemeteries; preparing sites for building. He laid out the township of Mungindi in northern New South Wales. Speculation occurred constantly during Mathews' surveying years; land was bought and sold according fluctuations of the market and the season. There was constant demand for his services. His daily routine was well adapted for his later ethnographic fieldwork. He led his team by day, attended to calculations and other paperwork by night. The rewards were substantial. Government work alone provided him with average returns of more than £2,000 a year in the period 1873-79.[92] To set that in context, a professor at the University of Sydney was paid handsomely at £900. Little wonder that Mathews was in a position to invest substantial sums. He lent £2,000 in cash to a building society in 1880;[93] acquired an interest in a property called Goorangula, 24 miles north of Singleton; he owned another farm closer to the town called Springwood.[94] Diarised complaints about recalcitrant tenants reveal other investments in property.[95] As he became wealthier, however, his interest in surveying lessened. In February 1882 he resigned as district surveyor for Singleton and sold his horses and equipment. The time had come to reap the rewards of success, and in May that year he and Mary set sail for San Francisco on the *City of New York*. By this time they had three girls and two boys, all of whom were left in the care of a nanny and a governess. A budget of £1,500 was allocated for the trip.[96] This was £300 more than Mathews later paid in cash for the family's house in Parramatta.[97]

A day in the life of a colonial surveyor—R. H. Mathews and theodolite, together with members of his team. This unique photograph from the family album was probably taken in the 1870s or early 1880s when his surveying business was at its peak. By permission of Jane Mathews.

Robert and Mary's round-the-world trip, which lasted from May 1882 until March 1883, is a matter of particular interest in thinking about his overseas publishing and correspondence. His diary for the period indicates that he kept a separate journal during the period abroad, but it has not survived.[98] William Mathews provides detail of the early part of their travels. They stopped in New

Zealand and Honolulu en route to California where they visited Yosemite Valley and other attractions, before heading for Salt Lake City, where Mary 'derived a good deal of entertainment watching Robert and others—particularly a very fat man—bathing in the dense water of the Lake ... and next day they attended service in the Mormon Tabernacle'.[99] Sadly, the greater part of William's account of the tour is also missing. He takes us as far as Chicago. From there the records are fragmentary. A letter of credit reveals that they drew funds in New York from where, presumably, they sailed for England. The next withdrawal was dated 12 October 1882 from the Midland Grand Hotel, London. Later that month they drew £119, a substantial sum, which probably funded a tour of the Continent. (Mathews' obituary claims that he travelled in America, Europe and Africa.)[100] The financial records show that they visited Edinburgh and Inverness in the early days of 1883. On return to London they booked their passage back to Australia via the Suez Canal.[101] Records of the trip are slight, but it must have been formative in many ways. Mathews' profession had demanded extended absence from his family. This was the longest period that he and his wife had spent together. Even less is known of Mary than Robert. How did she cope with a husband always fixated, by his profession and then his scholarship? Gregory writes of her briefly but romantically. She was a 'very beautiful woman,' he says, 'the belle of the district' as a girl. He considered his parents 'a splendidly matched couple,' but beyond that he says almost nothing about his mother. The voyage home from Europe could not have been easy for Mary. Just a few weeks after they returned in March 1883, she gave birth to William Mathews. Their youngest child, Robert, followed in 1886.

There is nothing to suggest that Mathews visited the anthropological societies of Vienna, Paris, Washington or London—all future publishers of his work—during the period abroad. His anthropological interests remained inchoate. Presumably he and Mary visited the attractions favoured by prosperous Victorians. They visited galleries, saw the sights. A later article mentions a boomerang exhibited in the British Museum.[102] Although he was not active in anthropology during this period, it is significant that he had firsthand, if only brief, acquaintance with Britain, Europe and the United States, the destinations for his anthropological writings and correspondence. His transmission of data from the Australian backblocks to the great international centres—places he had read about and briefly encountered—expresses his position on the edge of the empire. As someone personally known in Aboriginal communities, he picked his way around the insights, assumptions and prejudices of 'armchair anthropologists' in Europe. His attitude to these theorists is sometimes expressed in the agitated marginalia that crowd his copies of Lang and the British kinship scholar, N. W. Thomas. Yet Mathews also craved validation from such authorities, as can be seen in his letters to Hartland.

I am very anxious to know whether my views have any points of value in them, or whether I am thought by ethnologists to be altogether wrong. If I am entirely in error I do not wish to publish any further particulars until I see the views of my critics and gain enlightenment from them. On the other hand, if my views are upheld by competent authority, it will give me courage to go on in the work I am engaged in.[103]

The time in Europe raises the question of Mathews' multilingual ability. The project of retranslation establishes conclusively that Mathews did not write in French or German. With the French publications this is immediately apparent. A Germanically-named Oscar Schmidt is credited with translating six of the nine French articles. No German translators are acknowledged, but they certainly existed as we know from footnotes added by and attributed to these anonymous scholars. Mathews certainly knew some German and by his own account more French. A letter to Mary dated 1872 states: 'I know a little of French and German myself, but have not had sufficient practice to engage in much conversation, although I can read French books pretty well.'[104] Instruction in these languages might come from his father or the wayward tutor. He could have had private lessons, studied at a school of arts, or taught himself with dictionaries and primers. That his French was not strong is revealed in his surviving correspondence with Oscar Schmidt and another more celebrated Parisian, the ethnologist Arnold van Gennep. Both wrote to him in English and van Gennep suggested that his article 'Does Exogamy Exist in Australian Tribes?' be published in that language, four tongues being admissible in his journal *Revue d'Ethnographie et de Sociologie*.[105] Mathews' competence in German is indicated by the correspondence with the Frankfurt-based Baron Moritz von Leonhardi, editor and supporter of Carl Strehlow (see 'Correspondence', this volume). Each wrote to the other in his own language.

Apart from his time in Europe, Mathews had limited opportunities for practising French and German. But this did not lessen his interest in the multilingual dimension. While it was certainly a compliment that Europeans regarded his work as worthy of translation, it opens important issues, exemplified by his correspondence with the remarkable van Gennep who drew upon the initiation rituals described by Mathews and other Australian anthropologists in his seminal book, *Les rites de passage* (*The Rites of Passage*) (1908). Van Gennep was born in Germany to a Dutch father and a French mother. He lived most of his life in France, spoke the major European languages, studied Egyptian culture and was fluent in Arabic.[106] It is revealing that Mathews, who was so heavily spurned by British anthropologists, should find a sympathetic ear in the person of van Gennep and, more generally, a readership in Europe. In charting the histories of empire, it is convenient—and indeed sometimes appropriate—to lump Britons and Continentals together under the descriptor 'Europeans'.

However the linguistic dexterity of a scholar such as van Gennep is a reminder of differences *within* Europe and *between* Great Britain and its neighbours across the Channel. Europe, as a linguistically crowded place, suggests certain parallels with the Aboriginal world in which Mathews worked. Recall him as a young surveyor struggling with the limits of his English notation. His interest in recording the sound of Aboriginal tongues epitomises the difference between him and most of his contemporaries in colonial Australia. In a settler society, dominated by British values, it was normal to be monolingual. To be interested in Aboriginal language was doubly aberrant, as can be seen in a letter from an irate farmer whom Mathews petitioned for assistance in grammatical inquiry.

> I certainly have not time to spare to sit in office with a blackfellow or gin to talk patiently with him or her … If you can send a few inches of rain I might then have time to go into the question of niggers' grammar but under present conditions am not interested.[107]

Non-Aboriginal Australians now have some idea of the linguistic diversity that once prevailed. Prior to colonisation there were some 250 languages. This diversity was not recognised in colonial times, and since then more than two-thirds of the languages have become extinct or have only a few elderly speakers. The very fact that I can cite such a statistic is due to the foundational work of Mathews and others like him.[108] For decades, white people derided Aboriginal speech as 'black mumbo jumbo'. Managers of Aboriginal institutions discouraged the use of Indigenous language, partly because it threatened their own authority. Frequently the word *dialect* was improperly applied to discrete languages, a practice so widespread that many Aboriginal people themselves adopted the term. In Aboriginal circles, loss of language is often mentioned in the same breath as loss of land—a logical connection. Languages are associated with particular territories; land and language are integral to one's sense of being. When traditional languages are lost, the colonised must express themselves in the words of their colonisers and for the most part, their world becomes monolingual.[109]

One of the great revelations of Mathews' work is the degree of differentiation within Aboriginal Australia. He was interested in the languages of various regions, and other distinguishing cultural traits. Mathews came to realise that Aboriginal people were often proficient in negotiating these differences. Many lived outside their traditional territory—by choice or necessity. In Mathews' descriptions of ceremonial life and in his more limited discussion of trade, he showed how diverse communities congregated for ritual and celebration. This can be seen, for example, in 'The Mŭltyerra Initiation Ceremony' (this volume), described by Kurnu people on the Darling River in the vicinity of Bourke. The organisers of the ceremony dispatched messengers to summon the surrounding tribes.

> The bearers of the message on approaching the boundaries of the camp of the foreign tribe sat down in view of the dwellings of the single men and made friendly signs. Some of the old men then walked over to them and led them to the special meeting place of the initiated men where they were brought before all the chiefs and warriors.[110]

Similar deputations are described scores of times in the Mathews opus. Frequently, as occurred with the Bunan ceremony of the Shoalhaven district, the messengers followed a particular route, advising each tribe along the way of the impending ceremony. The most distant tribe would join the messengers immediately, and then the next tribe, and the next, so the mass of people grew continually throughout the homeward journey.[111] The gatherings were celebratory occasions. Much partying and revelry occurred as the mobs assembled. The hosts occupied the centre of the campground, while each group of visitors was 'situated in the direction of the region from where it has come', as the anthropologist-surveyor never failed to point out.[112] It is not always clear what Mathews meant when referring to a 'tribe'. Sometimes, as suggested here, it refers to localised groups that might comprise several families. At other times 'tribe' referred to an entire language group, a large mass of people. While the ceremonies described by Mathews were usually associated with particular language groups (Kamilaroi, Wiradjuri, Muruwari, etc), there are strong indications that the presence of 'foreigners' was a feature of these gatherings. In a description of the initiation ceremony of the Darkinung people (a relatively small language group north of Sydney), Mathews was at pains to point out that the ritual was influenced by their more populous Kamilaroi and Wiradjuri neighbours.[113] Given that the rituals were secret-sacred, 'influence' would only be possible if visitors were admitted. The ceremonies as Mathews described them showed remarkable consistency across much of Victoria, New South Wales and Queensland. This in itself is evidence of their inter-communal quality. Mathews' fastidiousness in documenting the social and co-operative aspects of Aboriginal life forms a marked contrast to the emphasis on tribal enmity that saturates so many observations of the colonial period.

*

A decade passed from Mathews' return from Europe in 1883 until the issue of his first publication in anthropology. In many ways it was an unsettled period, a time of restlessness and searching. He did some part-time surveying and explored other interests, intellectual and religious. While he usually attended a Presbyterian service each Sunday morning, he now strayed in his evening worship, sometimes to the Wesleyans and even the Catholics. Often he took the train to Newcastle and then a steamer to Sydney, where he saw to business and attended meetings of the Royal Society of New South Wales. Since 1875 he had been a member of this small but influential scientific body, modelled on (though independent of) its London namesake. But until the 1880s he had been a fairly passive member. Now that he had the opportunity to attend meetings, he could hear presentations by members and participate directly in the scientific culture of the colony. The society encouraged research into all branches of science including archaeology and ethnology (as anthropology was often known). While inquiry into matters Aboriginal was hardly a major concern, it did appear in the occasional paper, as Mathews noted in 1885 when he heard a presentation 'by Rev. McPherson on Implements of the Australian Aborigines'.[114] After he emerged as an anthropologist, the Royal Society of New South Wales became enormously important to him. This was the chief forum for presenting and publishing his research. It also provided members with access to its library containing periodicals from around the world. There Mathews discovered the major journals for which he wrote.[115]

Ness House, Singleton, NSW. The Mathews family lived in the Hunter Valley township from 1880 until 1888, when they moved to Parramatta. The girl in the foreground is Mary 'May' Mathews, the fifth of Robert and Mary's children. Standing is the family nurse, Tilly, and their 'lady help', Miss Agnes Beck. By permission of Jane Mathews.

During this period Mathews often served on the magistrate's bench. Salaried or 'stipendiary' magistrates were uncommon throughout the colonial period. Untrained Justices of the Peace presided over local courts, and this gave the office 'JP' considerable cachet. It is a mark of Mathews' wealth and gentlemanly standing. He was first made a Justice of the Peace by the Queensland government in 1875; and by New South Wales after he returned from Europe in 1883. In his frequent travels during this 1880s, he often served at local or police courts in the towns he visited. It brought some income, for he received a sitting fee for his service. As a magistrate he was also entitled to preside over coronial inquiries, and in 1886 he was appointed District Coroner of Singleton. The court experience also played a role in his anthropological career, for his status as JP made him known among policemen, some of whom assisted him greatly as correspondents. It also marked his debut as an author. He became sufficiently versed in legal practice to publish *Handbook to Magisterial Inquiries in New South Wales* (1888), a how-to manual for gentlemen new to the bench.

Mathews' court work occurred alongside various business dealings, one of which had unfortunate repercussions. In June 1884 his diary mentions that while in Sydney 'in search of employment' he formed an arrangement with a man named McCulloch to go to Silverton for £150 'to look at land for mining purposes'.[116] Silverton, near Broken Hill in southwest New South Wales, had been founded as a silver town just five years earlier. To get there required a lengthy journey. He travelled by train to Melbourne, steamer to Adelaide and then took the train to the railhead at Terowie, some 200 km north of the South Australian capital. The final leg he did by coach. While in Silverton he pegged out claims for McCulloch and officiated at various court proceedings. Then, on 8 August,

> Got telegram from Dr Read telling me my dear little daughter Australie was dead, – died on 3rd instant and was to be buried on the 5th. She died from inflammation of the brain brought on by knocking her head accidentally against a door on the 15th July.[117]

In the emotionally sparse terrain of Mathews' diary this entry stabs deeply. They are perhaps the most expressive words he recorded. Despite being so affected by the news, he could not return to Mary and the children. He had come down with measles a few weeks earlier, and for obvious reasons he was not prepared to take the risk of infecting the rest of the family.[118] Instead, he remained in Silverton for a further three months. In that time he surveyed a small township and continued to officiate at the police court where a large and thirsty population of miners was creating a steady stream of business. Not until late November did Mathews begin the return trip. He stopped at Kingston in South Australia where he was sworn in as a magistrate for that colony. He stopped again, with cousins in Ballarat. When reunited with the family at Singleton, his diary records various activities with the children—days in Sydney; a cruise up the Hawkesbury. The death of five-year-old Australie must have been bitter blow to them all.

Robert and Mary's fourth child, Australie Matilda, was five years old when she died from a head injury. This is how she was memorialised in the family album. By permission of Jane Mathews.

Great difficulties resulted from his business dealings with Andrew Hardie McCulloch, who became an ogre in the family history. He was a solicitor, property developer, pastoralist and, for 11 years from 1878, a member of parliament. He was at the centre of many public controversies, including that surrounding the development of the Blackfriars Estate in the Sydney suburb of Chippendale, a sub-division that flaunted the town-planning laws of the day.[119] McCulloch was also the reluctant father-in-law of Dowell O'Reilly, the poet, fiction writer, and left-leaning MP—and thus the grandfather of the novelist Eleanor Dark.[120] His business dealings with Mathews involved a mining syndicate and a speculative land company which Mathews managed. He also advanced McCulloch considerable sums of money. These ventures crashed in the late 1880s and McCulloch was declared bankrupt. According to William Mathews, R. H.'s losses amounted to approximately £30,000.[121]

It is an indicator of Mathews' wealth that he was not ruined by this experience. He could still afford to send his children to elite schools. Indeed they moved from Singleton to Parramatta in 1888 so the boys could attend The King's School, the elite military-style academy frequented by many scions of the pastoral dynasties. Mathews avoided future investments to do with mining and as a consequence he declined an invitation to acquire for £105 a one-fourteenth share in the mine that became Broken Hill Propriety Company (BHP). Had he done so, he would soon have been numbered among the wealthiest men in the country.[122] Instead, he returned to his former occupation, fleshing out his surviving investments with survey work. His monetary losses proved to be anthropology's gain.

It was a routine survey, commissioned by a farmer named Benjamin Richards, that took Mathews and his son Hamilton to their old stamping ground in the Hunter Valley in 1892. Richards owned land at the hamlet of Milbrodale, about 20 kilometres south of Singleton. They were going about their business when someone on the farm told them 'of the existence of a rather striking aboriginal painting of a human figure in a cave in the vicinity'.[123] In this way Mathews' attention was drawn to one of the great Aboriginal art sites of eastern Australia, a representation of the creation hero or 'great spirit' known as Baiame. It is not altogether surprising that Mathews, on seeing this huge, painted image, was inspired 'to make an accurate copy of it '.[124] Few observers would be unaffected by the painting in that sandstone shelter. Baiame is stunningly depicted in red and white ochre. His eyes are large and almost luminous, and his arms are extraordinary. They are greatly exaggerated in proportion to the rest of him, extending laterally from the torso, reaching across the wall of the cave, so as to measure five metres from fingertip to fingertip.

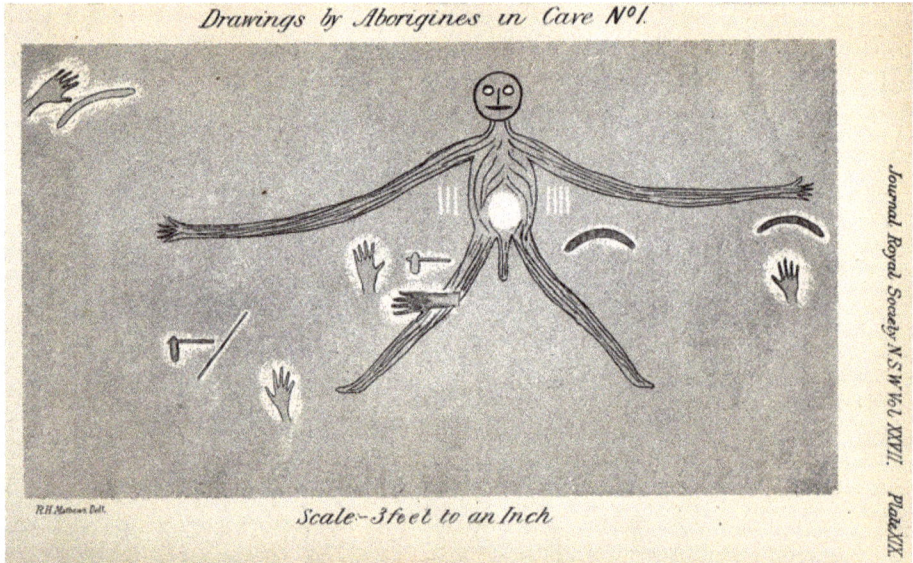

Drawings by Aborigines in Cave Nº1.

Scale—3 feet to an Inch

Journal Royal Society N S W Vol. XXVII.   Plate XIX

A cave painting of a giant figure, identified by R. H. Mathews as the creation hero, Baiame, prompted his first anthropological publication in 1893. Mathews and his son Hamilton visited the site at Milbrodale in the Hunter Valley, NSW, during a routine surveying job. Reproduced from 'Rock Paintings by the Aborigines in Caves on Bulgar Creek, near Singleton' (1893). By permission of the National Library of Australia.

Mathews' observations of the Baiame painting and some other less dramatic art sites in the area became the basis for a short presentation, delivered to the Royal Society of New South Wales in 1893. It was his first paper in 17 years of membership. While revealing some residual knowledge of Aboriginal customs, this first ethnological publication is quite prosaic. Mathews states unashamedly that he has confined himself 'as much as possible to descriptions only of these drawings, and have not attempted to connect them with the myths and superstitions of the Australian aborigines'. With the benefit of hindsight there is a certain humour in his remark that he will leave these more detailed questions 'for those better qualified to follow them than I am, or have more time at their disposal'.[125] Soon he was feverishly visiting rock art sites within and beyond Sydney, gathering information for the Royal Society's essay prize, which had as its topic for 1894 the rock art of the Australian Aborigines. He won the prize, a bronze medal and a cheque for £25—perhaps the one time he made money from anthropology. With the essay prize in the bag, the man with little time at his disposal soon discovered how little time he had for anything else.[126] He turned 52 the year that first article went to press. By the time of his death 25 years later he had clocked up 2,200 pages of published work. Starting with rock art, he turned his attention to ceremonies, kinship, mythology, material culture, and more. He came to realise that his entire former life had prepared him for this particular vocation. The rush was on.

*

Interpreting the produce of that 25-year period is no simple matter. While we turn to Mathews for his portrayals of Aboriginal life, we must read them with caution. Like any documentary project his writings are only a partial representation. The problem they pose is reflected in the scenario with which I started: Mathews as a young surveyor recording language at Narran Lakes, unable to 'find letters in our language to express the proper sounds'. Such perplexity is more than a hindrance to ethnographic documentation; *it is integral to its meaning*, as Franz Boas, the German-American anthropologist, argued in a seminal essay titled 'On Alternating Sounds', published in 1889. Analysing the very problem Mathews experienced, Boas quoted from his own notebook to show how he had failed to differentiate between phonetic variants that were recognised as discrete sounds in the ears of his Eskimo instructors. He recommended study of the philologist's notebook as a key to the linguistic and cultural background of its author who 'apperceives the unknown sounds by the means of the sounds of his own language'.[127] This nascent awareness of cultural relativity had profound ramifications. As the historian of anthropology George Stocking glosses its eventual impact, Boas began to question 'whether the cultural practices of savages were to be treated as imperfect approximations of those of European civilization, or rather as quite differently constituted cultural categorizations that were at best problematically commensurable to a Eurocentric evolutionary standard'.[128]

This is to say that Mathews' writings can feed into different forms of cultural and historical inquiry. They inform localised Aboriginal histories; they open up debates about anthropology as a discipline; and they colour understandings of colonisation and the spread of modernity. It is the first of these that gives Mathews the bulk of his current readership. He provides information on languages and traditions that have been modified, and in some cases lost, in the period since he recorded them. As suggested above, we must always read him cautiously. Often it is beneficial to consult his correspondence or notebooks in order to identify the locations where he worked or the individuals with whom he spoke. Where possible, his work should be evaluated in the light of other evidence. To say this is not to downplay his integrity as an ethnographer, as has often happened. Mud flung by Spencer and others stuck and hardened, and it lasted for generations. Unfortunately for his reputation, many of the anthropologists who admired Mathews did not say so publicly, perhaps in an effort to differentiate their newly professionalised discipline from the world of their amateur forebears. Elkin claimed that Radcliffe-Brown's use of Mathews bordered on plagiarism, and it is likely that others have been similarly grudging in their attribution.[129] Elkin's own writings on Mathews are the most sustained homage from within the profession. Many others expressed their admiration privately. Norman Tindale, who often cited Mathews when mapping Australia's tribal boundaries, came to think of him as 'our greatest recorder of primary anthropological data'.[130] W. E. H. Stanner expressed delight at Elkin's work on Mathews. 'It is something I had always hoped to do myself'.[131] These comments by leading authorities might temper the arguments of critics such as Diane Barwick who claimed (without substantiation) that Mathews was a plagiarist and a fraud.[132] Although he could exaggerate the extent of his personal inquiries, and sometimes suppressed the names of correspondents, I can find nothing to suggest that he invented or pirated data. As he said to Hartland in 1907, 'I have a large mass of information regarding all the states which has not yet been published anywhere'.[133] He suggested publishing a book on mythology and another on languages. He could have proposed a substantial tome on ceremonial life. As we now know from his unpublished papers, Mathews had no need to pillage from other writers, and given the loathing between him and Howitt it is hard to believe that either could have plagiarised from the other.

While Mathews has, for some time now, been cited as a standard reference in community histories, native title claims, cultural heritage projects and attempts to revitalise Indigenous language, there are strong arguments why the cross-cultural project of his formative period should be read more broadly, rooted as it is in the history of modernity and empire. The historian Patrick Wolfe presents a more extreme version of this argument, proposing that anthropological theory of this period should be read *solely* for its insights into the colonial imaginary. Anthropology, he says, 'begins to emerge as a kind of soliloquy—as Western discourse talking to itself'.[134] To me this argument is not ultimately sustainable, principally because it replicates the colonial paradigm that it criticises. Anthropology can only be regarded as a soliloquy if it ignores the input, actions and agendas of colonised people, many of whom find the work of Mathews and other researchers sufficiently accessible and convincing to make use of it in their own political and cultural projects. Still, Wolfe's position is instructive in that it points to the value of intercultural investigation in elucidating narratives of nation and empire. As Barry Hill points out in his study of T. G. H. Strehlow, the few histories of anthropology we have in Australia 'have not fully attempted to put the individual lives of anthropologists into the field of cultural history'.[135] Reading Mathews has convinced me that all its layers of significance must be recognised and interpreted with reference to one another. As much as they evoke the Aboriginal world that so intrigued him, they are expressions of his own culture and, more obliquely, expressions of himself. Like the moraine that marks the passage of a long-thawed glacier, these writings chart a personal quest, an intellectual journey, as much as they evoke the wider milieu. Mathews has left us a swarthy monument, as difficult to come to grips with—and almost as intriguing—as the land he measured for a living.

ENDNOTES

[1] Mathews to Bartlett, 17 March 1872, R. H. Mathews Papers, National Library of Australia (henceforth NLA) MS 8006/7/8.

[2] RHM 1903, 'Das Kumbainggeri, eine Eingeborenensprache von Neu-Süd-Wales', *Mitteilungen der Anthropologischen Gesellschaft*, vol. 33, p. 321. Trans. Christine Winter.

[3] This experience was related in an interview with Frank Mathews, 1971, Australian Institute of Aboriginal and Torres Strait Islander Studies (henceforth AIATSIS) Audio Archive, A1954.

[4] 'Late Mr. R. H. Mathews', *Sydney Morning Herald*, 28 May 1918, p. 8.

[5] RHM 1910, 'Some Articles used in Burial and other Rites by the Australian Aborigines', *Queensland Geographical Journal*, vol. 24.

[6] Ibid, and RHM 1903, 'The Aboriginal Fisheries at Brewarrina', *Journal and Proceedings of the Royal Society of New South Wales*, vol. 37.

[7] RHM 1904, 'Ethnological Notes on the Aboriginal Tribes of New South Wales and Victoria', *Journal and Proceedings of the Royal Society of New South Wales*, vol. 38, p. 209.

[8] RHM 1906, 'Bemerkungen über die Eingebornen Australiens', *Mitteilungen der Anthropologischen Gesellschaft*, vol. 36. Reproduced this volume.

[9] RHM 1904, 'Ethnological Notes on the Aboriginal Tribes of New South Wales and Victoria', p. 209.

[10] RHM 1904-5, 'Ethnological Notes on the Aboriginal Tribes of Queensland', *Queensland Geographical Journal*, vol. 20, p. 74.

[11] Spencer, Baldwin 1921, 'Blood and Shade Divisions of Australian Tribes', *Proceedings of the Royal Society of Victoria*, vol. 34, no. 1, p. 2.

[12] RHM 1906, 'Notes on Some Native Tribes of Australia', *Journal and Proceedings of the Royal Society of New South Wales*, vol. 40, p. 99.

[13] Spencer, Baldwin 1904, 'Totemism in Australia', *Report of the Australasian Association for the Advancement of Science*, vol. 10, p. 380 (note).

[14] Lang to Hartland, 19 October [year not stated], Letters to E. S. Hartland, National Library of Wales (henceforth NLW) MS 16889C.

[15] Spencer to Howitt, 15 August 1907, A. W. Howitt Papers, State Library of Victoria (henceforth SLV) MS 9356/Box 1049/7(b). The content of the letter clearly indicates that Spencer was referring to RHM and not Rev John Mathew, another anthropological contemporary.

[16] One letter from their correspondence survives: Mathews to Spencer, 24 September 1896, Sir Walter Baldwin Spencer Papers, Mitchell Library (henceforth ML) MSS 29/9.

[17] RHM 1896, 'The Burbung of the New England Tribes, New South Wales', *Proceedings of the Royal Society of Victoria*, vol. 9 (new series), 1896 and RHM 1896, 'The Bora of the Kamilaroi Tribes', *Proceedings of the Royal Society of Victoria*, vol. 9 (new series).

[18] RHM 1896, 'The Bŭrbŭng of the Wiradthuri Tribes', *Journal of the Anthropological Institute*, vol. 25, p. 313.

[19] Mathews to Hartland, 10 August 1907, Letters to E. S. Hartland, NLW MS 16889C. Reproduced this volume.

[20] Mathews to Hartland, 9 April 1907, Letters to E. S. Hartland, NLW MS 16889C. Reproduced this volume.

[21] Howitt and his collaborator Lorimer Fison were encouraged and supported by Morgan. See Stern, Bernard J. (ed.) 1930, 'Selections from the Letters of Lorimer Fison and A. W. Howitt to Lewis Henry Morgan', *American Anthropologist*, vol. 32 (new series).

[22] RHM 1898, 'Divisions of Queensland Aborigines', *Proceedings of the American Philosophical Society*, vol. 37, p. 330.

[23] Howitt, A. W. 1996, *The Native Tribes of South-East Australia*, Aboriginal Studies Press, Canberra [1st pub. 1904], pp. 43-4.

[24] Mathew to Mathews, 11 December 1907, R. H. Mathews Papers, NLA MS 8006/2/11.

[25] Mathew to Mathews, 11 February 1909, R. H. Mathews Papers, NLA MS 8006/2/11.

[26] See Jones, John, 'Federation and the Dalungbara', viewed 30 March 2007. <http://brumbywatchaustralia.com/WelcomeFraser06.htm>

[27] Aldridge to Mathews, 10 September 1898, R. H. Mathews Papers, NLA MS 8006/2/6.

[28] The extent of this reliance is becoming more apparent with the publication of several volumes of anthropological correspondence. See, for example, Mulvaney, John, Morphy, Howard, and Petch, Alison (eds) 2001, *My Dear Spencer: The Letters of F. J. Gillen to Baldwin Spencer*, Hyland House, Melbourne [1ˢᵗ pub. 1997] and Mulvaney, John, Morphy, Howard, and Petch, Alison (eds) 2000, *From the Frontier: Outback Letters to Baldwin Spencer*, Allen & Unwin, Sydney.

[29] Miller to Howitt, 13 August 1907, A. W. Howitt Papers, SLV MSS 9356/Box 1049/7(a).

[30] Spencer to Howitt, 15 August 1907.

[31] RHM 1904-5, 'Ethnological Notes on the Aboriginal Tribes of Queensland', p. 74.

[32] RHM 1907, 'Ethnological Notes on the Aboriginal Tribes of New South Wales and Victoria [Letter to the Editor]', *Nature*, vol. 76, no. 1958.

[33] Howitt, A. W. 1907 'Literature relating to Australian Aborigines [Letter to the editor]', *Nature*, vol. 77, no. 1987, p. 81.

[34] Howitt, A. W. 1908, 'The Native Tribes of Southeast Australia', *American Antiquarian*, vol. 30, and RHM 1909, 'Sociology of some Australian Tribes', *American Antiquarian*, vol. 31.

[35] Howitt, A. W. 1908, 'A Message to Anthropologists', *Revue des Études Ethnographiques et Sociologiques*, vol. 1.

[36] See Thomas, Martin 2005, 'Looking for Mr Mathews: Uncovering the traces of an early Australian anthropologist', *Meanjin*, vol. 64, no. 3.

[37] Biographical and Historical Notes of the Mathews Family, R. H. Mathews Papers, NLA MS 8006/7/8.

[38] Interview with Frank Mathews, 1971.

[39] Mathews to Strehlow, 14 November 1905, Strehlow Research Centre Manuscripts, Alice Springs.

[40] Diary 1893-1907, R. H. Mathews Papers, NLA MS 8006/1/2.

[41] Spencer to Frazer, 13 June 1903, Sir Baldwin Spencer Manuscripts, Pitt Rivers Museum (henceforth PRM) MSS Box 5/Frazer 51.

[42] Frazer to Spencer, 19 April 1908, Sir Baldwin Spencer Manuscripts, PRM MS Box 5/Frazer 70.

[43] Lang, Andrew 1903, *Social Origins*, Longmans, Green, and Co, London, p. 38.

[44] Lang to Hartland, 19 October [year not stated].

[45] The paper referred to by Roth is in fact co-authored. See RHM and Everitt, M. M. 1900, 'The Organisation, Language and Initiation Ceremonies of the Aborigines of the South-East Coast of N. S. Wales', *Journal and Proceedings of the Royal Society of New South Wales*, vol. 34. Records of the Royal Society of New South Wales indicate that the two were still friendly in April 1901 when Mathews presented two papers on Everitt's behalf. This was necessary because women were not admitted as members. See Records of Council Meetings, Royal Society of New South Wales Minutes 1894-1903, 13 March and 24 April 1901.

[46] Roth to Spencer, 8 February 1903, Sir Baldwin Spencer Manuscripts, PRM MSS Box 1A/Roth 14.

[47] See Thomas, Martin 2004, 'R. H. Mathews and anthropological warfare: On writing the biography of a "self-contained man"', *Aboriginal History*, vol. 28.

[48] Executive Committee Minutes, 9 February 1904 and 20 October 1903, Records of the Royal Anthropological Institute, London, F 80 and F 90-1.

[49] RHM 1904, 'Ethnological Notes on the Aboriginal Tribes of New South Wales and Victoria', p. 204.

[50] Elkin, A. P. 1975, 'R. H. Mathews: His Contribution to Aboriginal Studies: Part II', *Oceania*, vol. 46, no. 2.

[51] Ferguson to Mathews, 19 March 1918, R. H. Mathews Papers, NLA MS 8006/8/544.

[52] 'A Noted Ethnologist: Robert Hamilton Mathews', R. H. Mathews Papers, NLA MS 8006/7/8.

[53] Bates to Mathews, 13 June 1905, R. H. Mathews Papers, NLA MS 8006/2/10.

[54] Mathews to Bates, 13 April 1905, Daisy Bates Papers, NLA MSS 365/970/250-381.

[55] R. H. Mathews Papers, NLA MSS 8006/2/11.

[56] Mulvaney, D. J. and Calaby, J. H. 1985 *'So Much That is New': Baldwin Spencer, 1860-1929: A Biography*, Melbourne University Press, Carlton, p. 370.

[57] Prentis, Malcolm 1998, *Science, Race and Faith: A Life of John Mathew*, Centre for the Study of Australian Christianity, Sydney, p. 136. Lang expressed disbelief at the rejection, declaring that 'very few *theses* are so well deserving of a degree'.

[58] Lévi-Strauss, Claude 1992, *Tristes Tropiques*, Penguin, Harmondsworth [1ˢᵗ pub. 1955], p. 383.

[59] RHM 1896, 'The Bora of the Kamilaroi Tribes', p. 137.

[60] Belmont, Nicole 1979, *Arnold Van Gennep: The Creator of French Ethnography*, University of Chicago Press, Chicago [1st pub. 1974], p. 27.

[61] RHM 1907, 'Beiträge zur Ethnographie der Australier', *Mitteilungen der Anthropologischen Gesellschaft*, vol. 27, p. 34. Reproduced this volume.

[62] Elkin 1976, 'R. H. Mathews: Part II', p. 132.

[63] Mathews to Bates, 29 August 1905, Daisy Bates Papers, NLA MSS 365/970/250-381.

[64] See Donaldson, Tamsin 1985, 'Hearing the First Australians' in Donaldson, Ian and Donaldson, Tamsin (eds), *Seeing the First Australians*, George Allen & Unwin, Sydney, p. 85.

[65] Diary 1879-90, entry for 22 April 1884, R. H. Mathews Papers, NLA MS 8006/1/1.

[66] Atchison, John, 'Hamilton Bartlett Mathews', *Australian Dictionary of Biography*, Online Edition, viewed 28 June 2006. <www.adb.online.anu.edu.au/biogs/A100431b.htm>

[67] See Thomas, Martin 2003, '"To You Mrs Mathews": The Cross-Cultural Recording of Janet Mathews 1914-1992', *The Australasian Sound Archive*, vol. 29, Winter.

[68] Mathews, Janet 1994, *The Opal that Turned into Fire*, Magabala Books, Broome, WA, pp. 161-2.

[69] Interview with Herbert Chapman, AIATSIS Audio Archive, J11 - 01019B.

[70] F. A. Ray to Elkin, 26 August 1936, Elkin Papers, University of Sydney Archives (henceforth USyd Archives), P130/41/53.

[71] Elkin to F. A. Ray, 10 September 1936, Elkin Papers, USyd Archives, P130/41/53.

[72] Enright, W. J. 1899, 'The Initiation Ceremonies of the Aborigines of Port Stephens, N. S. Wales', *Journal and Proceedings of the Royal Society of New South Wales*, vol. 33, pp. 115-16.

[73] RHM 1897, 'Bullroarers used by the Australian Aborigines', *Journal of the Anthropological Institute*, vol. 27, p. 58.

[74] RHM 1896, 'The Bora, or Initiation Ceremonies of the Kamilaroi Tribe (Part II)', *Journal of the Anthropological Institute*, vol. 25, p. 319.

[75] Mathews' copy of *Native Tribes* is Item 262, Elkin Collection, Fisher Library Rare Books, University of Sydney.

[76] Ibid, p. 391.

[77] Ibid, p. 389.

[78] Ibid, pp. 390-93.

[79] Biographical and Historical Notes of the Mathews Family.

[80] Ibid.

[81] Interview with Frank Mathews, 1971.

[82] Koch, Harold 2007, 'R. H. Mathews' schema for the description of Australian languages' in McGregor, William (ed.), *Excavating Australia's linguistic past: Studies in the history of Aboriginal linguistics*, Pacific Linguistics, Canberra.

[83] Biographical and Historical Notes of the Mathews Family.

[84] RHM 1904, 'Ethnological Notes on the Aboriginal Tribes of New South Wales and Victoria', p. 203.

[85] Biographical and Historical Notes of the Mathews Family.

[86] RHM 1910, 'Does Exogamy Exist in Australian Tribes?' *Revue d'Ethnographie et de Sociologie*, vol. 5, p. 1.

[87] RHM, Survey Book. Collection of Susan Upton.

[88] Mathews, Gregory M. 1942, *Birds and Books: The Story of the Mathews Ornithological Library*, Verity Hewett Bookshop, Canberra, p. 12

[89] Ibid, p. 12.

[90] Biographical and Historical Notes of the Mathews Family.

[91] Amount earned by Licensed Surveyor Mathews from the Government in Six Years, from Official Records, R. H. Mathews Papers, NLA MS 8006/7/2.

[92] Ibid.

[93] Diary 1879-90, entry for 11 November 1880.

[94] Mathews, G. M. 1942, *Birds and Books*, p. 15.

[95] Diary 1879-90, entries for 28 July 1895 and 23 November 1888.

[96] Letter of Credit, 9 May 1882, R. H. Mathews Papers, NLA MS 8006/7/4.

[97] Diary 1879-90, entry for 28 August 1889.

[98] Ibid, entry for 15 May 1882.

[99] Biographical and Historical Notes of the Mathews Family.

[100] 'Late Mr. R. H. Mathews', *Sydney Morning Herald*, 28 May 1918, p. 8.

[101] Letter of Credit, 9 May 1882.

[102] RHM 1907, 'Beiträge zur Ethnographie', p. 30 (note). Reproduced this volume.

[103] Mathews to Hartland, 27 September 1908, Letters to E. S. Hartland, NLW MS 16889 (see 'Correspondence', this volume).

[104] Mathews to Bartlett, 18 February 1872, R. H. Mathews Papers, NLA MS 8006/7/8. This early correspondence between Robert and Mary is evidentially problematic in that we do not have originals but only copies in William Mathews' hand. Still, I see no reason to doubt their veracity. In documenting his father, William copied many pages from his publications and other documents, always with fidelity to the original.

[105] Van Gennep to Mathews, 28 October 1907, R. H. Mathews Papers, NLA MS 8006/2/13.

[106] Belmont, *Arnold Van Gennep*, and Zumwalt, Rosemary 1982, 'Arnold van Gennep: The Hermit of the Bourg-la-Reine', *American Anthropologist*, vol. 84 (new series), no. 2.

[107] McLean to Mathews, 8 December 1905, R. H. Mathews Papers, NLA MS 8006/2/7.

[108] Schmidt, Annette 1993, *The Loss of Australia's Aboriginal Language Heritage*, Aboriginal Studies Press, Canberra, p. 1.

[109] I acknowledge that in northern and central parts of Australia, a tongue is sometimes replaced by pidgin or a more dominant Aboriginal language. These remarks apply principally to the areas where Mathews worked in southeast Australia.

[110] RHM 1904, 'Die Műltyerra-Initiationszeremonie', *Mitteilungen der Anthropologischen Gesellschaft*, vol. 34, p. 77. Reproduced this volume.

[111] RHM 1896, 'The Būnăn Ceremony of New South Wales', *American Anthropologist*, vol. 9.

[112] RHM 1904, 'Die Multyerra-Initiationszeremonie', p. 78. Reproduced this volume.

[113] RHM 1897, 'The Burbung of the Darkinung Tribes', *Proceedings of the Royal Society of Victoria*, vol. 10 (new series), p. 12.

[114] Diary 1879-90, entry for 4 November 1885.

[115] See Thomas, Martin 2007, 'The Ethnomania of R. H. Mathews: Anthropology and the rage for collecting' in Gretchen Poiner and Sybil Jack (eds), *Limits of Location: Creating a Colony*, Sydney University Press, Sydney.

[116] Diary 1879-90, entry for 6-14 June 1884.

[117] Ibid, entry for 8 August 1884.

[118] Ibid, entry for 11 July 1884.

[119] Fitzgerald, Shirley 1990, *Chippendale: Beneath the Factory Wall*, Hale & Iremonger, Sydney, pp. 54-64.

[120] Brooks, Barbara and Clark, Judith 1998, *Eleanor Dark: A Writer's Life*, Pan Macmillan, Sydney, p. 14

[121] Biographical and Historical Notes of the Mathews Family.

[122] Ibid.

[123] Ibid.

[124] Ibid.

[125] RHM 1893, 'Rock Paintings by the Aborigines in Caves on Bulgar Creek, near Singleton', *Journal and Proceedings of the Royal Society of New South Wales*, vol. 27, p. 358.

[126] Mathews to Bates, 14 November 1905, Daisy Bates Papers, NLA MSS 365/970/250-381.

[127] Boas, Franz 1974, 'On Alternating Sounds' in Stocking, George Jr (ed.), *The Shaping of American Anthropology 1883-1911: A Franz Boas Reader*, Basic Books, New York, p. 76.

[128] Stocking, George 1995, *After Tylor: British Social Anthropology 1888-1951*, University of Wisconsin Press, Madison, p. 12.

[129] Elkin, A. P. 1956, 'A. R. Radcliffe-Brown, 1880-1955', *Oceania*, vol. 26, no. 4, pp. 249-50.

[130] Tindale to McCarthy, 12 February 1958, Papers of Frederick D. McCarthy, ML MS 3188/1350, Box H 2313. I am indebted to Val Attenbrow for bringing this reference to my attention.

[131] Stanner to Elkin, 4 June 1975, Elkin Papers, USyd Archives, MS P.130/9/131.

[132] Barwick, Diane E. 1984, 'Mapping the Past: An Atlas of Victoria Clans 1835-1904 Part 1', *Aboriginal History*, vol. 8, no. 1-2, p. 102.

[133] Mathews to Hartland, 9 April 1907.

[134] Wolfe, Patrick 1999, *Settler Colonialism and the Transformation of Anthropology: The Politics and Poetics of an Ethnographic Event*, Cassell, London, p. 126.

[135] Hill, Barry 2002, *Broken Song: T. G. H. Strehlow and Aboriginal Possession*, Knopf, Milsons Point, NSW, p. 225 (note).

Part 1: Rock Art and Daily Life

Introduction

Martin Thomas

In these three texts we meet R. H. Mathews as a student of rock art and as a close observer of daily life in Aboriginal communities. Evidence of his surveying background is apparent in all three publications, though with very different effect. The two rock art papers reveal his determination to measure, record and physically locate each art site discussed. In contrast, 'Contributions to the Ethnography of the Australians' (1907) takes us into the domestic environment of Aboriginal camps. In all these papers Mathews reveals a keen interest in how Aboriginal people deal with the practical problems of sustenance, survival and self-expression. He also turns his attention to the much neglected subject of leisure and recreation.

I will start by considering the rock art documentation, which is integral to understanding Mathews as an anthropologist. It was a short paper on this subject that launched his ethnological career in 1893.[1] His son William records that this first paper, a discussion of art sites in the southern part of the Hunter Valley, was well received by the Royal Society of New South Wales. He received particular encouragement from W. D. Campbell, a fellow surveyor with an interest in ethnology, whom Mathews quotes in the 1910 article, reproduced here. Campbell was already collecting material for the Royal Society's 1894 essay competition, which had as its topic 'the Aboriginal Rock Carvings and Paintings in New South Wales'.[2] Mathews prepared an entry at Campbell's suggestion—to the latter's disadvantage as events transpired. In late 1893 and early the following year, Mathews made a number of field trips, travelling as far west as Mudgee, and to Howes Valley on the Macdonald River, northwest of Sydney. He also visited a variety of locations in the Sydney Basin including the Botany Bay settlement of La Perouse. Mathews won the essay prize and this encouraged him to pursue his research further. His victory was blemished, however, by the refusal of the Royal Society of New South Wales to publish his paper, as was customary for a prize essay. To the irritation of the society's executive, it was discovered that Mathews had published a condensed form of his paper in the 1894 *Proceedings of the Royal Society of Victoria*.[3] There was little friendliness between the rival societies; all publications were supposed to be original and unpublished. So Mathews sought other forums for his extensive rock art documentation, sending submissions to journals in France, Britain and the United States. His work was widely welcomed, and he ultimately published 23 articles containing descriptions of rock art in the years between 1893 and 1912.

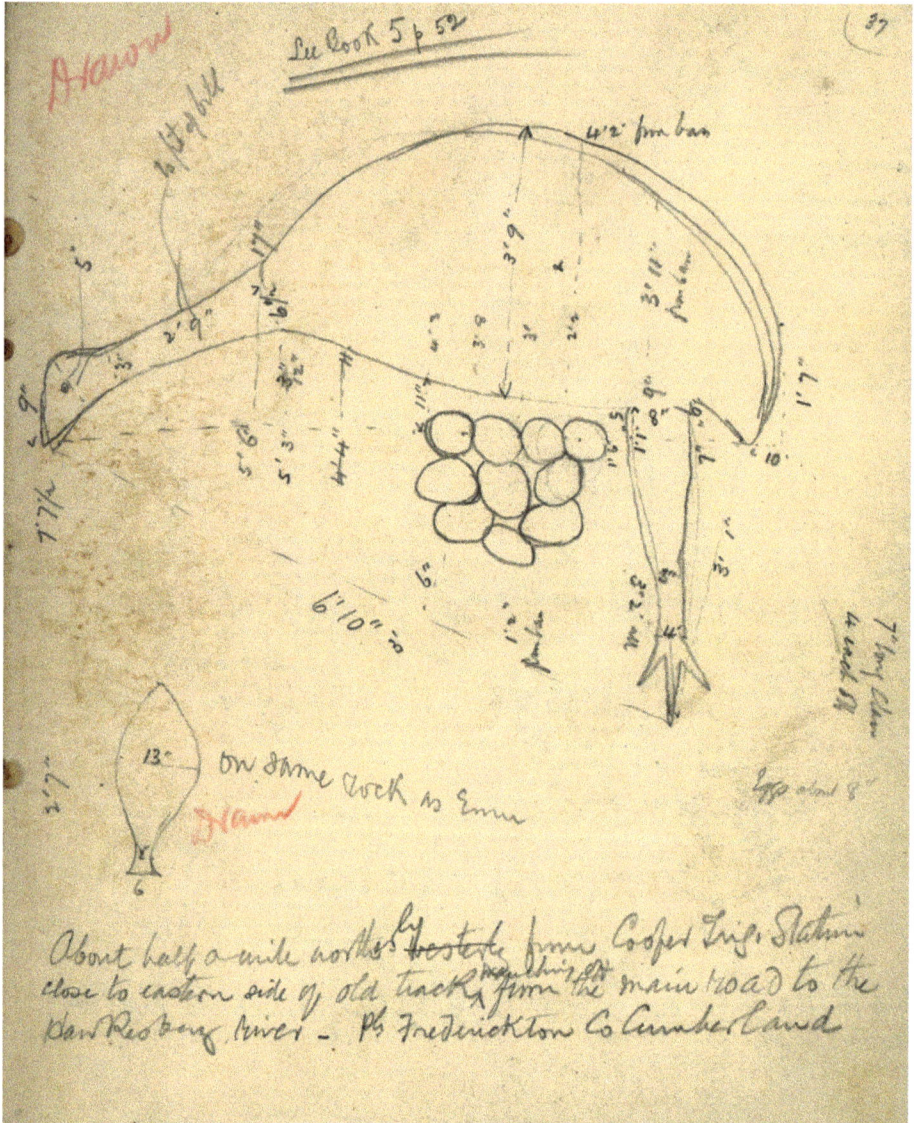

This drawing from a notebook shows how R. H. Mathews approached the documentation of Aboriginal rock art. The image drawn here is a rock engraving at the site known as Devils Rock near the Hawkesbury River, NSW. By permission of the National Library of Australia. (NLA MS 8006/3/2).

Translated here are the two rock art papers Mathews published in a foreign language. Both are pointedly directed at French anthropologists who (as we see in the discussion recorded at the end of the 1898 paper) discerned connections between Aboriginal art and ancient cave paintings in Europe and elsewhere. Three images of sea creatures, engraved in the sandstone at La Perouse, are described in the 1898 article, titled 'Rock Carvings and Paintings by the Australian Aborigines'. He also describes caves containing hand stencils. One, near Dural Creek, he could have reached by horse from his home in the western Sydney suburb of Parramatta. The other, at Coxs Creek, west of the Blue Mountains, he visited while researching his prize essay.[4]

Discussing the settlement of La Perouse, Mathews explains (perhaps unnecessarily with this audience) that it is named after the famed French navigator who stayed there briefly in 1788. This French connection inspires him to give a précis of La Pérouse's visit to Australia. For Mathews this was a rare segue into matters historical. Otherwise the article adheres to his usual formula for describing rock art.

Mathews was clearly intrigued by cave paintings, hand stencils and the spectacular representations of people, animals, artefacts and spirit ancestors that adorn so many sandstone platforms in the Sydney region. As he knew from his library-based research, Europeans from the time of the First Fleet had been moved to comment on, or reproduce in their notebooks, the rock art they observed along the Sydney foreshore. But little systematic documentation had been attempted. Mathews, Campbell and R. J. Etheridge Junior, a curator at the Australian Museum, were part of a small cluster of individuals who in the late nineteenth century began to document this art in a 'scientific' fashion.

Mathews would always try to identify the motifs depicted at an art site (animals, implements, men or women, etc). Using his surveyor's methods, he gave the county, parish and portion number so that others could readily find it. As we know from his notebooks, he measured each artwork carefully and copied it with a high degree of fidelity. He considered this method more accurate than photography. Eventually he worked his drawings into illustrative plates for an article.

Admittedly, there are limitations to what Mathews achieved in these papers. His illustrations reveal something about his assumptions, for despite his surveying background, suggestive of an interest in locality, he did not attempt to *map* the art site. That is to say, he did not analyse its location in relation to water supply, camping grounds, shelters, or other (possibly related) cultural sites—all of which might impact upon its meaning. Nor did he remark on the often stunning views obtained from many of the engraved rock platforms, which might also reflect on their significance. Rather, Mathews tended to treat the carved and painted motifs as specimens, arranging them in an almost ornamental fashion on the page. Similarly, he said little at all about the meaning of the art, or its possible connection with ceremonial life.

Possibly, this dearth of cultural information is due to the location of the sites discussed. The Sydney region is extremely rich in Aboriginal art. A total of 875 rock shelters containing painted motifs have been recorded; there are almost as many rock engravings.[5] But since this was the first area to suffer colonisation, the few Aboriginal survivors lost contact with many rituals and traditions. As revealed in 'Rock Carvings and Paintings by the Australian Aborigines', he spoke to Aboriginal people about their art where possible. Always curious about the age of the art, he was interested to hear that the engravings at La Perouse predated the arrival of the British. At the outset, Mathews was curious about whether Aboriginal art-making in Sydney had continued into the post-contact period. He came to realise that in parts of the Sydney Basin rock art traditions had survived and were possibly continuing. Charley Clark, who lived at the Sackville Reach Aboriginal Reserve near Windsor,[6] was introduced to him as a maker of hand stencils near the Hawkesbury.[7] Mathews also met a Darkinung man named Andy Barber who led him to a rock engraving that he remembered being made in the 1850s. Located in the parish of Wilberforce, it depicts a white settler wearing a cabbage-tree hat and carrying an axe. Barber testified that the artist was a man known as Hiram.[8] These are among the very few cases where works of Sydney rock art can be attributed to particular individuals.

Poignantly, Mathews reported that when Hiram depicted the foreigner striding into his territory, he made the carving with a European axe instead of traditional implements. Mathews was always interested in the practical business of how things were made and how people survived with the technological resources available to them. His own surveying experience, which involved camping out for extended periods, led him to respect the makers of traditional arts and crafts. Hence his interest in the technique used by Aboriginal artists to create smooth grooves in Hawkesbury sandstone, a medium likely to split and shatter. In the 1910 paper (reproduced here), Mathews accurately describes their production. First 'a row of holes was pierced with a piece of pointed stone, establishing the outline of the drawing, after which the intervals between these holes were cut in such a way as to produce an uninterrupted groove'.

In reading this work we must bear in mind that Mathews' enthusiasm for his subject is sometimes obscured by his desire to sound authoritative and scientific. For example, in an early article he describes rock art in the following way:

> Rude pictorial representations found on the walls of caves and on the smooth surfaces of rocks in various parts of Australia show that the aboriginal inhabitants were not altogether without appreciation of the beauties of art. Drawings more or less artistic and elaborate have been found in a number of places throughout Australia.[9]

R. H. Mathews observed this rock carving of a settler in the parish of Wilberforce, northwest of Sydney. Andy Barber, a Darkinung man, told him the artist's name was Hiram and he carved it with a steel hatchet during the 1850s. This is a rare case where an example of Sydney rock art can be attributed to a particular artist. By permission of the National Library of Australia. (Fieldbook No.5, NLA MS8006/3/3).

If the tone sounds condescending, or seems to damn with faint praise, we must keep in mind the context in which he was working. Mathews' choice of level-headed, unemotional language was integral to his argument that Aboriginal life was important and worthy of study. His diction set him apart in a society that positioned 'blackfellows' as objects of ridicule, even in supposedly scientific forums. Compare Mathews' description to that of his contemporary, Robert L. Jack, writing about rock art in 1896.

> The figures about to be described are not introduced to your notice on account of their artistic merits, which would hardly procure for them a place in the National Gallery. They are, in fact, not much above the level of the dawn of art displayed on school slates. As examples of the art of

a race in a stage of intellectual infancy, and which race will certainly die before attaining manhood, they possess, however, a certain interest for ethnologists.[10]

This was the prevailing culture of Mathews' epoch, the mores of which he subtly resisted. While it is unfortunate that his writings do not elucidate the cultural meaning of rock art in greater detail, his plain descriptions and illustrations afford it a dignity. It was his fascination with rock art that drew Mathews into anthropology and led him to explore his Aboriginal contacts and friendships in new ways. Soon he would be studying initiations, making careful observations of the ceremonial grounds and the designs marked on trees or carved directly into the earth. In his writings on ceremony the cultural meaning of art is seen from a very different perspective.

*

'Contributions to the Ethnography of the Australians' (1907), the first article presented here, was published by *Mitteilungen der Anthropologischen Gesellschaft*, a leading Austrian journal. Mathews published nine articles in this forum during the period 1903-10. This is an important article, unlike any other he published. Running to more than 11,000 words, it is his longest foreign-language publication. After its translation back into English, I discovered that the text is very similar to the chapter of an unpublished book by Mathews, a draft of which survives in the National Library of Australia.[11] This is probably the manuscript that Mathews tried unsuccessfully to publish in England (see letters to E. S. Hartland in 'Correspondence', this volume). So the article provides important insights into how Mathews intended to synthesise his observations on Aboriginal life for an international readership.

Superficially, the theme of the article is material culture. But it is very different to Mathews' other writings on the subject which typically consist of taxonomic descriptions of weapons, bullroarers, message sticks, etc. This article is very much concerned with material culture in its social context. Mathews gives fascinating information on subjects ranging from tool-making to ball games and other pastimes. He states that all information 'is the result of my own observations and visits to natives of various districts', although some data are drawn from published sources including E. M. Curr's *The Australian Race* (1886). Mathews says at the beginning of the paper that the 'geographic spread of the individual custom is in every case fixed', a promise not always fulfilled. Even so, the close observations of camp life in Aboriginal communities make this article especially valuable. It is Mathews' most sustained evocation of the communities where he sat, ate and talked for extended periods, studying language, kinship and other aspects of traditional life.

ENDNOTES

[1] RHM 1893, 'Rock Paintings by the Aborigines in Caves on Bulgar Creek, near Singleton', *Journal and Proceedings of the Royal Society of New South Wales*, vol. 27.

[2] Biographical and Historical Notes of the Mathews Family, R. H. Mathews Papers, National Library of Australia (henceforth NLA) MS 8006/7/8.

[3] Thomas, Martin 2004, 'R. H. Mathews and anthropological warfare: On writing the biography of a "self-contained man"', *Aboriginal History*, vol. 28.

[4] Diary 1893-1907, entry for 3 January 1894. R. H. Mathews Papers, NLA MS 8006/1/2.

[5] Attenbrow, Val 2002, *Sydney's Aboriginal Past*, UNSW Press, University of New South Wales, p. 146.

[6] RHM 1897, 'The Burbung of the Darkinung Tribes', *Proceedings of the Royal Society of Victoria*, vol. 10 (new series), p. 1.

[7] Red notebook, R. H. Mathews Papers, NLA MS 8006/3/11, p. 1.

[8] RHM 1896, 'Rock Carving by the Australian Aborigines', *Proceedings of the Royal Society of Queensland*, vol. 12, p. 97 and Red notebook, p. 1.

[9] RHM 1894-95, 'Aboriginal Rock Pictures of Australia', *Proceedings and Transactions of the Queensland Branch of the Royal Geographical Society of Australasia*, vol. 10, p. 46.

[10] Jack, Robert L. 1896, 'On Aboriginal Cave-Drawings of the Palmer Goldfield', *Proceedings of the Royal Society of Queensland*, vol. 11, p. 91.

[11] *Australian Aborigines* [manuscript of book], R. H. Mathews Papers, NLA MS 8006/5/6.

Contributions to the Ethnography of the Australians

R. H. Mathews

First published as 'Beiträge zur Ethnographie der Australier' in *Mitteilungen der Anthropologischen Gesellschaft*, vol. 27, 1907, pp. 18-38. The article was written in English and translated into German by an unnamed translator. This version was retranslated into English by Christine Winter.

Mutilations and other customs of Australian natives; their dwellings, utensils, and daily life

The Anthropological Society of Vienna has, in earlier issues, included some of my contributions, in which I have provided information about the natives of Australia, and which deal with sociology, language, initiation ceremonies and vendettas.

In this article at hand I will provide a short outline of some particular mutilations, as well as other customs, including piercing of the nasal septum; extraction of teeth; amputation of fingers; *mumbirbirri* or scarification design; and dried hands as amulets. Further, I will deal with canoes and rafts, then give an account of dwellings, weapons, utensils, clothing, games, fire-making and other customs of daily life.

All information contained in the following pages is the result of my own observations and visits to natives of various districts. Where I refer to work of other authors the location is indicated from where the relevant statement is taken. The geographic spread of the individual custom disclosed is in every case fixed.

The work at hand is intended to deliver, together with my earlier contributions, an introduction to the customs of the natives of Australia, and I hope to have rendered a service to German ethnographers and to those who live in colonies where similar races exist.

The mutilations connected with circumcision and the splitting of the urethra for men and the widening of the orficium vaginae for women, which is practised in some parts of Australia I have already described in other works and I will therefore not repeat myself here.[1]

Piercing of the nasal septum

This custom is spread very widely, and is practised in various parts of Australia. Among the native tribes of the southeast coast of New South Wales this act occurred after the initiation of a young man, during the colder months. It is generally done with a sharp pointed bone or a piece of hard wood. During ceremonial occasions a wing bone of *uroaetus audax* [wedge tailed eagle] is carried in the hole and forms part of the gala decorations.

Of course, injuring such a sensitive organ as the nose causes considerable swelling, so that the patient has to breathe mainly through the mouth. In some cases the swelling is so great that the skin stretches so far that the cartilage of the septum breaks through at the bottom side and the inserted pin is pushed out. In my youth I saw old blacks whose nasal septum showed clear signs of such a rupture.

A thin piece of wood, bone, a feather, a grass stalk or the like is put into the freshly made wound and turned at intervals over and over again—a painful operation. The hole was widened bit by bit, until it was wide enough to take in a peg of proper size, which then had to be carried constantly for ceremonial occasions or when a person was not working.

In all the regions of Australia I have had the opportunity to visit, the piercing of the nasal cartilage was customary for men and women. Looking through various works about the natives I find that nearly all observers report seeing natives who carried some ornament in the nose. It is practised in the whole of New South Wales and Victoria, also in Queensland, South Australia and in the Northern Territory. In regard to Western Australia I have asked some of my friends who reside there to inquire into this matter, and they now report that most of the tribes practise nasal piercing, although some tribes in the southern part of this state are said to have intact noses.

As already mentioned with some tribes of New South Wales, a youth cannot have his nose pierced before undergoing his initiation ceremony; but there are other areas in Australia where the operation is performed on very young boys and girls and apparently is not accompanied by any further ceremony.

Extraction of teeth

In an article published in this journal[2] I described the Mŭltyerra ceremony. In it I gave precise details of the procedure whereby a tooth is extracted by the natives. This custom prevails in the greater part of Australia without, however, being universal. Sometimes it is the right upper incisor which is extracted, sometimes the left one, and in other cases both middle incisors are removed. Then there are areas where the women, too, are operated upon, while elsewhere the custom is restricted to men. In the eastern part of the continent the operation was usually connected with initiation ceremonies, which was not necessarily the case in the central and western regions, even though the operation is usually accompanied by some ritual.

The most southern part of the Australian mainland where incisors were extracted was the central and northern parts of the state of Victoria. I dealt with this extensively in my report on 'The Wonggumuk Ceremony of Initiation'.[3] In New South Wales we find the custom in various places, in the interior and along the coast; examples are contained in my description of 'The Bŭnān Ceremony of New South Wales'.[4]

In 1900 I mentioned the extraction of an incisor in my description of the *Toara* or *Dora* ceremony, which can be encountered along the Mary, Dawson and other rivers in southern Queensland.[5] After enquiries I made to individuals residing at various places it seems that, as is mentioned above, the extraction of teeth on the Australian continent is a common, but not a general, phenomenon.

Amputation of phalanges

Another curious mutilation occurs which is not practised universally, but it is widely spread over the Australian continent. The following short report will show the occurrence of the custom in parts of New South Wales, Queensland, the Northern Territory and Western Australia. It was mainly in vogue amongst women near the coast, but its appearance was observed amongst individual inland tribes. As far as I am informed it was usually the little finger that was amputated, but occasionally one of the other fingers instead. Then we will see that in most cases where such mutilations have been reported they are solely restricted to women, but in some parts of Australia the loss of a phalanx is also claimed by men.

Amongst the Thurrawal speaking tribes, from Port Hacking down to the Shoalhaven River, there are certain women who are missing two phalanges, though sometimes only one, of the little finger of one hand. Mostly it was the right hand, but it also occurred that the little finger of the left hand was mutilated in this way. Out in the scrub there are large spiders that spin a strong thread from tree to tree or from bush to bush. Some of these spider's threads were collected by a native and put together as a fine string, which was wound as tight as the twine permitted around the finger at the phalanx, the amputation of which was intended. Thus the circulation of blood was stopped and the distal end of the finger died off. The wound then healed very quickly.

According to my own observations, I can state that this custom existed everywhere along the coast of New South Wales from Tuross River to the Manning. During my official travels in this region as surveyor, and also during special excursions amongst the natives, I undertook examinations into the causes of these mutilations. Insofar as I could inform myself about them from old natives, they carried the character of magic with them, because a woman who was mutilated in this way was supposed to have more skilfulness and success catching fish than other women who were not. The amputation was carried out on very young girls in the described manner to appoint them as fishers with rod and line. It also served to distinguish the respective woman from others who had different occupations.

E. M. Curr says that in Queensland, from Brisbane to Gympie, '[m]others used to bind round at the second joint, the little finger of the left hand of their daughters when about 10 years old, with coarse spider's webs so as to stop circulation and cause the two joints to drop off.'[6] The same author reports that between the Albert and Tweed rivers the girls during childhood have the small finger of the left hand cut off.[7] He also says that at Halifax Bay the women have a phalanx of the right thumb amputated.[8] Where Curr talks about the natives of Fraser Island, from the mouth of Mary River up, he says: 'Women have the first phalanx of the little finger of the right hand amputated during their youth.'[9]

The late Edward Palmer told me that he noticed the loss of a finger with blacks around Tower Hill and the surrounding area, between Maghenden and Muttaburra. He had observed the same mutilation with tribes at Mitchell River on the Cape York Peninsula, but he was unable to remember which finger was missing there.

In the Northern Territory Reverend Donald MacKillop observed this custom at Daly River. Talking about the women he said: 'When young girls they remove the two first joints of the right forefinger. The operation is most artistically performed, judging by results. Yet they use no knife or, as when circumcising, sharp stone. They find in the jungles a very strong cobweb, and with a thin skein of this they tie tightly round the joint. The circulation is, of course, stopped, and after a time the dead joints fall off. This custom is far from universal.'[10]

From Beagle Bay in Western Australia Captain J. L. Stokes reports on the appearance of the natives: 'All of them had lost one of the front teeth, and several one finger joint; in this particular they differed from the natives seen in Roebuck Bay, amongst whom the practice of this mutilation did not prevail.'[11]

Mumbirbirri or scar drawing

Raised scars as a consequence of incisions into the flesh on the shoulders, breast and arms is a custom widely spread amongst the natives of Australia. The effect of the scarification is so conspicuous and noticeable on the nude body of the savage, that nearly every author who met Australian natives observed the scars, but their meaning has not been secured and remains unknown.

I was lucky to be the first to discover the interesting details of this custom and reported them in a paper presented to the Royal Society of New South Wales on 5 October 1904. I have reprinted this article together with a number of others in the form of a book titled *Ethnological Notes on the Aboriginal Tribes of New South Wales and Victoria*. I can therefore refer my readers here to this work, where a short report of the *Mumbirbirri* ceremony can be found.[12]

Dried hands as amulets

A universally practised custom amongst the natives of New South Wales and Victoria was also to carry the dried hand of a deceased person around, in some cases of a friend or relative, in other cases of an enemy. Indeed, all Australian tribes I have met have an unshakable believe in the helpful influence of some part of a human corpse in everyday life as well as during hunting undertakings or raids on their enemies. First the results of my own observations are recounted, followed by reports of early colonists, which go back to the 1860s and 70s.

Some old men of the Darkiñung and Thurrawal tribes in New South Wales have told me that their forefathers used to have the firm belief that the wearing of dried or preserved hands was an effective protection against their enemies. Such an amulet was carried in a small bag, which was tied over one shoulder and hung under the armpit of the other. Sometimes a dried hand was tied to the neck with a string and hung down to the chest. Another dried hand could also be attached to the neck band and hung on the back of the wearer between the shoulder blades.

When an evil-minded individual or a hostile gang of several people came to inconvenience the wearer of this amulet, he assumed he was scratched by the preserved hand, or had the skin made mangy, on the side of the body from which the enemy had come. For example, if a man thus equipped was scratched by the dried hand which he wore on his chest, then he knew that an enemy was somewhere in front of him. If the hand hung between the shoulder blades pinched the wearer, then the enemy was somewhere at the rear. Then, if the amulet he carried under the armpit showed signs of agitation, an adversary was nearing from this direction, and so forth. A sudden twitching of the muscles or an irritation of the skin, the blacks would understand to have been brought about by the preserved hand, and it gives them a warning towards that side. If a man wears only one such appendage it is believed that it has the power to give him the signal, from whichever side of the body danger might come, without him being aware that it has moved from its usual place as its movements are regarded as invisible.

These dried hands in the same way have the power to give warnings about harmful magic of a hostile wizard, whether he is located far or near, and enable the wearer of the amulet to fend off the intended misdeed. When the wizard performing the magic is near, the hand is clearer in its warning than when he is far away. The proximity of game and its direction are also indicated in the same way.

It is not absolutely necessary that the amulet consist of a hand; parts of a foot or a hand, parts of flesh from arms and legs or the back are regarded as a very effective protective magic in different ways, as is reported below.

Searching for usable grazing land in Gippsland, Victoria, A. MacMillan suddenly came upon an old black, who was not to be got rid off. 'The only ornaments he wore were three hands of men and women, beautifully dried and preserved.'[13]

W. J. Mollison from Pyalong, Victoria, learned that '[t]here are traditions of portions of the body, usually hands or fingers, being observed in the lubras' bags ... Certainly, in conversation, they admitted the fact'.[14]

Hugh Jamieson[15] from Mildura, Victoria, said under a report dated 10 October 1853, but concerning much earlier experiences amongst the natives: 'On some occasions, in accordance with superstitious rite, they carry about with them the legs, arms, and pieces of the skin of their victim, not for the purpose of eating these, but with the view of distribution as charms for fishing operations.'

Dr J. Fraser from Maitland said in his report about the murder of some white shepherds many years before at the upper Williams River, New South Wales: 'One old gin [woman] carried about with her in her shoulder-net a hand of one of these shepherds; she would bring it out at times, and pulling the sinews make the fingers move, and say "Bail (no) you make doughboy any more". For this murder one of the blacks was afterwards hanged at Dungog.'[16]

Canoes

When bark of the red gum tree is available it is always used for canoe making because it withstands the weather without rolling or splitting. A canoe is mostly made from one single sheet of bark. When trees are available with a natural bend these are chosen, because canoes thus attained do not require so much work to give them the peculiar shape. When the bark is peeled from the tree, spreaders are at once inserted at intervals of a few feet to avoid rolling in, for as long as sap is still in the bark. Short props are also stuck under the bow and stern so that they might not drop too much under their own weight.

Then the vessel is left to dry for about 14 days, and when it has dried properly it keeps its shape. After a duration of two or three years such a canoe becomes heavy and macerated and accordingly inflexible; then it is necessary to replace it with a new one. The tree from which the bark is taken is chosen according to the size one wants to give the canoe.

The pole or oar that drives the canoe is about 10 or 12 feet long and two or three inches wide. At the other end three sharp tines are attached, two of which have barbs. With one side of this instrument the native drives his boat through the water; with the other he spears a fish coming his way. The oar is made out of pine wood if such is attainable, or from other light timber.

Sometimes a lump of clay is put on the bottom of the canoe to serve as a stove on which a small fire is kept; it serves the double purpose of keeping the native warm and of cooking some of the fish caught. The canoe is, for the natives who live in the vicinity of rivers or great deep expanses of water, a highly prized possession.

Although trees with a natural bulge are preferred, they are not always available, as mentioned above. Stringybark and the bark of the tree known by the name of 'grey box' are often used. When the bark is stripped from the tree some of the outer, rougher layer is split off at the end for a width of about a foot, so that only the flexible inner bark remains. The thus thinned out endings of the bark piece are then folded lengthwise and wrapped with a strong string, which is made out of the fibres of kurrajong or stringybark. Firm ropes made from this tough stringy bark or from thin tendrils are then tied at two or three locations from one side to the other across the vessel to prevent expansion sideways. Spreaders of the same number are attached at the inside of the canoe to serve as ribs and secure the sides of the boat from falling inwards. The folding of the bark does not only hold it straight, but causes it to bend upwards, so that when the binding is finished and the vessel is launched, the ends are a little higher than the sides of the canoe and jut above the water line.

In New South Wales, Victoria, southeastern Queensland and South Australia, and in parts of the Northern Territory, one piece of bark is used to make a canoe. In certain parts of the north the natives use two, three or more pieces of bark, and it is notable that such craft are made more skillfully than those usual in the south, a fact from which one might surmise foreign influence, such as Malays and Papuans, in relatively recent times. In my opinion the canoe made out of one piece of bark is a pure Australian development, as I was unable to detect its occurrence in any other region. The thick, smooth trunks of the eucalypt trees in Australia might easily have suggested to the mind of the natives the use of the bark for huts and canoes. Owing to the warmth of the climate the saps are, during a large part of the year, in ascending and descending circulation, so the stripping and removal of the bark from the trunk becomes a simple and easy task, even with so rough a tool as the stone axe.

Rafts

Along most of the bigger rivers of Australia as well as in the bays of the sea coast the use of rafts was known to the natives. On the Shoalhaven River on the southeast coast of New South Wales the trunk of the cabbage tree palm, a light and strong wood, was used for building rafts. Usually two, sometimes three, dried beams of this wood 15 to 20 feet in length, selected straight, symmetrical and of the same size, were tied together with ropes from stringybark fibres or with tough vines and thus had the ability to carry two or three people over rivers, small bays, and the like. The raft was moved by a paddle or rod, which the boatman, standing on the vessel, plunged into the water on both sides. In shallow waters he drove his raft forward by setting the rod against the bottom of the river.

Occasionally I have seen young boys using one dry plank on which they were sitting with sprawled out legs, feet in the water, and paddling with their hands or a piece of bark. On the Lachlan River, New South Wales, where big reeds grow amass, these were dried and used for building rafts. Bundles of these reeds were tied together with cords, and then three, four or more such reed bundles were treated like the above-mentioned planks by attaching them together with stronger ropes. From weeds or green grass covered with moist soil a place was prepared on which a small fire could be kept. Moving forward was done as with the wooden raft.

The rafts of the natives are frequently in their general principle of construction the same in all parts of Australia and Tasmania where they were observed and described, and likewise the mode of moving forward. The use of rafts is known amongst various primitive peoples across the whole world, and many of these rafts do not differ significantly from those of the Australians.

Although the canoe is used for the same purposes as the raft, the latter has the advantage that it is not so exposed to damage during an accident. To hit a sharp rock or a simple obstacle may damage a plank or bundle, without seriously impeding the raft's ability to float. With a canoe such an accident can, however, cause damage, which cannot be repaired and can even lead to its sinking. Perhaps this is the reason why rafts are so widely in use.

The catamaran and dug-out used by the natives of the Cape York Peninsula, Port Darwin and other northern parts of Australia are not mentioned here, as I do not regard them of pure Australian origin, but as Malayan and Papuan imports. I refer in this regard to works about the Malayan Archipelago and New Guinea.

Camps and dwellings

Their huts are of the roughest kind, rarely more than windbreaks or shelters. First a frame of sticks was put up, to which twigs, reeds or grass were fixed angularly. During wet weather this rough building was covered with bark, if it could be easily obtained from trees at the respective place. Bark can of course only be stripped during the season when the saps are in circulation. A part of one side, or a whole side of the roof, was left free as an entrance, which was always situated on the opposite side from where the wind came. In front of the entrance a fire was kept.

Their dwellings were rarely lived in for more than a few days, as the stay depended on the fecundity of the location. When camping at a river or lagoon, or at an estuary where fish were plentifully available, or during a season when affluence of vegetable food abounded, they stayed longer than when sustenance was sparse.

Along the Hawkesbury, Shoalhaven and some other big rivers, the shores of which consisted of Hawkesbury sandstone, the natives often dwelt in caves or under rock eaves, where they found easy and comfortable accommodation.

As soon as that offered by nature as food was depleted, they were forced to move to a new camping place. Or when a death occurred in one part of the camp everybody had to leave and hurry to another location. During these travels from camp to camp the men usually take a detour or an irregular course, travelling in individual sections,[17] to reach the envisaged camping place by different routes. It would not be advantageous for hunting game or finding any other food if they all travelled together. The women were led in as direct a march as possible, as they were burdened with the children and the luggage.

The location of the huts or roofs in the camp is regulated by certain laws. When a camp is chosen at the shores of a waterhole or river, the older people begin taking up land for their dwellings at the water, while the others put up camp a bit further back. The entrances to the dwellings are situated to the north or northeast, so as to admit the rays of the morning sun, unless the wind comes from that direction. If there is a meeting of the community for a corroboree, or for an initiation ceremony, the local people set up camp first, and the visiting tribes take that side of the general camp for themselves which lies in the direction in which their home is situated. As far as the condition of the ground allows, they take exactly the same position to each other as in their own land, in a kind of miniature depiction of the home camps.

When the men are not searching for meat, which naturally occupies the greater part of their time and thoughts, their main occupation is the production of weapons and utensils or the preparation of skins for sheltering against the weather. The women have the task of searching for plant food, collecting wood for the fire, and creating nets, bags and the like.

Boomerangs, clubs, containers, bags, and so on, are left somewhere on the ground around the dwellings of the owner, but spears are either leaned against a nearby tree or stuck vertically into the soft ground to avoid the danger of injury to the shaft or spearhead.

Stretching or bending of wood is often necessary for the making of weapons or utensils. Green wood is put into hot ash to make it bendable. Rubbing with fat or exposure to fire has the same effect on dry wood. Softening in water is also used to bend wooden things into shape.

Body painting

The beautification recipes of the natives consist of ochre, pipe-clay, charcoal and fat; the latter constitutes the base of all artful lines and scribbles with which they decorate their person. As a protection against the cold in winter and against the bites of mosquitoes, ants and other insects in summer, the fat proves to be very useful. Its application during very hot weather also provides relief. The pipe clay is made from plaster [gypsum] which is burned in the fire and then mixed with enough water to form a tough thin paste.

During the preparations for a corroboree one of the very important moments in the process of the ceremony is the 'arranging' or 'making up'. The men adorn face, body and limbs with lines and fantastical drawings in white and red. This requires some hours of patient work and great care and effort are spent on the details. The men carry a feather quill or a piece of grass or bone in the nasal septum and their heads are decorated in a tremendous and wonderful way.

Corroborees

These national dances are performed on ceremonial and festive occasions. The night was always the time chosen for these entertainments, and the light for it was given by the moon or the campfire or both. During these friendly meetings one party from every tribe takes turns performing a nightly corroboree, while the other tribes form the audience. Mixing of members of different tribes amongst the performers was never admissible.

The women represented the orchestra beating with their flat hand onto a folded skin-blanket. An old man conducted the music by performing songs peculiar to this performance and clapping two short dry sticks or boomerangs. Occasionally the songs were indecent and the performance obscene.

The corroboree was always held on a level spot of earth, free of trees and bushes, after all loose sticks, stones and the like had been diligently removed. The different tribes present took their seats around this cleaned place, each on the side turned towards its territory.

Games and entertainment

Amongst the amusements of the men, wrestling always takes a pre-eminent place and is also practised during ceremonial meetings. According to native legends this game was common among the mythic ancestors. Another game is performed with a ball consisting of pieces of wallaby or possum skin, tightly rolled and sewn together with sinews. Before the game starts two or three parties are formed, each of which consists of those men and women who belong to a particular range of companions. The ball is thrown in the air and the aim of the game is to keep it continuously moving without touching the ground. When somebody catches the ball he throws it to one of his party, while the opposing team tries to catch it in mid-flight. The game continues until the people are tired or become too hot.

Wity wity throwing is another game. The wity wity is made from an oblong piece of wood, five or six inches long and one inch thick in the middle, petering out towards both ends into a point. A thin, tough rod about 20 or 30 inches long was fixed to one end with string or gum. The player throws the wity wity in such a way that it touches the ground a few feet before him and then jumps away for some distance in the grass. The person who is able to throw his projectile the furthest in that way is the winner. Often a *nulla nulla* [club] was used as a wity wity and the game played in exactly the same way.

Spear exercises are conducted as follows: a disc of green, hard bark, about a foot in diameter, is removed from a tree. The participants are placed in a row, all facing the same direction and one strong man takes his place about 10 or 15 yards in front of one end of the row. When all men are holding their spears in balance a signal is given and the man throws the bark disc on its edge over the ground in front of the participants and parallel to them. When it is rolling along like a boy's hoop, every man hurls his spear at it as soon as it passes his sight line. The best hit is rewarded by the applause of the audience.

During the warmer months of the year swimming in deep waters offered a good pastime. Most of us have entertained ourselves as boys by seeing who, during diving, could stay longest under water. The young blacks do the same as well. On a given sign the competitors dive at the same time, while some old men wait for their resurfacing. The blacks always dive with their feet ahead, just the opposite to the European way of diving.

Weapons

(a) Spears The spear is without doubt the main deadly weapon of the natives, and its manufacture often requires a great deal of time, especially when the wood has to be hewn off from one side of the tree with a stone axe. Fighting spears are made from thin small trees of hard wood, seven or more feet long, put into hot ash and prepared to the same thickness. The thick end of the small tree was hardened and sharpened in the fire. Sometimes on one or both sides of the spear barbs were attached close to the tip.

Hunting spears were lighter, about seven feet long, made out of firm reed or from the trunk of the grass-tree. The spearheads were produced from hard, heavy wood and carefully tied to the shaft with string and gum. There were two types of spear used to kill fish. The one used for spearing flathead, bream and such like has three or four prongs on one end. A bigger spear made from a small tree with only one head, or perhaps two, was used to kill the kingfish, the *cossyphus* or other big fish.

During hunting the spears were usually hurled with a *wommera* or spear thrower, but some heavy ones made from hard wood were thrown directly from the hand by balancing them in the middle. Serrated spears were used for fighting and spearing emus. A deep hole was made at the blunt end of the spear into which the tooth of the spear thrower was inserted when the hunter aimed at a distant object.

When the natives make a spear, a wommera, a shield, a boomerang or any other weapon for which lightness is an important requisite, they first carve it raw into the form wanted and then let it soak for one or two days in water to extract the saps and thus make it lighter. This is particularly so with the long spears made from hard wood, which more than once during the period of their making have to be soaked in water.

(b) Wommeras The *wommera* or spear thrower is a piece of wood little more than two feet in length, two thirds of an inch thick and two or three inches wide in the middle, running out at one end in a long rough handle, while the other end thins out into a hook or protrusion at the upper side. The surface of the shaft of the wommera is held horizontally when it is put against the end of the spear ready for hurling. The above mentioned hook is sometimes completely cut from the wood like a normal crochet hook. In other cases it is formed from a special piece of hard wood or bone, which is fixed into place with gum and entwined by sinews from wallaby, kangaroo or other animals. When a piece of human bone is used as the hook the natives believe this increases the accuracy and might of the spear.

Apart from being used to throw spears, the wommera also serves in some districts as a chisel and its upper surface is used as a container for blood or other liquids. For the former use the gripping end is furnished with an adze-sharp stone, while, for the latter, the middle part of the utensil is shaped as a leaf, wider in the middle than at the ends. The flat upper side on which the hook is attached is slightly hollowed. Finally, the handle of the weapon can serve to loosen the ground when searching for roots or digging out small animals from their burrow.

In parts of Queensland and at other places the shaft of the wommera is held vertically during use. When such use is intended the hook or pin, which grips into the hollowed end of the spear, is attached on the upper edge of the shaft of the wommera at the distal end (in contrast to the weapon described previously). In North Queensland my son saw some wommeras of a kind that show a bend similar to that of a boomerang with the pin or hook attached to the concave edge of the weapon.

(c) Shields There are two kinds, one for defence during spear fights, the other for skirmishes with clubs. The former consisted of a light piece of wood or bark with a special handle, which was attached on the back in the middle. Sometimes the handle was also carved from the same piece of wood as the shield.

The club shield was thick and hard and made from fine-grained tough wood so that it did not easily crack. The timber left for the handle was cut out from the whole and recessed all around to take in the hand. Some shields, the ones for spears as well as those for clubs, were roughly ornamented with differing recessed patterns cut into the surface. The spear shields were of oval shape with a convex outer and flat inner surface.

(d) Clubs Clubs are of varying kinds and size and can be used in scuffles (hand to hand fights) or for throwing after game. The proximal ending is slightly curbed to provide a firmer grip for the hand.

(e) Axes The stone axe was an indispensable tool. Some of these axes were artfully beaten into shape from pieces of rock formed by the influence of weather and picked up by the native for their appropriate shape. Others were apparently only well-rounded smooth pebbles of the desired size and form, found in the bed of a stream or river. In every case, however, the stone was ground on one end into a cutting edge.

The grinding and sharpening of these axes was done on sandstone rocks at places close to water for easing the work. The grooves resulting from the grinding of the axes on the rocks can be seen at numerous places in different parts of the country. The blacks often also carried a flat piece of sandstone or other suitable stones with them, five to six inches long, three to four inches wide and about one inch thick, which they used as a whetstone to renew the blades of their axes.

The handle of the utensil was made from a flexible wooden slat of any kind or a piece of creeper, cut flat on one side. It was heated up in warm ash, oiled, and then wound around the stone like a sling. The two loose ends of the wood or vine were placed on top of each other and firmly tied together with a string or some animal sinews. A strong coat of putty prepared from gum over and around the wooden sling served to fasten them. When the gum loosened due to the beating it was softened over the fire and pressed back in its place.

To give the handle a better grip the upper part of the axe where the handle was wound around was roughened up. This was usually done by pecking or beating with a piece of sharp stone, which the worker held in his hand. In some cases this was continued until a groove was formed all around the end of the axe, the depth of which—for a width of one inch—varied in the middle line from about one-eighth to half an inch. A piece of flexible wood or vine was wound around this groove or around the roughened part and bound as already described.

With these rough tools the native gained the material for his shields, spears, clubs, and so on; he peeled bark with it for his *gunyah*; he cut the branches for his wind-roof; he climbed trees and hewed holes into them to get out animals or bees' nests. Occasionally the axes were also used as weapons during fighting. When the hunter hewed holes into the trunk or cut branches of trees he always hit parallel to the grain of the wood instead of across the grain as the European would, widening the opening sideways until it was big enough for the desired purpose. This method was followed because it was easier to remove splinters in this way than when hitting across the grain, which would also have been harder with such a primitive tool.

(f) Boomerangs The returning boomerang is a unique weapon. The natives of India and some other regions produce a weapon somewhat similar to the boomerang, which they use for hunting or during war,[18] but no other region in the world has the quality of this instrument, that, after it is thrown, flies through the air and comes back to within a few feet of the thrower. The returning boomerang mostly serves as a toy, but sometimes it is used to kill ducks and other small animals. Keep in mind, however, that the boomerang, in order to return, must not touch anything after it is thrown; as soon as it touches any object it ceases to turn and falls to the ground.

The feature of returning is created by a light, but very distinct, turning on both ends. It can be characterized by imagining that the maker grabs the boomerang at both ends and then turns it, the left hand to the front, the other to the back. In practice the swinging is produced, if it is not already present naturally in the grain of the wood, by heating one side of the weapon, so that it curls in the desired direction. The maker helps the process by using his hands. He scrapes and polishes the wood, testing it repeatedly and altering it until the boomerang is ready. The finished weapon is flat on the underside, the upper side is slightly rounded. The edge of the outer curve, the back of the boomerang, is slightly thicker than the inner edge.

The turning of the wood, together with the flatness of one side and the convexity of the other, produces a difference of air pressure at specific places, which serves to work against gravity so that the boomerang, when the force given to it by the thrower is spent, continues its flight, but in a course towards the point of origin in a downward direction.

There is another kind of boomerang used for hunting and fighting, which in no case returns to the thrower. It is considerably bigger and heavier than the returning one and has a more open curve. It reminds one of the blade of a sabre and its inner edge is sharp and dangerous. It is a very effective weapon when thrown amongst some animals or used in war; it bounces back in a straight line.

The late Edward Palmer stated in his report concerning natives along the Mitchell, Palmer and Walsh rivers of the Cape York Peninsula, that boomerangs are used 'more for killing wild fowl than for fighting; they are made with only a slight curve, and do not return as do those used by the Wide Bay blacks'.[19] One of my correspondents living on the peninsula wrote to me that the returning boomerang was not produced between the Mitchell River and Cape York. They were unknown there until they were brought in as trading goods during the occupation of the area by whites.

The *warridilla*, a hunting boomerang about two feet long, is produced by the natives from Sturt Creek and Victoria River in the Northern Territory. It consists of a bent, flat piece of wood with a protruding hook on the end of the convex edge (the back) of the weapon. The hook, which is about five inches long, goes backwards, forming an angle at the nadir of about 30 or 40 degrees. This utensil is in use by the tribes from the Western Australian border, through the Northern Territory and into Queensland, where it was encountered by Dr Roth.[20] It is then mentioned by D. W. Carnegie, who saw it amongst the natives of Western Australia.[21] I myself have described this weapon previously in 'Ethnological Notes on the Aboriginal Tribes of the Northern Territory'.[22]

Utensils

(a) **Yam sticks** This utensil, used solely by women, was made from a small hard tree and was about four or five feet in length and about one or two inches in diameter. The thick end was cut to a wide, sharp, cutting edge hardened in fire; the thinner end terminated as a point. The main function of the thing was to dig out yams and other roots, or to rummage out small animals that dwell in the ground. With the help of their yam sticks the women provide the vegetable food of the camp. During domestic scenes in the camp the yam stick was a terrible weapon.

(b) **Stone knives** The production of the knives is essentially the same as that of axes, only the stone need not be as hard, and smaller pieces can be used. When they had been beaten into the right shape a sharp edge was produced by grinding. Smaller knives simply consisted of pieces that had broken off during the production of the cutting edge by beating. Handles were not attached, but one held the stone tight between the thumb and the other fingers. These knives were used for skinning and eviscerating animals, for scraping and marking wooden utensils, for cutting scars on the human body and for any other purpose.[23]

(c) **Chisels** The chisel was produced by attaching onto the end of a short stick with string or gum a sharp flint, a quartz splinter or a piece of hard stone sharpened to a cutting edge. It was of great use for sharpening spearheads, for cutting grooves into shields and clubs, for the making of wooden water containers and for various other tasks. Sometimes the whole chisel was made from a long bone of the leg of a kangaroo, which was sharpened at one end to a cutting edge. A double bladed chisel is used on the Victoria River in the Northern Territory. This tool is made from a piece of hard wood, one end of which is equipped with a small cutting stone while at the other end a stone with a wide blade is attached. Both then serve different tasks.

(d) **Containers** Bark containers to take in water, honey, food or other things are obtained in the following way. The native seeks a small tree with a natural bend and from the convex side a piece of bark about 18 inches long and nine inches wide is peeled off. This is done in such a way that the bark is severed with an axe around the edge of the selected piece of bark and is then lifted off by sliding a pointed stick between bark and wood. The stripping of the bark can only be undertaken at the season when the saps are circulating in the trees. When no suitable tree with a natural bend could be found a piece of thin bark was cut from a straight tree and tied together on both ends in the same way as the canoes were made.

Wooden containers are often also made in the following way. When a tree or branch is found which is hollow and has a well-marked bend, a container is hewn out from the convex side with an axe. Rotting or disintegrating wood that might be sticking to the inside is cut out and the whole is smoothed through scraping and rubbing. The outside is usually decorated with carved parallel lines going around the container.

(e) *Berl-ye* A small wooden utensil called a *berl-ye*, about the size of a pencil, and similarly pointed, is used for combing hair and to eradicate vermin on the head.

(f) **Awls** Awls, used for pricking or drilling, were generally made from the fibula of the kangaroo or emu, which was ground to a fine point.

(g) **Bags** Bags, neatly woven from strings, twisted bark fibres, tough grass and vines, were used to carry small animals, roots, small utensils and odds and ends of all kinds. Nets with different patterns for catching fish were made of similar materials. Two or three kinds of stitches are employed for weaving bags or nets.

(h) **Calabashes** Calabashes cut from wood as already described serve for storing and carrying water. Cleaned human skulls, the seams of which are clogged with gum, are used for this by some tribes. Sacks for transporting water over greater distances are made from the skin of the kangaroo, wallaby or similar animals, with the fleshy side of the skin turned inwards. With some coastal tribes of New South Wales and Queensland water sacks are also produced from leaves of the bangalow tree or from palm leaves sewn together with animal sinews.

Bigger bags or satchels consisted of a rough net made from fibres of bulrushes or from bark of certain trees and were hung over the shoulder or carried on a breast band diagonally across the chest. In these diagonal sacks heavy utensils, such as stones for grinding seeds, stone scrapers or knives, tools, and such like were carried.

(i) Fishing hooks In the coastal districts of New South Wales, from Sydney southwards, the natives formerly fished with fishhooks they made themselves. It is reported by Collins that at the time of first occupation of the area by Governor Phillip the natives in the vicinity of Sydney used lines from the bark of small trees and hooks from the shell of oysters, which they rubbed on a stone until they obtained the desired shape.

Presently, the steel hooks of the whites are used by all natives, but I have spoken to old men and women in native camps who still knew how the hooks were made and occasionally manufactured them when the hooks of the whites were not available. They took the shell of the *dhūlla* (*turbo stamineus*) [heavy turban shell] and struck the outer part off until only the firm spiral part remained, which was formed as a rough hook. By rubbing on a stone it was ground until it obtained the right thickness. It was simply pointed without barbs. The hook was usually swallowed by the fish together with the bait, and was then hauled in.

Fire-making

The natives produce fire by means of two pieces of dry wood, of which one, that can be described as the 'stationary board', is mostly soft, and the other, the 'drill stick', consists of a piece of harder material. Into a totally dry, soft piece of wood, maybe half of a split branch, a small notch or dent is cut. This is then put flat on the ground, notch up, and the fire maker, sitting in the usual posture of the natives, holds it firmly with his feet in front of him.

A round, straight stick, roughly tapered at the thick end, is put upright onto the notch or cut in the 'stationary' piece of wood. Now this vertical 'drill stick' is vigorously whisked forwards and backwards between the palms of the hands with the hands constantly pressing firmly down. By exercising this pressure the hands can easily glide down the drill stick, but the man then lifts them up immediately to the upper end of the stick and continues to whisk.

In the course of one or two minutes smoke rises from the point of contact of the woods, followed by red glowing of rubbed off dust particles on which the tinder, made from rolled up bark fibre, dry grass or any other easily flammable material, which had been wound around beforehand, can now easily ignite. Careful blowing produces a flame. Usually two men sit opposite each other; one turns the stick quickly, and the other one organises the tinder.

Another method of fire making consists of putting a piece of soft wood on the ground, which is split at one end. Into this split, which is kept open by a wedge jammed in, finely ground bark or dried grass is placed. A transverse notch is cut into both sides of the split wood and a piece of harder wood with an angular edge fitted into the notch is quickly rubbed in a sawing motion with some pressure through this notch, back and forth. The wood in the notch is pulverised by this and heated up, and by falling down onto the tinder in the split can easily be blown into a flame by the man making the fire.

When the natives travel anywhere they always carry a burning stick in their hand. In a hunting party there will always be one or two thus equipped, so that all the culled game can be roasted. But to safeguard against any mischance with this kind of fire making, some men also carry the rubbing wood.

The women, too, carry a piece of smouldering wood from the grass tree or honeysuckle or another suitable tree so as to be able to make fire immediately when the troop halts. This was done partly for comfort, partly to cook any provisions; it was also totally independent of the temperature. The fire was carried on the hottest summer day as well as in winter.

Cooking

A usual way of cooking the flesh of animals was to make a round pit in the ground, varying in depth and diameter depending on the size of the animal to be cooked in it. Stones were put onto the ground and within the sides of this pit as a kind of pavement or tiling on which a big fire was lit. Further stones and the soil gained by excavating the pothole were likewise placed beside the fire to heat. When the fire had burned down, the ash and the superfluous stones were scuffed out. Damp grass was put onto the hot stones at the bottom of the pothole and onto it the animal together with its skin, and over the top more damp grass was scattered. Then the superfluous heated stones were first piled onto the grass layer, and the excavated hot soil was piled up as a cover. The heat of the stones and the closed-in steam combined to cook the meat. When the steam rising from the stones and the grass was considered insufficient for cooking, holes were made in the upper cover with a pointed stick, into which water was poured, thereby improving the conditions for a build-up of steam. With this kind of cooking the roast retains all its juices and when it is taken out of the oven the skin peels off easily. At places where stones were scant, clay was used as a paving for the bottom and the sides of the pothole to keep heat and steam enclosed. When there was no grass available, leaves were used instead.

Small birds, fish, opossums and all lighter mammals and reptiles were roasted simply by putting them on top of the coals. Roots, tubers, shellfish, eggs and so on were dug into hot ash until they were cooked through. In some localities the natives wrap small animals into a thick coat of clay and put them into the ashes of a big fire and keep them covered with hot ash until cooked. When they were taken out, the skin or feathers stuck to the hard clay crust while the animal remained clean and juicy.

Clothing and adornments

The only cover worn by the natives were the skins from animals, such as kangaroo, wallaby, opossum, bear, and the native cat. Blankets were mostly made from opossum fur, sewn together with the sinews of the animal from which they came, with a sharpened bone serving as needle or awl. The blankets held together with a string or pin were worn across the chest so that the right arm stayed free, very similar to the Roman toga, and reached mostly down to the knee. The hairy side was worn inside during cold weather, and during other weather the smooth one. During rain the hairy side was turned outside, as the coat otherwise, if the flesh-side got wet, would have become stiff and hard when later dried by the sun. Usually the men and women walked around in Adam's and Eve's costumes; the blankets were only used around the camp and at night time.

Significant work was required for the preparation of these blankets. About 30 to 40 opossum furs were needed for one blanket for an adult. When the fur is skinned from the animal it is put flat on a dry hard piece of earth and fastened around the edges with stakes, the fur being strenuously pulled to stretch it. When it is dry it is taken away and cut with a stone knife into a square shape by keeping the best part and throwing away the damaged edges. The surface of the skin is then worked with a stone scraper to remove all pieces of flesh, which might still adhere, in order to make it soft and flexible. Then it is rubbed with fat and red ochre.

When the necessary number of furs has been collected they are stitched together with sinews gained from the tails of marsupials; a sharp bone or wooden pin serves as an awl to make the holes through which the end of the sinew is pulled by hand. Some furs were decorated with rough drawings on the flesh side with a shell or sharp flint; the treatment with fat and ochre served to proof it and protect it against the influences of the weather.

The furs of the kangaroo, native bear and wallaby were prepared in a similar way and a smaller number of those were sufficient for this purpose. I have seen men who wore cloaks made from only one or two kangaroo furs with which they protected themselves during damp days against the rain. The skins of large birds, such as the pelican, emu and swan were occasionally used for the same purpose. Skins were also used as mats on the damp ground.

Instead of pegging the skin on the ground, as described above, the pelts of smaller animals were sometimes stretched on a smooth barked tree or a piece of bark forming the *gunya* or shelter. In both cases the nails used were made of hard wood or pieces of splintered bone.

Necklaces are made from short pieces of reed or grass stalks, which are cut up with a sharp shell or a stone knife into the length of about half an inch or more and are threaded onto a fur string like the necklaces made from tube pearls by our white children. At some places shells are strung together, at others quandong kernels.[24] At other places kangaroo and dog teeth are carefully attached to a fur string or a strip of kangaroo fur. The material of the necklaces changes with the locality.

During the making of shell necklaces a hole is ground or pierced into each shell and the string is pulled through the artificial hole as well as through the natural opening of the shell; because of this the shells are in symmetrical order to each other, but hang randomly on the string.

Around Moulamein, Swan Hill, Balranald and other nearby places, the natives make necklaces from the feelers of the Murray lobster, which, when cooked, have a light red coral color. They are broken into pieces half an inch in length and strung on the sinews of a kangaroo tail. All necklaces mentioned form a pleasant contrast to the ebony coloured necks and shoulders of the wearers. Some of these are worn singly, but more often in two or three windings around the neck. Fur string necklaces are only occasionally worn.

Headbands, made from tightly plaited strings or human hair, coloured with red ochre or pipe clay, are worn around the forehead. Sometimes feathers of birds are included in the head ornament. White downy feathers are often stuck to the forehead or to other parts of the body. Often a head frill was made from kangaroo teeth neatly and firmly strung together. The tip of the tails of wild dogs were also worn attached to the hair with gum-like tassels or tied together with strings.

Armbands were worn around the biceps. These were made from strips of animal fur, the hairy side turned outside. Strings were tied around the knees and ankles, under which leaved twigs were inserted hanging down.

Belts or girdles, worn around the hips, were made from opossum skin, human hair or plaited or twisted strips of skin. An apron or pubic tassle was made by cutting a kangaroo rat fur into small strips, nine to 12 inches in length, depending on the size of the fur used. On one end of the fur a seam or band was left uncut from which all strips originate. This uncut seam was put under the hip girdle and the strips hung down over the male member like great tassels. The apron was so small that it rather served to draw attention to the pubic area than hide it. A similar cloth was placed at the back of the girdle, and one on each side, to make four in total. That is the custom of the Wirraidyuri; with the Thurrawal and related tribes only two loin cloths were worn, one at the front and one at the back over the crack between the buttocks.

During travels the men often carried some of their weapons, such as a boomerang, axe or other pieces of equipment deemed necessary in the hip girdle. Unmarried girls wore girdles around the hips, from which fringes of fur strips about a foot long and of a width of eight or nine inches hung down to cover the pudenda.

Trading

Meetings for exchanging articles and products occurred between tribes, which were scattered over a very significant stretch of land. Journeys to the region of neighbouring tribes were usually undertaken in connection with initiation ceremonies or they were linked with dances, songs and corroborees to increase game or induce rain or good weather. The travel routes taken on these occasions seem to be fixed and recognised from time immemorial.

In the territory of one tribe there might be an abundance of hard wood suitable for making certain weapons, while at another place there would be a great amount of stone for producing axes and knives or grinding seeds, and in such a case the mutual exchange of goods would be of benefit to both peoples. Those whose territory produced red ochre or other pigments, animal skins and so on, might exchange with tribes which had a wealth of rare feathers, grass tree wood for making fire by rubbing, or other products.

Craft products formed an object of trade exchange in the same way or were given away as presents. One group, for example, who were present at the big ceremonial meetings, might have had opossum fur strings, hip girdles from human hair, wristbands, grass necklaces or the like; others perhaps brought magnificent shields, stone knives and weapons of all sorts, while again others had dilly bags,[25] kangaroo teeth, fish nets and the like.

As a result of this trade, different articles found their way into areas that were relatively distant from their place of production or origin. The Murawarri natives from Culgoa River would, for example, attend a ceremonial meeting at the Darling River in the region of Brewarrina, where they would meet with the Ngeumba tribe from the Bogan, and numerous articles would be exchanged between them. We could assume that a boomerang cut from a special kind of wood, produced on the Culgoa River, came upwards along the Bogan to Nyngan. In the course of one or two years the then owner perhaps went to a meeting of the Wongaibon at Willandra Billabong and there traded the weapon with a man. The new owner could now carry it to a 'fair' at the Lachlan River and later it might perhaps be brought further to the Wirraidyuri tribe at the Murrumbidgee River.

Although the transactions at these native 'fairs' were for the most part restricted to the exchange of specific articles for others of a different kind, such as necklaces for boomerangs, it nevertheless happens, not too rarely, that some men, who had friendly relations with each other, or between whom a kind of kinship existed, exchanged similar articles, such as a shield for a shield, a spear for a spear, apparently as a memento. Also, here and there presents are made to relatives or men who have undergone particular rituals, without a counter gift.

These trade meetings also provided a suitable occasion for exchanging and spreading folklore of different tribes, as well as their superstitions, songs and corroborees. The traditional beliefs were transmitted from tribe to tribe over great distances, and even when the details were heavily altered so as to be in accord with the changed surroundings, the essential elements of many of these stories seem to have preserved the imprint of their shared origin.

In most of their legends there is a tendency to explain some peculiarity of animal burrows or particular characteristics, as well as to give reasons for unusual shapes of lakes, rivers, trees or other natural phenomena. In this way ideas were exchanged between distant tribes, which never associated with each other. Single words of a language could also be spread from district to district over long stretches of land.

ENDNOTES

[1] [Editor's note] See RHM 1900, 'Phallic Rites and Initiation Ceremonies of the South Australian Aborigines', *Proceedings of the American Philosophical Society*, vol. 39, pp.622-38.

[2] RHM 1904, 'Die Multyerra-Initiationszeremonie', *Mitteilungen der Anthropologischen Gesellschaft*, vol. 34, p. 77-83. Reproduced this volume.

[3] RHM, 'Some Initiation Ceremonies of the Aborigines of Victoria', *Zeitschrift für Ethnologie*, vol. 37, 1905, p. 874.

[4] RHM 1896, 'The Būnān Ceremony of New South Wales', *American Anthropologist*, vol. 9, p. 338.

[5] RHM 1900, 'The Toara Ceremony of the Dippil Tribes of Queensland', *American Anthropologist*, vol. 2 (new series), pp. 142-3.

[6] Curr, E. M. 1886-7, *The Australian Race, etc.*, John Ferres, Government Printer, Melbourne, vol. 3, p. 139.

[7] Ibid., p. 231.

[8] Ibid., vol. 2, p. 425.

[9] Ibid., vol. 3, p. 144.

[10] Mackillop, Rev Donald 1892-3, 'Anthropological Notes on the Aboriginal Tribes of the Daly River, North Australia', *Transactions and Proceedings and Report of the Royal Society of South Australia*, vol. 17, p. 257.

[11] Stokes, J. Lort 1846, *Discoveries in Australia with an Account of the Coasts and Rivers, etc.*, Boone, London, vol. 1, pp. 92-3.

[12] RHM 1905, *Ethnological Notes on the Aboriginal Tribes of New South Wales and Victoria*, F. W. White General Printer, Sydney, pp. 60-8.

[13] Bride, Thomas Francis (ed.) 1898, *Letters from Victorian Pioneers, etc.*, Trustees of the Public Library, Melbourne, p. 258.

[14] Ibid., p. 184.

[15] Ibid., p. 273.

[16] Fraser, John 1882, 'The Aborigines of New South Wales', *Journal and Proceedings of the Royal Society of New South Wales*, vol. 16, p. 207. The expression of the women during the apostrophising of the dried hand means that it would bake no more bread. Perhaps this is an allusion to the fact that the man was busy baking at the time when he was killed, and had dough stuck on his fingers.

[17] [Editor's note] The reference to 'sections' (*Abteilungen* in German) suggests that the men formed groups according to their kinship affiliation.

[18] The British Museum keeps an ancient Egyptian boomerang, which is very similar to the Australian variety.

[19] Palmer, Edward 1884, 'Notes on some Australian Tribes', *Journal of the Anthropological Institute*, vol. 13, p. 287.

[20] Roth, Walter E. 1897, *Ethnological Studies among the North-West-Central Queensland Aborigines*, Edmund Gregory, Government Printer, Brisbane, p. 145, fig. 353.

[21] Carnegie, David W. 1898, *Spinifex and Sand*, C. Arthur Pearson, London, p. 343.

[22] RHM 1900-01, 'Ethnological Notes on the Aboriginal Tribes of the Northern Territory', *Queensland Geographical Journal*, vol. 16, p. 84.

[23] Occasionally the returning boomerang was used to skin larger animals. After the skin was opened with the stone knife, one end of the boomerang was pushed between skin and flesh and the skin thus flayed.

[24] *Santalum acuminatum*. Note—German translator.

[25] *Dilly* is the name of all small bags carried by the blacks; the word probably originates from a native language of the Sydney area.

Rock Carvings and Paintings by the Australian Aborigines

R. H. Mathews

First published as 'Gravures et peintures sur rochers par les Aborigènes d'Australie' in *Bulletins et Mémoires de la Société d'Anthropologie de Paris*, vol. 9 (4th series), 1898, pp. 425-32. The article was written in English and translated into French by an unnamed translator. This version was retranslated into English by Mathilde de Hauteclocque.

For more than 20 years, a colony of Aborigines has lived near the hamlet of La Perouse, situated on the northern shore of Botany Bay, about 16 kilometres south of Sydney, New South Wales, which today numbers about 40 people of both sexes, most of them half-castes. They are the last descendants of the aboriginal race who have lived in the area since the occupation of the country by the English in 1788. The government of New South Wales, while providing a weekly allowance for the elderly and disabled, demands that the others look after themselves. During my visit to this settlement, in order to research the habits of the natives, they showed me drawings of three large fish carved into smooth slabs of Hawkesbury sandstone (which surrounds the bay), adding that it was the work of their ancestors before the arrival of the white man. Thinking that the members of your society would be interested in these sketches (found next to the monument erected in memory of La Pérouse), I have done a drawing which carefully reproduces them and to which a map is attached, showing the area where they are found.

The short extract that follows, from the official history of News South Wales,[1] will perhaps be of interest to your society.

The ships of the French expedition under the command of La Pérouse sailed from Botany Bay on 10 March 1788. During their stay Father Le Receveur, who had come out in the 'Astrolabe' as a naturalist, died. His death was occasioned by wounds he received in an unfortunate encounter at the Navigators' Islands. A monument was erected in his memory, with the following inscription:

HIC JACET LE RECEVEUR.
EX F.F. MINORIBUS GALLILAE SACERDOS
PHYSICUS IN CIRCUMNAVIGATIONE MUNDI,
DUCE DE LA PEROUSE
OB. 17 FEB. 1788.

This monument having been destroyed by the natives, Governor Phillip caused the inscription to be engraved in copper and affixed it to a nearby tree.

Neither La Pérouse nor his ships were seen again. An expedition charged with finding out about their disappearance was unable to discover anything. It was only 40 years later that Captain Dillon of the vessel *Research,* belonging to the East India Company, recorded that the *Astrolabe* had been shipwrecked on a coral reef and that most of the crew had perished. The survivors were washed ashore on the Mallicolo Islands and died many years before the arrival of Captain Dillon. A monument, bearing the following inscription, was erected at Botany Bay in memory of La Pérouse, and is still standing to this day:

To the Memory of Monsieur de la Pérouse
This country, which he visited in 1788, is the last from which he sent
news. Erected in the name of France, under the care of Messrs
Bougainville and Ducampier, commanders of the frigate La Thétis and
the corvette L'Espérance off duty in Port Jackson in 1825.
Foundation laid in 1825.
Raised 1828.

In many parts of Australia, the Aborigines customarily paint, in different colours, representations of hands, tools, human beings and various animals. These paintings are found on the walls of natural rock shelters, at the foot of large rocks, which protect them against the rain.

After familiarising myself with the literature on this subject, I judged it appropriate to add to this descriptive note a drawing (see Figure 4) reproducing the paintings which I copied from two of these caves.

The process used by Aboriginal artists in executing the carvings and paintings described here is amply described in an essay which I forwarded to the Anthropological Institute of Great Britain.[2]

FIGURE 1. This enormous fish seems to represent a shark. It is carved into the horizontal face of a mass of Hawkesbury sandstone, which surrounds Botany Bay, at the hamlet of La Perouse, and is 11.78 metres long. The two eyes are placed on the same side of the head, which, however, is frequently seen in aboriginal paintings of various animals. This carving is found about 160 metres southwest of the La Pérouse monument.

FIGURE 2. Inside the outline of the front part of the first figure, we see another fish, 4.52 metres long. One can ask if the artist wanted to give the impression of the bigger fish swallowing the other, or whether he put the smaller fish there because the surface of the rock in that position was more suited to his work.

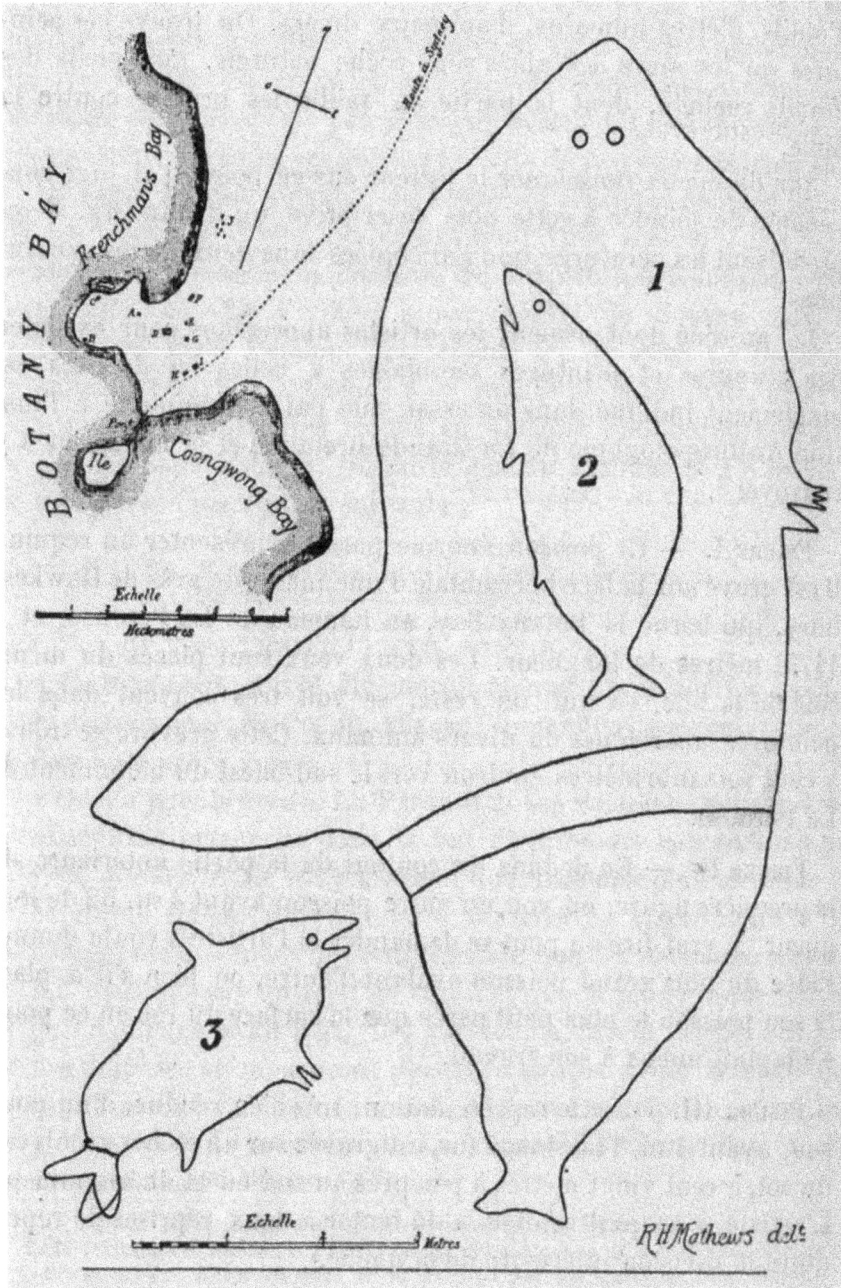

Fish engraved on rock at La Perouse, Botany Bay. Reprinted from *Bulletins et Mémoires de la Societé d'Anthropologie de Paris*, vol.9.

FIGURE 3. This well-made representation of a fish, 4.14 metres long, is carved on a rock at ground level, approximately 100 metres southwest of the monument.

The artist, it would seem, must have made two attempts to create the lower division of the tail.

Explanatory note on the map adjoining the carving

To the northwest of the southern headland on which the hamlet is built, is Frenchmans Bay, so named in honour of La Pérouse.

A. Point where the monument was erected in his honour.
B. Location of the rock showing the two carvings (1 and 2).
C. Location of the second rock, carrying Figure 3.
D. Telegraphic office from where the underwater telegraph to New Zealand departs.
E. Tomb of Le Receveur: a slab carries the aforementioned inscription, surrounded by an iron fence.
F. Restaurant.
G. Post Office.
H. Public School.
I. Customs.
J. Site of the Aboriginal community mentioned above.

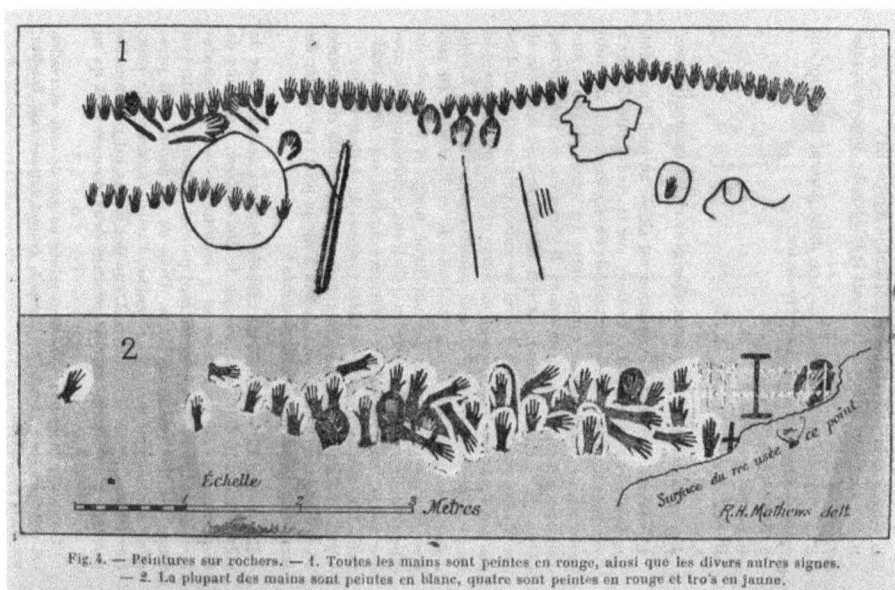

Fig. 4. — Peintures sur rochers. — 1. Toutes les mains sont peintes en rouge, ainsi que les divers autres signes. — 2. La plupart des mains sont peintes en blanc, quatre sont peintes en rouge et tro's en jaune.

Paintings on rock: 1. All the hands are painted in red, as are the various other motifs. 2. Most of the hands are painted in white, four are painted in red, and three in yellow. Reprinted from *Bulletins et Mémoires de la Societé d'Anthropologie de Paris*, vol.9.

CAVE 1. This cave is situated at the foot of a tall escarpment of Hawkesbury sandstone on the right bank of Coxs Creek, parish of Coolcalwin, county of Phillip. We see 64 hands, printed in red, as well as more or less distinct traces of 25 other hands. There are seven more, painted the same colour, making 71 visible hands in total. In the midst of the other paintings, we can distinguish an oval figure, sketched in red and from which a red mark extends right up to what seems to represent an aboriginal *waddy*, painted on the rock. To the right of this *waddy* we see two shorter ones, each indicated by a red line, and right next to the smallest of these are three lines in red, also short. Above these last ones, we see an indistinguishable figure of an irregular outline, also red in colour. Further on is the clear imprint of a left hand surrounded by a red line. The last drawing to the right could represent an aboriginal bag, with loose strings.[3]

CAVE 2. This engraving is carved into a large sandstone rock, situated near the left bank of Dural Creek, parish of Coonbaralba, county of Hunter. We see 38 representations of hands, most of which are painted in white, others in red and others in yellow. Three of these hands are almost marked in a white line, the artist perhaps having wanted to distinguish them from the others. One of the hands is particularly noticeable because it has two thumbs, an effect which seems to have been produced by first placing the right hand on the rock and spraying around it with a coloured liquid, and then putting the other hand there, in order to represent the other thumb, in a similar way. In certain figures, the arm has been reproduced up to the elbow or as far as is necessary. The most remarkable drawing at this location is one made up from a combination of white and red lines and two rows of white dots. It is regrettable that most of these unusual inscriptions have disappeared as a result of the crumbling of the rock surface on which they were carried out. The opening of the rock at this location has allowed the rain to get in, crumbling the sandstone, which does not resist the effects of humidity well.

The monument erected in memory of La Pérouse, of which I am sending a photograph which I took especially for you, is seen from the eastern side. The gate of the enclosure is open so that the pedestal may be seen more clearly. The southern side bears the inscription reproduced at the beginning of this article, minus the date of the erection, which was engraved in the eastern side; the northern and western sides bear the English translation of the inscription. The monument is surrounded by a low stone wall, topped with an iron fence; this wall is interrupted by a gate on the side. The officers and crews of passing French ships often visit the monument. On one of these occasions, the crew of a war ship marked their visit by screwing onto the base of the monument a metallic plaque bearing the following inscription:

"LE BRUAT"

TO LA PÉROUSE AND HIS MEN

1884

Discussion

[By] M. Capitan

This article is of real interest and is above all topical. Because of the particular interest these days in rock carvings and paintings from prehistoric times, it is vital to record this precious information.

These paintings and carvings on the faces of Australian rock shelters reveal ethnic customs similar in all respects to the prehistoric inhabitants of the grottos of Pair-en-Pair in France or of Mouthe or even the Altamira Cave in Spain. They are also reminiscent of the carvings recently studied in the grottos of the Yucatan by American scholars.

The comparison of these relatively recent customs, which have already been detected in all parts of the world, with similar ones from prehistoric periods, throws a strong light on these ones and helps us understand their genesis.

ENDNOTES

[1] Richards, Thomas 1883, *An Epitome of the Official History of New South Wales, etc.*, Thomas Richards, Government Printer, Sydney, pp. 20-1.

[2] RHM 1896, 'The Rock Paintings and Carvings of the Australian Aborigines', *Journal of the Anthropological Institute*, vol. 25, pp. 147, 150.

[3] The drawings of 40 hands painted on the wall of this cave have already been published. See RHM 1896, 'The Rock Paintings and Carvings of the Australian Aborigines', *Journal of the Anthropological Institute*, vol. 25, pp. 145-163, fig. 4.

Plan of some Drawings carved or painted on Rock by the Natives of New South Wales, Australia

R. H. Mathews

First published as 'Relevé de quelques dessins gravés ou peints sur rochers par les indigènes de la Nouvelle Galles du Sud (Australie)' in *Bulletins et Mémoires de la Société d'Anthropologie de Paris*, 11 (5th Series), 1910, pp. 531-35. The article was written in English and translated into French by Oscar Schmidt. This version was retranslated into English by Mathilde de Hauteclocque.

In 1898 I sent to this Society a short article on a few prehistoric rock carvings and paintings, executed by the natives of New South Wales.[1] This article was well received and, in discussing it, our colleague, M. Capitan, expressed the opinion that these paintings and carvings bore great similarity to those found in certain districts of France and Spain, as well as the Yucutan. He added that their comparison with similar customs could only serve to shed more light on the subject.

In the hope that a new study would be appreciated by the members of the Society, I have laid out a certain number of drawings, engraved on the faces of flat rocks at different locations in the County of Cumberland, New South Wales. All of them have been reproduced exactly to scale, based on measurements taken conscientiously by myself, the location of each drawing being well indicated on the descriptive maps printed by the Government, so that they may be easily found again in the future by all who might wish to see them.

With the examples chosen, I have tried to give an idea of the typical human figures, animals and monsters. Likewise, I chose some gigantic specimens (see Figure 1) while others are minuscule, like those of the small fish in Figure 8. All the dimensions are given in English feet and inches.

I have already described similar carvings and drawings which I found in Queensland[2] and Western Australia.[3] No matter where in Australia they have been found, they have all been made in the same manner. Firstly, a row of holes was pierced with a piece of pointed stone, establishing the outline of the drawing, after which the intervals between these holes were cut in such a way as to produce an uninterrupted groove. This tends to prove that either all indigenous artists came from common ancestors, or that the same practices evolved in similar areas.

It would perhaps be useful to point out, for those who have not attached much importance to these Australian artists, that they used two processes: one by *cutting into the surface of the rock*, as is the case for the drawings described in the present article; the other by *painting* the designs on smooth rock surfaces with white, red or black pigments, as I described in the previous article.[4] These paintings can be found scattered across extensive parts of all the Australian states, while the carved drawings are found only in a few rare locations, far removed from each other. That is why I have chosen a few specimens for the current paper.

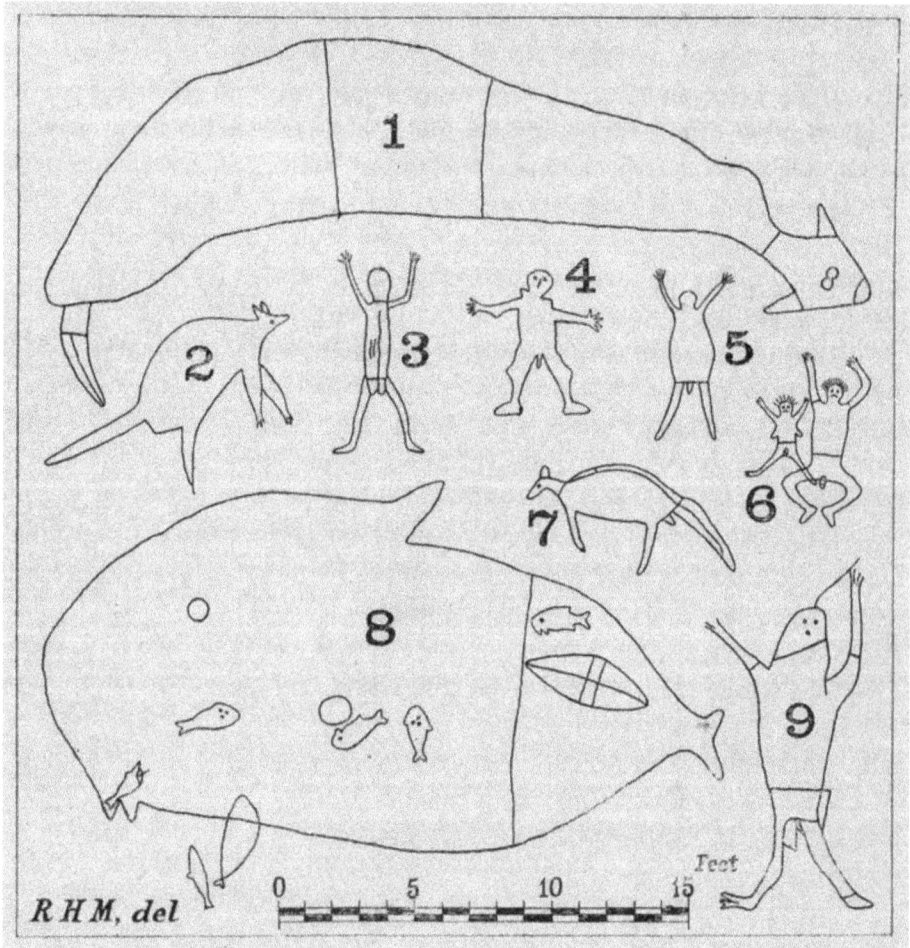

Rock carvings from the Sydney basin. Reprinted from *Bulletins et Mémoires de la Société d'Anthropologie de Paris*, vol.11.

FIGURE 1. This remarkable drawing is carved on a large overhanging ledge of Hawkesbury sandstone, elevated only a few feet above the surrounding ground and near the southern border of Portion 99 of 100 acres, in the Parish of Maroota,

County of Cumberland. It is close to the well known rock Lovers Leap, a steep precipice on the banks of the Hawkesbury River. The total length of the beast, taken from the tip of the nose, right along the middle of the body, up to the point of the appendage, in the form of a tail, is roughly 37 feet. The eyes are very close together and there is a band around the neck. Two similar bands or belts are carved across the body and there is another one on the tail. The largest part of the body measures 6 feet 3 inches.

FIGURE 2. This excellent reproduction of a male kangaroo is engraved on a sandstone rock at Point Piper, on a fairly low promontory on the south side of Port Jackson, between Rose Bay and Double Bay, in the Parish of Alexandria, County of Cumberland. Its total length, from the nose to the end of the tail, is 10 feet 5 inches. The two front paws are shown, but each of them has only three digits, instead of five. In 1847 G. F. Angas published an inexact drawing of this animal which he described as being 'nearly nine feet long'. His drawing also shows it on the move in a direction contrary to that which appears on the rock—that is to say moving to the left instead of to the right.

FIGURE 3. This human form, quite unique, is carved on a flat rock, at ground level, within Portion N°. 40 of 600 acres, in the Parish of Maroota, County of Cumberland. It is 6 feet 7 inches in height, from the top of the head to the heels. Apparently, it is the back of the man, the buttocks and the dorsal spine being marked. This type of depiction is rare because it is nearly always from the front that a man is drawn.

FIGURE 4. This grotesque sketch of a man is found on a flat rock, about 5 yards from Figure 2. He is 5 feet 2 inches tall and, with his arms extended, he measures nearly 5 feet from fingertip to fingertip. Mr Angas also laid out this engraving in 1847. He gives it a height of 5 feet and adds a few other details which are not entirely exact.[5]

FIGURE 5. Another sketch of a man, 5 feet 4 inches tall, carved on a sandstone rock within Portion N°. 32, of 60 acres, in the Parish of Maroota, County of Cumberland. The trunk is very large in relation to the limbs.

FIGURE 6. This group can be found on a nearby flat rock, to the west of the road which goes from the train station of Turramurra to Cowan Creek and roughly half a mile south from the surveyor's benchmark at Bobbin, in the Parish of Gordon, County of Cumberland. It shows a man about 5 feet high, if his legs were straight, and a woman of about 3 feet. The eyes and the mouths are shown, but the nose is missing from them both. They wear belts around the smalls of their backs and the man has a band around his arms, near his shoulders. 17 lines rise from the head of the man, like rays, and eight from the head of the woman. They could represent either hair or an ornament which has been attached there. Mr R. D. Hay was the first to publish, in 1892, a basic sketch of this group.[6]

An inexact drawing was later published by Mr R. Etheridge, his principal error being to have put the woman on the wrong side of the man.[7]

I published an exact drawing of it in 1895[8] and Mr W. D. Campbell published one in 1899.[9] I thought it a good idea to reproduce the group in this present treatise, it being difficult to access the different works cited.

FIGURE 7. Shows another male kangaroo, measuring 7 feet 10 inches, in a direct line, from the nose to the end of the tail. A double line is seen going from shoulder height, down the length of the back, until about 8 inches from the bottom of the tail, seemingly there to add to the size of the animal, although it would have significantly added to the work of the native artist. This kangaroo is found in the same Portion as Figure 3 and only a short distance from it.

FIGURE 8. A large fish, measuring 25 feet 3 inches long, cut into a slightly convex sandstone rock, three quarters of a chain northwest of Figure 2. The body is 12 feet at the largest part; 5 feet from the nose, we see a circular incision of 9 inches in diameter, marking the eye. Seventeen feet from the nose, in the direction of the tail, a band or a type of belt is engraved across the body and is 9 feet 8 inches long. Between this belt and the tail we see a shield 4 feet 8 inches long and a small fish, a little over 2 feet. Between the band and the nose four small fish can be seen and to the side of one of them, an engraved disc, about one foot in diameter. On a part of this whale's stomach, and going beyond its outline, there is a fish 3 feet 4 inches long and to the left of that, another smaller one. Mr G. F. Angas published in 1847 an inexact drawing of this whale; in it, he noted the length as 27 feet.[10]

Although the sketches of Figures 2, 4 and 8 made by Mr Angas have a number of flaws in the details, they are good enough, after 63 years, to identify them, without hesitation, with my own.

FIGURE 9. This enormous and rudimentary reproduction of a man is carved on a fairly large rock, at ground level on the side of the old road from Peats Ferry to Sydney, about half a mile north of the surveyor's benchmark at Vize, in the Parish of Cowan, County of Cumberland.[11] Its height, from head to toe, measures 10 feet 8 inches. The eyes are marked and we see a point that could indicate either the mouth or the nose. There are lines on the lower part of the figure, at the waist, across the body, on each arm near the shoulders, and across the left hip and ankle. An oblique line runs off the top of the head, going up beyond the index finger of the outstretched left arm. This image is one of many drawings on the same rock, reported by Mr W. R. Govett in 1836, that is to say 64 years ago. He said of them: 'The summit of the bank is a large, flat rock, on whose surface different figures are carved or dug out, representing a strange assembly of hands, arms, legs, men and animals.'[12] Since Mr Govett, other authors have reported these native carvings.

ENDNOTES

[1] RHM 1898, 'Gravures et peintures sur rochers par les aborigènes d'Australie', *Bulletins et Mémoires de la Société d'Anthropologie de Paris*, vol. 9 (series 4), pp. 425-32 with illustrations. Reproduced this volume.

[2] RHM 1901, 'Aboriginal Rock Pictures in Queensland', *Proceedings of the American Philosophical Society*, vol. 40, pp. 57-8.

[3] RHM 1903-04, 'Ethnological Notes on the Aboriginal Tribes of Western Australia', *Queensland Geographical Journal*, vol. 19, pp. 46-50, table 1.

[4] RHM 1898, 'Gravures et peintures', pp. 429-31, fig. 4. Reproduced this volume.

[5] Angus, George French 1847, *Savage Life and Scenes in Australia and New Zealand*, Smith, Elder & Co., London, vol. 2, p. 275, table 1, fig. 2.

[6] Hay, R. D. 1892, 'Native Carvings', *Journal of the Institute of Surveyors, New South Wales*, vol. 5, p. 193 with drawing.

[7] *Records of the Geological Survey of New South Wales*, vol. 4, 1894, p 57, table 9, figs 14 and 15.

[8] RHM 1894-5, 'Aboriginal Rock Pictures', *Proceedings and Transactions of the Queensland Branch of the Royal Geographical Society of Australasia*, vol. 10, p. 68, table 5, fig. 4.

[9] Campbell, W. D. 1899, *Aboriginal Carvings of Port Jackson and Broken Bay*, Government Printer, Sydney.

[10] Angus, *Savage Life and Scenes*, vol. 1, p. 24, table 1, fig 9.

[11] A very disappointing reproduction of this drawing appeared in the *Records of the Geological Survey of New South Wales*, vol. 3, p. 80, table 15, fig. 12. The observer missed many of the lines engraved on the rock, and others were reproduced inexactly, the outcome being that this native drawing of a man was taken to be a drawing of a fish.

[12] *Saturday Magazine* (London), vol. 9, 3 December 1836, p. 223.

Part 2: Kinship and Marriage

Introduction

Martin Thomas

W. Baldwin Spencer dismissed R. H. Mathews' work on kinship as 'an interminable series of papers dealing almost exclusively with the class names & marriages of tribes galore.'[1] While some readers might concur with this assessment, I would encourage patience in considering the kinship writings, despite the challenges they pose. This aspect of Mathews' work is the least accessible to a contemporary audience. Yet for him it was the most important. No less than 71 of his 171 publications discuss marriage customs. Disagreements about kinship rules were at the heart of his dispute with Spencer and A. W. Howitt (see my general introduction to this volume). So familiarity with Mathews' work on this subject is integral to an appreciation of his larger project. Although anthropological understandings of kinship have undergone several revolutions since Mathews' time, his writings on the subject reveal much about his thinking and methodology—and the milieu in which he worked.

Mathews' first publication on kinship was read before the Brisbane branch of the Royal Geographical Society of Australasia in 1894.[2] It concerns the Kamilaroi people of New South Wales whose country he knew well from his surveying days. In tackling this subject, Mathews was contributing to an established literature. The clergyman William Ridley did pioneering research on Kamilaroi language and marriage rules in the 1860s,[3] while Howitt and his collaborator Lorimer Fison had discussed Kamilaroi kinship at length in their book, *Kamilaroi and Kurnai* (1880).

In *Arguments About Aborigines* (1996) L. R. Hiatt shows how the rise of anthropology in the last quarter of the nineteenth century was affected by the publication of Darwin's *On the Origin of Species* in 1859. 'In the context of inescapable questions about the natural history of our own species, Australian Aborigines were assigned the role of exemplars *par excellence* of beginnings and early forms.'[4] Many anthropologists of this period assumed that the principles of natural selection were as fundamental to the formation of social structures as they were to the development of organisms. Just as marsupials and monotremes had survived under conditions of geographic isolation, it was thought that Aboriginal Australia possessed 'primitive' forms of social organisation, long superseded in other parts of the world. As Hiatt describes the international interest in Aboriginal kinship, 'European scholars bent on discovering the origins of social institutions began a rush on Australian material'. From these data they 'fashioned some of the most celebrated and influential works in the history of anthropology'.[5]

The works of Fison, Howitt and especially Spencer (who worked collaboratively with F. J. Gillen, postmaster at Alice Springs) can be counted among these celebrated treatises.[6] Mathews read them closely as his anthropological interests developed in the 1890s. Since Howitt and Fison were major voices in the field when Mathews began publishing, a perspective on their work helps in understanding the intellectual context for his own project. As D. J. Mulvaney glosses Howitt's approach, he sought 'to lay bare the essentials of primeval society, on the assumption that Australia was a storehouse of fossil customs'.[7] The articles translated here establish that Mathews reacted strongly against this approach. The most pronounced difference was in the area of evolutionary theory. Mathews was a sceptic, whereas Howitt and Fison were enthusiasts. Their position was endorsed by strong relationships with social evolutionists in both Britain and the United States.

Fison's research into marriage customs began in 1869 in Fiji where he was stationed as a missionary. A questionnaire from the American evolutionist Henry Lewis Morgan prompted his fledgling inquiries into family organisation, first in Fiji and then in Australia where he teamed up with Howitt, a public servant and magistrate based in Gippsland, Victoria (who had risen to considerable prominence in 1861 when he led the search for the missing explorers Burke and Wills).[8] Their patron Morgan began his research into kinship with Iroquois Indians, whom he had known as a youth in New York State. In *Ancient Society, Or Researches in the Lines of Human Progress from Savagery through Barbarism to Civilization* (1877), he advanced a theory about the evolution of society, establishing a historical hierarchy that began with the inchoate family structure of 'primitive man' and culminated with the putatively monogamous family unit of the industrialised capitalist state.

Mulvaney notes that Howitt was critical in his implementation of Morgan's ideas.[9] But the glee with which he and Fison sought to identify developmental phases in Aboriginal social structure is nonetheless overwhelming. It is evident in the extensive correspondence between Howitt, Fison and Morgan,[10] and in the journal articles they wrote in the 1880s and 90s, published mainly in *Journal of the Anthropological Institute*—a publication readily accessible to Mathews. Morgan had argued that in the most primitive societies (thought to be incognisant of the relationship between sexual intercourse and pregnancy) hunting rights and kinship affiliation descended through the maternal (or uterine) line. In more evolved societies, the transmission of both property and kinship between generations was patrilineal (or agnatic). Howitt and Fison were preoccupied with this issue, and were always eager to find evidence of the transformation from one evolutionary stage to the next.[11] Like Morgan, they drew extraordinary parallels between disparate cultures. For example, in 1885 Howitt and Fison argued for a direct correlation between ancient Attican society and the 'low savagery of Australia'.[12]

The prevalence of such theories explains the eagerness of Mathews to establish whether descent in Australian communities was patrilineal or matrilineal, just as it explains why anthropological disagreements on the subject were so fervent. It also contextualises Mathews' arguments against the institution of 'group marriage', a notion proposed by Morgan and which Howitt, Fison and Spencer discerned in the Australian data they gathered. Hiatt describes Morgan's thinking about this in the following terms:

> The Iroquois system makes sense, he argued, if we assume that it originated in circumstances where men who were related to each other as brothers commonly cohabited with women who were related to each other as sisters, so long as the partners were not related to each other as brother and sister. Within the limits of what may be referred to as 'group marriage', sexual intercourse was promiscuous. The resulting offspring, who were reared together in a communal family, referred to each other as 'brother' and 'sister'; and they referred to all the male adults as 'father' and all the female adults as 'mother'. In the course of social evolution, group marriage eventually gave way to marriage between pairs; but, although sexual mores were thus transformed, the old terminology persisted as a survival from a past era in which it faithfully reflected the actual conditions of reproduction.[13]

As we read in the works presented here, Mathews was a staunch opponent of the group marriage theory, a position he shared with his near-namesake, John Mathew, a Presbyterian minister and anthropologist, based in Melbourne. As Elkin pointed out, Mathews 'was not concerned with the current theories or arguments'.[14] He never argued for evolutionary stages or developmental hierarchies. For the most part, he saw his role as a gatherer of primary data, not as a theorist. In this regard he was an ideal fieldworker according to the model laid down by Sir James Frazer of Cambridge. As the anthropologist Frances Larson describes Frazer's position, he was convinced

> that the separation of data gathering and intellectual analysis reinforced anthropology's scientific integrity, since those collecting information in the field remained indifferent to theoretical bias, while the theoreticians were obliged to consider the whole range of data available to them regardless of their own intellectual prejudices.[15]

Naïve as he was to assume that fieldworkers in the colonies would or could operate in a theoretical vacuum, Frazer applied his standard unevenly. He gave short shrift to Mathews, despite his lack of theoretical pretensions, and lavishly supported Howitt, Fison and Spencer who broadly endorsed his own position.[16]

Mathews' attempt to sidestep evolutionary theory led him to think about Aboriginal kinship in historical terms. As explained below, he was convinced that the system of moieties, sections and sub-sections was the residue of successive waves of migration and intertribal amalgamation.[17] His idea that the institutions of kinship were historically determined—and thus bore no resemblance to biologically engrained attributes—was a minority position that won him limited acceptance in an era dominated by evolutionary theory.

*

The reader will notice how many of Mathews' kinship publications conform to the mould of scientific writing of his period. Often just a few pages in length, his reports list the names of moieties (which he called 'phratries' or less often 'cycles') for a particular district. He included a table listing the sections or sub-sections (sub-divisions of the moieties) and often provided a list of totems. He also tried to establish how totems and sections passed from parents to children—whether the system was matrilineal or patrilineal. Although often modest, such a report was sufficient to rate as a publishable 'discovery'. Letters to Mathews from the German ethnologist Moritz von Leonhardi show how closely such work was read outside Australia (see 'Correspondence', this volume).

The three translations published here show various faces of Mathews' work on kinship. 'Social Organisation of the Aboriginal Tribes of Australia' (1902) concerns the Yangman people (known as Yungmunni to Mathews), occupants of 'an extended area on the plateau which separates the sources of the Roper and Daly rivers in the Northern Territory'. Using tables, Mathews explains the names of sections and which of them are permitted to intermarry. These are the rules governing regular or what Mathews describes as 'direct' marriages. He points out that polygamy is acceptable and that sometimes the second wife belongs to a different section from that of the first. This was another aspect of Mathews' kinship study that drew the ire of contemporaries who believed that such unions were either illegal or else a sign that the culture was in decline. Mathews, however, was convinced of the antiquity and legitimacy of these 'irregular' marriages, which seemed to be tolerated by the community, although they transgressed the normal rules. He argued they did not contravene the ancient laws; instead a further set of rules came into play when such unions were being considered. He emphasised that 'irregular' marriages are fairly rare and that when they do occur, 'one of the spouses must come from a distant family, to avoid close blood relationship between the parties to the union'. Throughout his writings on moieties and sections, Mathews maintained that they were not designed to prevent inbreeding. He argued that the genealogy of each individual was well known to the elders of a community, and that inbreeding was prevented by their refusal to tolerate any marriage of close relatives.

How Mathews obtained such information reveals much about his kinship study—its strengths and limitations. As he points out in the 1902 article translated here, 'more urgent matters' had prevented him from ever going to the Northern Territory. He relied on correspondents to interview Aboriginal people whom they employed or knew in other ways. This was also true of Cape York Peninsula in North Queensland, a location discussed in 'Remarks on the Natives of Australia' (1906), the second translation published here. No correspondent is credited, but in an earlier article on Queensland, Mathews had acknowledged the assistance of Reverend Nicholas Hey, superintendent of the Presbyterian Mission at Mapoon, on the west coast of the cape.[18] Letters from Hey in Mathews' correspondence files reveal that he was the source of the Queensland data reported in 'Remarks on the Natives of Australia'.[19]

Missionaries, who were usually well educated, were obvious points of contact for someone like Mathews. In 1901 Hey was reputedly the only European within 90 miles of the Batavia River.[20] He knew the local language sufficiently well to publish a treatise on the subject.[21] Although missionaries were often more sympathetic to Aboriginal people than were the settlers who displaced them, they carried a generous share of cultural baggage. Many considered themselves duty-bound to eliminate the 'heathen' customs that so interested Mathews. In an early letter Hey warned him that the range of any ethnographic inquiry would be strictly curtailed.

> [I]n order to become well acquainted with the old customs of the blacks it is essential to enter into all their little doings & know their traditions & there is always a great deal of filth & other obscene ideas connected with them, & it is not in our interest to show any great desire to enter into, but rather to abhor these things.[22]

Despite this unpromising beginning, Hey became a valuable source of information. But his comments are indicative of the difficulties Mathews encountered on an almost daily basis. He quickly realised that the rules of marriage represented one of the more acceptable faces of Aboriginal society. Despite the very great differences between the cultures, the institution of marriage was common to both. Mathews had considerable respect for Aboriginal unions, which might explain the contemptuous tone in which he writes about the theory of group marriage.

Mathews also knew that moiety and section names were not secret-sacred. Quite the reverse. Knowledge of where each person (and indeed each element of the cosmos) fitted in terms of kinship was fundamental to almost every activity and social interaction. That is one of the reasons why many white people, including a number of Mathews' correspondents, were given a 'skin' name, section or totem. Sometimes this was presented as an honour or a form of induction into the Aboriginal community. But it was also to do with Aboriginal people's need to situate the settlers of their acquaintance within *their* system of classification. Awareness of this made Mathews confident that if properly directed a diligent correspondent from anywhere in Australia could gather a basic set of data. His own role was to efficiently 'manage' his precious volunteers, as he explained to E. S. Hartland in England.

> I referred and re-referred the information sent me by old residents of Central Australia back to them for further sifting and inquiry. Half a dozen of my best correspondents were and are located in different parts of the Chingalee, Binbingha, Wombaia and Inchalauchu country peopled with tribes of the eight-section system and they all gave the same results, quite unknown to each other. I also had two excellent men among the tribes of the Victoria river and three more in the Kimberley district of Western Australia where the 8-section system prevails. I was the 'head and front' of the investigation and my men worked and re-worked under my directions.[23]

Persons willing to become entangled in Mathews' research were comparatively rare. Should they volunteer a reply to his letters, he bombarded them with requests for information and offprints of his publications (perhaps in the hope of creating a reciprocal obligation). Mathews was well aware of the extent to which he pushed his correspondents, as can be seen in a letter he wrote to Daisy Bates that acknowledges the death of his correspondent Thomas Muir in Western Australia.

> I am sorry to hear of Mr Muir's death. Poor old Muir must have been dreadfully bored by my letters, but he took them in good part, and tried his best to help me. But I only published his statements for what they were worth.[24]

Limited by what he could expect of correspondents who invariably complained about lack of time, many of Mathews' writings on kinship do little more than report the names of sections and totems. But there are hints of a more complex understanding, as can be seen in 'Remarks on the Natives of Australia' (1906) where he comments on the Nawalgu, Milpulo and Marawara tribes of western New South Wales. Mathews reports that they have 'blood' and 'shade' divisions in addition to moieties, sections and totems. As I explain in my general introduction to this volume, the 'blood' and 'shade' castes or divisions influenced marriage arrangements and also governed where a person sat in relation to others. His report here is consistent with his documentation of the Kurnu, Ngemba, Kamilaroi and other communities of inland New South Wales. They did of course live in places that he could get to in person. So it is not surprising that his most original and reliable kinship study concerns these areas. As the astute Moritz von Leonhardi rightly diagnosed in his letters (see 'Correspondence', this volume), Mathews was far from correct in reporting matrilineal descent among the Arrernte people of Central Australia, a part of the country that he never visited.[25]

In 'The Natives of Australia' (1902), the third translation presented here, we get a sense of how Mathews synthesised the information he was assembling from so many parts of the continent. Atypically, the reporter becomes interpreter. He opens by expressing his ideas about the original population of the country, surmising that this occurred in the distant past when Africa, Asia, Australia and Papua formed a great southern land mass. The 'first human beings', who were of a 'negroid type', spread across this territory during successive phases of migration. In later periods the original 'primitive race' was invaded 'by hostile tribes of a higher character and a more advanced civilisation'. These new arrivals were superior fighters who displaced the original inhabitants. The later immigrants, however, never reached Tasmania 'which had become an island following the subsidence of a strip of land which became Bass Strait'.

Mathews was convinced that the descendants of these first inhabitants also survived on the mainland, particularly in the mountainous and coastal regions of South Australia, Western Australia, Victoria and New South Wales. His argument for this is that they lack the complex kinship system found across most of the continent. Instead of moieties and sections, they have what Mathews termed the *Tooar* marriage system, in which 'old men assembled in council to appoint the women to the boys'. Mathews writes that in both their physical appearance and cultural practices, the *Tooar* communities 'greatly resemble the Tasmanians'.

Mathews then discusses the more orthodox kinship and marriage systems found elsewhere in Australia—those involving moieties divided into either two or four sections. He hypothesises that these systems are the residue of various tribal amalgamations. He cites certain legends to support his case and argues that the historical experience of migration and inter-tribal merging can be discerned in initiation ceremonies. Commenting on the Kamilaroi ceremony at Tallwood, New South Wales, which he documented in 1896,[26] Mathews proposes that the removal of the novices from their mothers 'may be a symbol of what happened in the past'. During an enemy attack, he conjectures, 'a group of men may have taken charge of the women while the others took the young people away to bring them up in the traditions of the conquerors'. This article is unusual amongst Mathews' writings because of its interpretive approach. Some of these ideas were also advanced in 'The Origin, Organization and Ceremonies of the Australian Aborigines' (1900)[27] and 'Australian Tribes—their Formation and Government' (1906).[28] He discussed the *Tooar* marriage system in 'The Organisation, Language and Initiation Ceremonies of the Aborigines of the South-East Coast of N. S. Wales' (1900).[29] These 'overview' type articles give important insights into how Mathews thought about the notion of kinship. He treated it historically—as evidence of Aboriginal migration into Australia.

The vehement arguments fought out by Mathews and his contemporaries are largely due to the fact that none of the combatants was prepared to recognise the possibility of cultural transformation and adaptation. In contrast to the turn-of-the-century observers, who regarded kinship classification as timeless and immutable, it is now acknowledged that the systems of moieties, sections and sub-sections have undergone major and continuing modifications. Working from linguistic data, Patrick McConvell argued in 1985 that the patrilineal system of eight sub-sections, found in such diverse locations as Central Australia, the Kimberleys, Arnhem Land and further east in the Gulf country, originated from a fairly limited area in the Lower Victoria River Basin.[30] The spread of this system did not necessarily displace older systems; in contemporary Arnhem Land, for example, the patrilineal sub-sections determine marriage, yet they co-exist with the older matrilineal moieties. McConvell suggests that these transformations were occurring at the time when Mathews and Spencer were pursuing their inquiries and that in some cases this explains their often divergent findings.[31]

ENDNOTES

[1] Spencer to Roth, 30 January 1903, Sir Baldwin Spencer Manuscripts, Pitt Rivers Museum MSS Box 1A/Roth 13.

[2] RHM 1894-95, 'The Kamilaroi Class System of the Australian Aborigines', *Proceedings and Transactions of the Queensland Branch of the Royal Geographical Society of Australasia*, vol. 10.

[3] Ridley, William 1866, 'On the Kamilaroi Tribe of Australians and their Dialect', *Journal of the Ethnological Society of London*, vol. 4, and Ridley, William 1875, *Kamilaroi, and other Australian Languages*, Thomas Richards, Government Printer, Sydney.

[4] Hiatt, L. R. 1996, *Arguments about Aborigines: Australia and the Evolution of Social Anthropology*, Cambridge University Press, Cambridge, p. xii.

[5] Ibid.

[6] Spencer and Gillen rose to international prominence with the publication in 1899 of their *The Native Tribes of Central Australia*, Dover, New York, 1968.

[7] Mulvaney, D. J. 1971, 'The Ascent of Aboriginal Man: Howitt as Anthropologist' in Walker, Mary Howitt (ed.), *Come Wind, Come Weather: A Biography of Alfred Howitt*, Melbourne University Press, Melbourne, p. 290.

[8] Walker, *Come Wind, Come Weather*, ch. 11.

[9] Mulvaney, 'The Ascent of Aboriginal Man', p. 289.

[10] Stern, Bernard J. (ed.) 1930, 'Selections from the Letters of Lorimer Fison and A. W. Howitt to Lewis Henry Morgan', *American Anthropologist*, vol. 32 (new series).

[11] See Howitt, A. W. and Fison, Rev. L. 1883, 'From Mother-Right to Father-Right', *Journal of the Anthropological Institute*, vol. 12.

[12] Howitt and Fison 1885, 'On the Deme and the Horde', *Journal of the Anthropological Institute*, vol. 14, p. 165.

[13] Hiatt, *Arguments about Aborigines*, p. 39.

[14] Elkin, A. P., 'R. H. Mathews: His Contribution to Aboriginal Studies' (MS draft of Part IV), Elkin Papers, University of Sydney Archives, MS P130/9/138.

[15] Larson, Frances 2007, 'Anthropology as Comparative Anatomy?: Reflecting on the Study of Material Culture During the Late 1800s and the Late 1900s', *Journal of Material Culture*, vol. 12, no. 1, p. 97.

[16] Frazer's support of Spencer and Gillen is described at length in Mulvaney, D. J. and Calaby, J. H. 1985, *'So Much That is New': Baldwin Spencer, 1860-1929: A Biography*, Melbourne University Press, Carlton. For his attitude to Howitt and Fison, see his joint obituary of them: Frazer, J.G. 1909, 'Howitt and Fison', *Folk-Lore*, vol. 20, no. 2.

[17] Mathew also viewed the moiety system as the residue of tribal (or in this case *inter-racial*) amalgamation. See Mathew, John 1899, *Eaglehawk and Crow: A Study of the Australian Aborigines including an Inquiry into their Origin and a Survey of Australian Languages*, Melville, Mullen and Slade, Melbourne and Prentis, Malcolm 1998, *Science, Race & Faith: A Life of John Mathew*, Centre for the Study of Australian Christianity, Sydney, ch. 6.

[18] RHM 1900, 'Marriage and Descent among the Australian Aborigines', *Journal and Proceedings of the Royal Society of New South Wales*, vol. 34, p. 132.

[19] Hey to Mathews, 26 October 1899, R. H. Mathews Papers, National Library of Australia (henceforth NLA) MS 8006/2/5.

[20] Hey to Mathews, 26 January 1901, R. H. Mathews Papers, NLA MS 8006/2/5.

[21] Hey, Rev. N. 1903, *An Elementary Grammar of the Nggerikudi Language*, George Arthur Vaughan, Government Printer, Brisbane.

[22] Hey to Mathews, 4 August 1899, R. H. Mathews Papers, NLA MS 8006/2/5.

[23] Mathews to Hartland, 10 August 1907, Letters to E. S. Hartland, National Library of Wales, MS 16889C. Reproduced this volume.

[24] Mathews to Bates, 16 July 1905, Daisy Bates Papers, NLA MSS 365/970/250-381.

[25] An entry in Mathews' diary for 1907, 'Left Adelaide 25th Feby–arrive H'burg 14th March', led Elkin and others to assume that Mathews made a short visit to Carl Strehlow in Hermannsburg that year. In fact, the diary refers only to the progress of *letters* between Sydney and Hermannsburg (which received mail just once a month). Mathews made no claim to have visited the Centre, even in writings that post-date 1907. Carl Strehlow's 'Mission Chronicle', in which he detailed all visits to the station, makes no mention of Mathews. I am indebted to John Strehlow for checking the Chronicle on my behalf.

[26] RHM 1896, 'The Bora of the Kamilaroi Tribes', *Proceedings of the Royal Society of Victoria*, vol. 9 (new series), and RHM 1896,'The Bora, or Initiation Ceremonies of the Kamilaroi Tribe (Part II)', *Journal of the Anthropological Institute*, vol. 25.

[27] RHM 1900, 'The Origin, Organization and Ceremonies of the Australian Aborigines', *Proceedings of the American Philosophical Society*, vol. 39.

[28] RHM 1906, 'Australian Tribes—Their Formation and Government', *Zeitschrift für Ethnologie*, vol. 38.

[29] RHM 1900, 'The Origin, Organization and Ceremonies of the Australian Aborigines', *Proceedings of the American Philosophical Society*, vol. 39, 556-78.

[30] McConvell, Patrick 1985, 'The Origin of Subsections in Northern Australia', *Oceania*, vol. 56, no. 1, p. 16.

[31] Ibid., p. 18.

Social Organisation of Some Australian Tribes

R. H. Mathews

First published as 'Organisation sociale de quelques tribus australiennes' in *Bulletins et Mémoires de la Société d'Anthropologie de Paris*, vol. 7 (5th series), 1906, pp. 165-74. The article was written in English and translated into French by Oscar Schmidt. This version was retranslated into English by Mathilde de Hauteclocque.[1]

In 1901 I contributed to this society an article containing certain rudimentary remarks on the social state of the Yungmunni and some tribes allied to them who occupy a large region of the plain separating the sources of the Roper and Daly rivers of the Northern Territory, the name given to the northern and central portions of South Australia.[2]

Since that time, I have been able to procure for myself some more complete details on the sociology of the native tribes in question which I consider my duty to communicate to the society.

More urgent matters have prevented me from going personally among these tribes, but I had the good fortune to make the acquaintance of owners and managers of many 'runs'[3] of this part of Australia. I sent them very precise lists of all the subjects about which I wished to be informed, as well as giving them some indication of the manner in which to proceed with their investigations. The confidence with which my correspondents inspire me, and the personal knowledge I have on the subject, allow me to assert that the information contained in these pages can be safely accepted.

To clarify the subject, I remind the reader of Table 1 from my preceding paper, reproduced on page 415. The only difference between the present table and the preceding one is that the 'Wives' column is placed first and the 'Husband' one after it. This arrangement makes the cycle of the women stand out better.

The whole tribe is divided into eight sections, each one having a distinct name, which allows the members of each division to be easily recognised; the identification is, in addition, made easier by the masculine or feminine form of each of the eight names.

Table 1

Cycle	Wife	Husband	Son	Daughter
	Inkagalla	Eemitch	Uwallaree	Imballaree
A.....	Imballaree	Unmarra	Urwalla	Imbawalla
	Imbawalla	Uwannee	Uwungaree	Imbongaree
	Imbongaree	Tabachin	Yungalla	Inkagalla
	Immadenna	Yungalla	Tabachin	Tabadenna
B.....	Tabadenna	Uwungaree	Uwannee	Imbannee
	Imbannee	Urwalla	Unmarra	Inganmarra
	Inganmarra	Uwallaree	Eemitch	Immadenna

The above table shows the mother, father, son and daughter on the same line from left to right. Note that the eight sections of women are classed in two distinct series which have been called 'cycles',[4] each cycle being composed of four specific categories of women, repeating itself continually as follows.

Let us examine the upper moiety of the table—the A Cycle. We will find that the women from the 'Wife' and 'Daughter' columns reproduce each other in a certain rotation. For example, Inkagalla is the mother of Imballaree and she has a daughter Imbawalla; Imbawalla, in turn, produces Imbongaree who becomes the mother of Inkagalla; now, Inkagalla is the name of the section with which we started. This series is continually repeated, no matter which name we commence with. Let us call this series of women 'Cycle A'.

If we take the women from the lower moiety of Table 1 (Cycle B), we find that Immadenna is the mother of Tabadenna; Tabadenna bears Imbannee and her daughter is Inganmarra; Inganmarra, in turn, produces Immadenna. This series, which we call 'Cycle B', repeats itself forever just as the first one does.

Let us come back to Table 1. Eemitch marries Inkagalla, Unmarra weds Imballaree and so on for all the others. Those are the normal and general alliances and can, as a result, be distinguished as 'tabular' marriages.[5] But more detailed investigations into the marriage laws of this tribe have shown that a man from any section is qualified to marry within three other sections of women who have been added to, or rather replaced by, those mentioned above.

To draw out all the possible marriages between sections, we must establish another table which will show that the four sections of women within which a man—Eemitch, for example—can marry, might also be claimed by three other sections of men. For instance, Uwannee, Urwalla and Yungalla, as well as by that same Eemitch. The following table indicates a category of four sections of women from whom four categories of men are required to take their wives, in accordance with the rules which will be explained in detail in Tables 3 and 4.

Table 2

Cycle	Husbands	Wives	Offspring
	Eemitch	Inkagalla	The children of each
A	Uwannee	Imbawalla	woman, taken individually,
	Urwalla	Imbannee	are the same as in Table 1, regardless of
	Yungalla	Immadenna	the name of her husband.
	Unmarra	Imballaree	
B	Tabachin	Imbongaree	
	Uwungaree	Tabadenna	
	Uwallaree	Inganmarra	

In all cases, the name of the section to which her offspring will belong depends irrevocably on the mother. If Eemitch marries Inkagalla, his children are Uwallaree and Imballaree; if he weds an Imbannee, they will be Unmarra and Inganmarra; if he takes an Imbawalla, they will be Uwungaree and Imbongaree and if he is married to an Immadenna, they will be Tabachin and Tabadenna. See in Table 1, the name of each woman's children and of all the sections of women.

A woman taken from the 'Wife' column of Table 2 can be married by any member of one of the four sections of men in the 'Husbands' column. Therefore it is obvious that the name of her child's father will not matter, because it will depend on which of the four sections she has taken him from.

For example, let us take Uwallaree, the first of the names in the 'Sons' column of Table 1. If his mother, Inkagalla, had married Eemitch, he would be the direct father or 'First Father' of Uwallaree (see Tables 3 and 4). If, on the contrary, Inkagalla married Uwannee, he would become the alternate father or 'Second Father' of Uwallaree. If she married with Urwalla, he would be the 'Third Father' and finally, if with Yungalla, this last one would be the 'Fourth Father' of Uwallaree. All of which goes to show that it matters little which of these four husbands Inkagalla will have chosen—her son will still be Uwallaree.

Let us temporarily admit the term 'phratry' to refer to each of the categories or groupings of women appearing in the 'Wives' column of Table 2. We notice that the men in the 'Husbands' column of Phratry A produce the men in the 'Husbands' column of Phratry B, not withstanding the fact that this filiation is limited by that which we have described as 'First Fathers' which we find on the same line from left to right. The 'Wives' of one of the phratry columns equally produce the 'Wives' of the other without limits, the descent in each section being ruled by the mothers. It is therefore obvious that just by alternating itself, one phratry stays related to the other.

I have shown on a preceding page that although a man can only have one real father, the name of this father's section would depend on the man whom his mother had married. It follows that a man from any section can have a different paternal grandfather. But in retracing the filiation of many families, thanks to the help of trustworthy correspondents who have resided in the district for years, I find that there are, so to speak, four sorts of men in each section; for example, there are four Eemitchs of different descents which we will distinguish with the Numbers 1, 2, 3 and 4.

Let us look at Table 3. We find, on the left, that the father of Eemitch No. 1 is Uwallaree and that the 'First Father' of Uwallaree is Eemitch. Eemitch No. 1 marries as his 'First Wife' Inkagalla, daughter of Tabachin, who is the son of his 'First Father's' sister; or he marries as his 'Second Wife' Imbannee, daughter of Tabadenna, daughter of his 'First Father's' sister.

Moving on in Table 3, let us take Eemitch No. 2 with a different descent; he marries as his 'First Wife' Imbawalla, daughter of the son of Imbannee, who is sister of Uwannee his 'Second Father' or alternate father; or, he marries as his 'Second Wife' Immadenna, daughter of Imbannee, who is sister of Uwannee, his 'Second Father'.

Now, let us take Table 4. Eemitch No 3, son of Uwallaree who, in turn, has Urwalla as 'Third Father', or let us also take Eemitch No 4, son of Uwallaree whose 'Fourth Father' is Yungalla. The other details are the same as those given in our explanation of Table 3.

Table 3

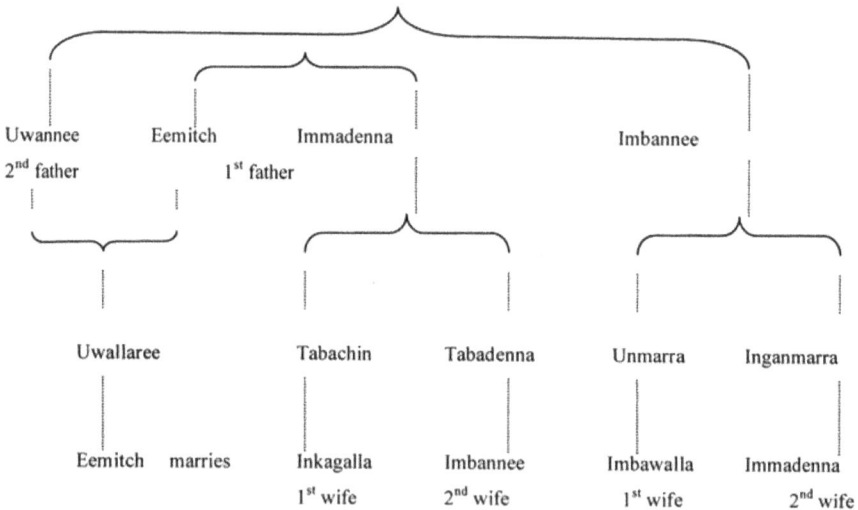

Table 4

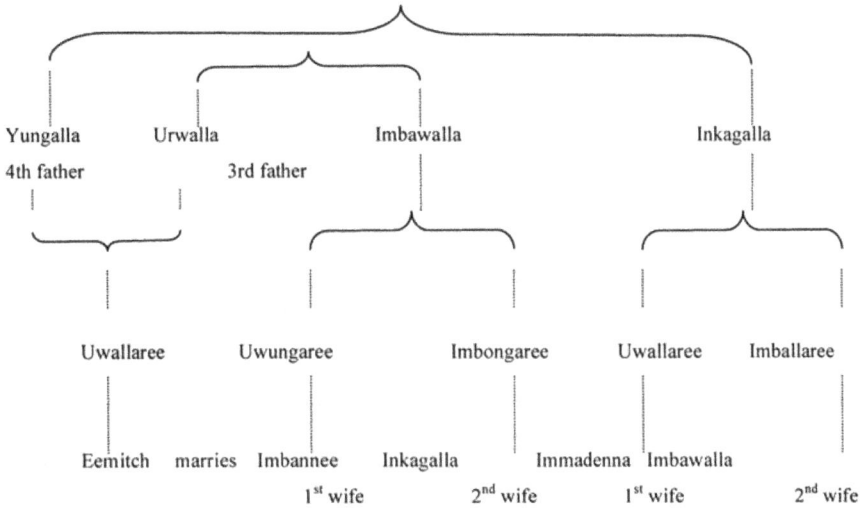

		Yungalla	Urwalla		Imbawalla		Inkagalla	

The diagram shows the following relationships:

Yungalla — 4th father
Urwalla — 3rd father
Imbawalla
Inkagalla

Uwallaree   Uwungaree   Imbongaree   Uwallaree   Imballaree

Eemitch   marries   Imbannee   Inkagalla   Immadenna   Imbawalla
                    1st wife   2nd wife   1st wife   2nd wife

The examination of these two tables shows that, whichever one of the four wives a man of any given section is permitted to marry, this wife is always related to him, although the filiation is different.

If, in Table 3, I have brought together Eemitch and Uwannee as grandfathers, it is because, in referring to Table 1, we find that these men, while belonging to two sections, take their wives directly and normally from the same cycle of women. I have, for the same reasons, brought together Urwalla and Yungalla as grandfathers in Table 4.

In Table 3 we see Eemitch No. 1 marrying an Inkagalla or an Imbannee as first or second wife. Eemitch No. 2 will take, in the same way, an Imbawalla or an Immadenna. Eemitch No. 3 (Table 4) marries an Imbannee or an Inkagalla and Eemitch No. 4 becomes tied to an Immadenna or an Imbawalla. Careful examination of Tables 3 and 4 shows that each of these four Eemitchs in our example can marry his 'First Wife' from among those in Cycle A, Table 1, and his 'Second Wife' from Cycle B of that same table. There are, however, certain customary extensions or variations to this last paragraph. An Eemitch can, for example, marry, in certain cases, an Inkagalla as 'first' wife and an Imbawalla as 'second' wife; in this case, the two wives would be taken from the same cycle (Cycle A, Table 1).

Although each section is comprised of four categories of men—four Eemitchs for example—they reduce themselves, in fact, to two, and it follows that they marry women from Cycle A or they take them from Cycle B, which in reality reduces each section to two parties instead of four.

In all Australian tribes, the children call their father's brothers by the same name as their father. Thanks to this custom, the Eemitch of our examples could trace his filiation back through one of his father's brothers who would have a 'Father No 2' by modifying the details.

In Table 3, we have shown that Eemitch No 1 marries Inkagalla, that is to say that if Tabachin weds Imbongaree, as in Table 2, his daughter will be Inkagalla and could be considered his 'tabular' daughter. But, let us suppose that this same Tabachin marries one of the three other women in Phratry A, his daughter could be Imbawalla or Imbannee or Immadenna; this daughter would therefore be 'first wife' to Eemitch. The same variant would happen for the 'first wife' of Eemitch's Nos. 2, 3 or 4. Other variants could be cited, but the fundamental principle remains immutable for all of them.

However, although the phratries recur, they have this particular characteristic of not marrying between themselves. Let us take, for example, the 'Husbands' and the 'Wives' of Phratry A, Table 2. Their 'sons' and 'daughters' become the 'Husbands' and 'Wives' of Phratry B, but they intermarry exclusively among themselves. Their offspring become, in turn, the 'Husbands' and 'Wives' of Phratry A, and intermarry among themselves exactly as their parents did. There is therefore no possible outside marriage, either within the sections or the Phratries, if we accept Table 2.

Returning to Table 1, it is clear that Eemitch can marry Inkagalla or Imbawalla from Cycle A, or he can take Imbannee or Immadenna as his wife, these unions being ruled as explained in Tables 3 and 4. That is to say that Eemitch will look for his wife in one of the two cycles, a custom which absolutely excludes all exogamy or outside marriage.

If we continue to scrutinise Table 1, it reveals to us the interesting fact that, taken as a whole, the four sections of the 'Husbands' column of Cycle A, are able to marry on average with all eight sections of women in the 'Wife' column. It is the same for an average of four men of Cycle B who can, in the same way, take a wife from all eight sections of the same table. The conclusion that can be drawn therefore, is that outside marriage does not exist in any of the tribes discussed in this article.

The preceding pages reveal the manner in which marriage is practised and perpetuated within the different sections. On this basis, unions between two given persons are ruled by a system of betrothal which takes place at the birth of a child and, often enough, before the event. The choice of a wife or husband is fixed by the grandparents of the future spouses.

The genealogical graphics which follow give a summary which will allow the reader to follow my paper.

A brief summary of the succession of the 'totems' is not without interest. The traditions of these tribes are full of fabulous stories concerning the ancestors of each totem. While some of them resemble men and women of present days, others are fabulous beings created by the native legends. In far off times, as in our days, the ancestors of the totems formed families, or groups of families, each possessing their own hunting ground in a part of the tribe's territory. Born in a particular place, they occupied it by birth right. Some were referred to, for example, as swans, others as dogs, or kangaroos, or snakes, or crows and so on. The members of each of these family groups were divided up into the same eight sections which exist among them today.

Some of the traditional totems were invested with a greater authority than others, as is true of the head men of certain totemic groups today. Some of these fabulous territories were large, others small. As soon as death removed one of these legendary men, his spirit was supposed to establish itself in a well known place within his hunting ground, such as a rock, or a tree, or a hill, or a pond or even to disappear underground. He could also, by virtue of his supernatural power, leave some parts of his spirit, as a special gift to his lineage, in different places, such as places where he had camped or accomplished a brilliant feat, or celebrated some initiation ceremony and so on. The places consecrated by these events were scattered across different areas of the place where he lived.

All the members of his family naturally possessed the same rights over the same hunting grounds and, in turn, their spirits haunted certain places in the same way. After a number of generations, all the camps, all the ponds, all the large rocks, the springs, the hills, the noteworthy trees etc. of this territory were packed, saturated, so to speak, with spirits. Thus, there were bandicoots in certain places, snakes, porcupines etc. in others. Some of these animals, more numerous than others, left a large number of spirit offspring, while others less common had only a limited number of representatives. The exact location of each of these familiar sites is made known by oral tradition to all the living natives, who are sure to adorn the great feats of these ancestors with all the virtues that their imagination can invent.

Whether they take a human form or whether they are monsters, these creatures, fantastical or exaggerated by native inspiration, possess supernatural powers. Some made springs or streams flow, others raised up hills and rocks in certain historical places.

All the natives believe firmly in the reincarnation of their ancestors' ghosts, the first phalanx of the spirits, reappearing continually from one human to the other. These natives ignore the natural laws of procreation and are convinced that conception is absolutely independent of sexual consent. When a women has felt, for the first time, movement within her, she remembers the place where the event took place and announces it to the people present. And so, the belief is, that it is the spirit or the soul of a late ancestor who, at that same moment, entered the body of the woman. This entrance could have taken place via one of the natural orifices or by some part of the skin.

When the child is born, it will be given the totemic name of the mystical ancestor attributed to this special place. If, for example, the foetus moved for the first time next to a remarkable rock, hill, pond or camp known for being haunted by the spirit of the galah, the child will belong to the galah totem, irrespective of the totem of its father or mother.

It is important to remember, as far as the succession of the totems is concerned, that in all our native tribes, the women are taken into the familial group or 'tribelet' of her husband and that she travels his country with him. If, for example, he is 'crow', he will spend a large part of his time, with his wife, in the places especially haunted by his ancestor. When his wife notices, for the first time, that she is pregnant, she will very probably find herself in a place consecrated to some crow of times gone by, because she lives in the country of the 'crow men'. In this case, the child will become a 'crow' like its father.

If, on the contrary, the foetus moves for the first time when she finds herself visiting her own people, that is to say in the district where she was born or where she grew up, it is very probable that the event will be related to one of her own ancestors. If it is 'porcupine' [echidna], the child will be 'porcupine' like its mother. If, at that critical moment, she found herself on a hunting ground haunted more particularly by the 'pigeon spirits', her child will become 'pigeon'. It could happen therefore that certain of her children have different totems; however, given that their parents will always live, by preference, in the 'crow' country as I have said, it is more than likely that the majority of the children will be 'crow'. It is thus by error that other investigators have been able to claim that the filiation of totems is made via the father.

Certain places, such as a rock, spring, tree etc, are supposed to be haunted by the spirits of animals of closely related species cohabiting together as they did when they were living. If a mother feels the first movement of her foetus in such a place, it would be impossible to decide which spirit had penetrated her body and it becomes very difficult for the elders of the tribe to determine the totem of the child.

The space in your journal being limited, I am obliged to bring to a close this interesting subject. Please recall that in preceding articles I have already proven that 'exogamy' does not exist in Australian tribes. In dealing, in 1894, with the laws of marriage in the Kamilaroi tribe, I pointed out that although a Butha woman was the normal wife of a man from the Murri section, a Murri could also marry a Martha;[6] which is to say, that a man from that section could take a wife from either phratry. In 1897, I again drew attention to a custom established in the Kamilaroi and Wirraidyuri tribes, allowing a man to marry in these two phratries.[7] It is thus obvious that exogamy cannot exist among the Kamilaroi, Wirraidyuri, Ngeumba or other similar tribes in New South Wales.

In 1898, I described the sociology of the Dippil[8] and other tribes occupying more than half of Queensland. In this article, I showed that a Barrang man married a woman from the same section. Since then, I have pursued my investigations throughout all of Queensland amongst the main tribes, and I have been able to assert authoritatively, in other papers, that exogamy did not exist there.

In 1904, I also made known a series of facts concerning the sociology of the native tribes of New South Wales and of Victoria, which refutes incontestably the existence of exogamy in these two states.[9]

If my preceding articles on this subject are put together side by side with this current paper, I can only draw one conclusion: that exogamy is absolutely impossible in the native tribes of the Northern Territory, New South Wales, Victoria, Queensland and eastern Australia. Therefore the fact emerges that after all the investigations which I have pursued, there is no evidence of exogamy among the native tribes of the whole of Australia.[10]

My study of Australian sociology over many years has convinced me that neither sexual promiscuity, nor what has been called 'group marriage', have ever existed within the Australian tribes. I am equally sure that the divisions into cycles, phratries and sections were not instituted to prevent intermarriages, but that they were gradually developed under the influence of the environment.

Spencer and Gillen drew up, in their *Northern Tribes of Central Australia* (1904), tables of tribes whose sociology resembles that of the Yungmunni, who divide their tribe into eight sections. The tables published by these two authors are unable to give any idea of a practical arrangement of the sections in cycles, phratries or whatever we call them, and are nothing but a confused and ill-assorted mix. It is a mistake to assert, as they do, that the filiation of the sections operates via the men and they are completely mistaken in declaring that the community is divided into 'two exogamous groups'.

In his book *The Native Tribes of South-East Australia*, Mr A. W. Howitt proves that he does not understand anything about the elementary principles of Australian sociology when he claims that 'all the Australian tribes are divided into two moieties and it is forbidden for each of these moieties to marry in their own group'. He is also completely mistaken in speaking of the 'division of the community into two exogamous moieties'.

ENDNOTES

[1] [Editor's note] An offprint of this article, containing pencilled corrections in Mathews' hand, is located at National Library of Australia MS 8006/8/307. These amendments have been incorporated in the text.

[2] RHM 1901, 'Organisation Sociale des Tribus Aborigènes de l'Australie', *Bulletins et Mémoires de la Société d'Anthropologie de Paris*, vol. 5, no. 4, pp. 415-19.

[3] 'Run' is the term given to define an area of land used for the raising of all sorts of animals.

[4] [Editor's note] Mathews usually referred to moieties as 'cycles' or 'phratries'. Both these terms are used in the article.

[5] [Editor's note] Described as such because they conform to those laid out in the table.

[6] RHM 1894-5, 'The Kamilaroi Class System of the Australian Aborigines', *Proceedings and Transactions of the Royal Geographical Society of Australasia*, vol. 10, p. 24.

[7] RHM 1897, 'The Totemic Divisions of the Australian Tribes', *Journal and Proceedings of the Royal Society of New South Wales,* vol. 31, pp. 156-76.

[8] RHM 1898, 'Divisions of Queensland Aborigines', *Proceedings of the American Philosophical Society*, vol. 37, pp. 328-30, with a map of Queensland.

[9] RHM 1905, *Ethnological Notes on the Native Tribes of New South Wales and Victoria*, F. W. White General Printer, Sydney, pp. 5-15 and 84-103. This is the book version of an article of the same title, first published in 1904.

[10] [Editor's note] That Western Australia and South Australia go unmentioned suggests the translator erred in writing 'all of Australia'. Tasmania is generally ignored in Mathews' writings.

Remarks on the Natives of Australia

R. H. Mathews

First published as 'Bemerkungen über die Eingebornen Australiens' in *Mitteilungen der Anthropologischen Gesellschaft*, vol. 36, 1906, pp. 167-73. The article was written in English and translated into German by an unnamed translator. This version was retranslated into English by Christine Winter with reference to Mathews' original draft in the National Library of Australia (NLA MS 8006/5/8).

Introduction

In 1903 I published in this journal a short grammar and vocabulary of the Kumbainggeri language spoken on the northeast coast of New South Wales.[1] The following year I dealt with the elements of the grammar of the Tyeddyuwurru language,[2] in use in the central parts of Victoria, and described the important ceremony of initiation known as the Mŭltyerra, which is practised by the Kurnū tribe in New South Wales.[3]

In the present article I shall describe the social organisation of a number of tribes inhabiting both sides of the Darling River in New South Wales. Then follows information on the sociology of some tribes of Queensland. A study of these organisations will exhibit the utter fallacy of the belief in exogamy which has been so tenaciously adhered to by all Australian writers who belong to the old school.

I am the first and only author to report that there is no exogamy among any of the tribes whose sociology I have investigated, neither in New South Wales, Victoria, Queensland, the Northern Territory, nor in Western Australia. The range of my investigations comprises extensive regions in all the states mentioned, and I feel sure that the publication of my work will completely dispel all the antiquated notions of previous writers.

My article concludes with a brief description of the *Gurē*, or Aboriginal method of inflicting the death penalty as it was practised in certain parts of Victoria.

Sociology of the Ngunnhalgu, Mailpurlgu and Maraura Tribes

Adjoining the Kurnū[4] people on the southwest are the Ngunnhalgu, reaching down the Darling River from Winbar to a point a little way beyond Wilcannia. From that locality onward, down the Darling via Menindie to Cuthero, was the habitat of the Mailpurlgu tribe. From Cuthero down the Darling river to its confluence with the Murray River at Wentworth, was the country of the Maraura tribe.

The social organisation of these three great tribes—Ngunnhalgu, Mailpurlgu and Maraura—may be briefly stated as follows. The community is segregated into two phratries, whose masculine appellations are Mukkungurra and Kilpungurra. The feminine of each of these names is formed by adding *ga* to the masculine. Arranged in tabular form, the rules of intermarriage of the phratries and the descent of the resulting offspring will be easily understood.

Table 1

Phratry	Husband	Wife	Son	Daughter
A	Mukkungurra	Kilpungurraga	Kilpungurra	Kilpungurraga
B	Kilpungurra	Mukkungurraga	Mukkungurra	Mukkungurraga

In addition to the above divisions, every man, woman and child bears the name of some animal, plant or natural object, as his or her totem, which is in all cases inherited from the mother. If the mother is, for example, a magpie, the sons and daughters will be magpies also. All creation, animate and inanimate, is divided between Mukkungurra and Kilpungurra—the former possessing a certain aggregate of totems and the latter another. Members of both phratries and the various totems are scattered through all the local divisions of the tribe.

In addition to the partitions of the community into phratries and totemic groups, there is a further subdivision of the people into Muggulu and Ngipuru, meaning sluggish blood and active blood respectively, which may for convenience of reference be called 'blood divisions'. These castes of 'blood' are not necessarily coincident with the other divisions. For example, a Muggulu man or woman may belong to either phratry, and the same can be said of a Ngipuru individual. Therefore the 'blood' castes are dispersed indiscriminately between the phratries.

There is still another repartition which can be designated 'shade' divisions, which are in reality an extension of the 'blood' castes, for the purpose of regulating where people rest under the shades of trees in the vicinity of water or elsewhere. For example, the people belonging to the Muggulu division sit down in the shadow thrown by the butt or lower partition of the tree, whilst the Ngipuru folk sit down to rest in the shade cast by the higher branches.

The castes of 'blood' and 'shade' must be considered in arranging the marriages. A man of the Muggulu blood and the butt shade marries a Ngipuruwoman of the branch shade. And in regard to the offspring, a Muggulu mother produces Muggulu children, who take their mother's butt 'shade'. A Ngipuru woman produces Ngipuru children, belonging to the 'shade' of the branches.

Some further illustrations of the intermarriages will be interesting. A Mukkungurra usually espouses a Kilpungurraga as in the table, and in that case a man's son's child marries a sister's son's child. But if a Mukkungurra takes a Mukkungurraga as his conjugal mate, that represents the marriage of a man's son's child to a sister's daughter's child. According to this law it is evident that any given man can take his wife either from his own phratry, or from the opposite phratry. Hence it becomes quite clear that there is no exogamy among the tribes we are dealing with. We have seen that the phratry and the totem are in all cases perpetuated through the woman but this does not constitute exogamy, inasmuch as a man can marry into either phratry and consequently into either aggregate of totems.

Intermarriage of individuals of the same totem is forbidden. When a Mukkungurra marries a Kilpungurraga there is no risk of a clash of the totemic prohibitions. But if a Mukkungurra marries a Mukkungurraga it would be possible for the parties to belong to the same totem. In consequence of the 'blood divisions' already described, a Mukkungurraga of the proper lineage could not possibly be of the same 'blood division' as the man. This matter is illustrated more fully in my article on the sociology of the Wongaibon tribe.[5]

The subdivisions 'blood' and 'shade' had altogether escaped the notice of all writers on the sociology of the Australian Aborigines, and was reported for the very first time by me in 1904, as discovered by me among the Ngeumba and Kamilaroi tribes.[6] It has also fallen on me to be the first author to report the non-existence of exogamy among the Ngeumba, Kamilaroi, Wirraidyuri, Wailwan, Wongaibon and kindred tribes in New South Wales.

Sociology of some Queensland Tribes

That portion of Cape York Peninsula extending from the Cape to about the fifteenth parallel of south latitude, in the state of Queensland, is occupied by a considerable number of Aboriginal tribes with different names. Of these tribes I am best acquainted with the Chūnkūnji people on the Batavia River. The Gamete tribe occupy the country to the north of the Chūnkūnji whilst the Tanegute tribe is to the South. The Ngerikudi language is spoken about Mapoon on the Batavia and as far south as Duyphen Point. Dialects of this language are used all the way from the Jardine River to the Archer River, or perhaps further south. In all these dialects there are two pronouns in the first person of the dual and plural—one that is used when the person addressed is included, and another which excludes the person addressed.

The community is divided socially into two primary phratries or moieties or groups—whichever of these names we choose to employ for purposes of distinction. These two divisions are named Chamakunda and Kamanutta; the former is again bisected into two sections called Lankenami and Nameguri, and the latter into two, called Pakwikki and Pamarung. In these names there is no distinction between the masculine and feminine.

Table 2

Phratry	Husband	Wife	Offspring
Chamakunda	Lankenami	Pakwikki	Pamarung
	Nameguri	Pamarung	Pakwikki
Kamanutta	Pakwikki	Lankenami	Nameguri
	Pamarung	Nameguri	Lankenami

In addition to the partition of the community into phratries and sections, there is a further subdivision of the people into lesser groups, which bear the name of different animals, plants or inanimate objects, to which the name of totems has been given by the anthropologists of America and Europe.

Intermarriages are regulated as follows: a man of the Chamakunda phratry and Lankenami section marries a Kamanutta woman of the Pakwikki section. This is the normal rule of marriage and is the one shown in Table II. In such a case, a man's son's child marries his sister's son's child. But it is quite lawful for a Lankenami man to espouse a Lankenami woman, which represents the marriage of a man's son's child with his sister's daughter's child.

Another variation of the intermarriages of the sections allows the Lankenami man of our example to marry a Pamarung or Nameguri woman. In other words, a man of any given section can marry into one or other of the three remaining sections, or else into his own. Or, to express it in another form, a man of any given section has potential marital qualifications over all the four sections of women. It is needless to add that these facts altogether disprove the existence of exogamy among the tribes with which we are dealing.

Reference to Table 2 shows us that the children follow the phratry of their mother, but they do not adopt the name of her section. They are Pamarung, being the supplementary section of their mother's phratry. That is to say, the section name of the progeny is invariably determined through the women. The totems remain constantly in the same phratry as the women and are accordingly transmitted from a mother to her children.

Although the totems as well as the sections and phratries are perpetuated through the women, this does not constitute exogamy. We have already shown that a man Lankenami, for example, can marry into either phratry.

The totems, called by the natives *idite*, are divided between the two phratries in the same manner as the people themselves. The totems of each phratry are common to the two sections of which it is composed; thus the totems attached to Chamakunda are common to the sections Lankenami and Nameguri, and the Kamanutta totems are common to the Pakwikki and Pamarung sections.

When the boys are about 12 years old, they are taken from the control of their mothers by the chief men, and are passed through a course of initiation formalities, analogous in their main features to those practised by the Kamilaroi and Kumbainggeri tribes and described by me elsewhere. Scars are raised upon their bodies, the septum of the nose is pierced and a front tooth punched out of each youth. The novices are required to pass through the ordeal of inauguration at not less than three meetings of the tribes called for that purpose, and on each occasion fresh scars are added to those previously made on the body of each novice.

In my 'Ethnological Notes on the Aboriginal Tribes of Queensland',[7] published by the Royal Geographical Society of Australasia, Brisbane, I detailed the sociology of a large number of important tribes in Queensland, the Northern Territory and Western Australia. The mass of information therein supplied will be sufficient to prove that exogamy is quite impossible amongst any of the tribes dealt with in this article.

Gurē or Revenge Expedition

When among the native tribes of that part of the state of Victoria through which the upper Murray, Mitta Mitta, Ovens, upper Goulburn and Yarra rivers flow, a member of a tribe was killed by anybody from a neighbouring tribe, the custom to avenge this wrong was known as *Gurē*. They believed that the soul of somebody whose death was not avenged would stray and bother relatives. In consequence of this superstition the punishment of the offender was carried out at the first opportunity presented.

The following is a short description of a Gurē expedition, as it was told to me by a native of the Mitta Mitta River in northeast Victoria.

The brothers and friends of the murdered person, accompanied by the older respected men, congregated at the *Ngulubul* or secret meeting place of the men and deliberated on the best way to retaliate against the guilty party. Some hair, or perhaps some skin taken previously from the body of the murdered person, was shown at this meeting to awaken in the souls of those present the desire for quick vengeance.

The population of a particular locality often consisted of a number of families who were sufficiently independent that they could be called sub-tribes. Sometimes there were feuds between these families, and occasionally murders. And when such injustice was done to a weak sub-tribe who were not able to take revenge, a messenger was sent with information concerning the incident to other familial groups, to ask for their assistance.

The messenger had a flat stick about 18 inches to two feet long and about one-and-a-half inches wide, decorated with lines and symbols inscribed with a marsupial tooth, and painted with red ochre. Instead of a wooden message stick, sometimes an emu tarsus or a kangaroo thighbone was used, decorated in the same way as the wooden one by use of a flint.

The neighbours so called upon usually answered because one day they might request similar help themselves. When the shared meeting ground assigned by the messenger was reached, a party of warriors was selected who had to advance into the territory of the offender. Then the spears were busily greased, straightened and sharpened; boomerangs, clubs, shields and other weapons were carefully checked, and all necessary preparations made for the planned attack.

Some of the most skilled sorcerers made ready with their magic decorations and deadly instruments. Every man took his beard into his mouth and bit on it making wild antics. When all these preparatory things had been finished, the chosen troop specially besmeared and painted left for their mission. The smaller details of the expedition are so similar to that of the 'Pirrimbir', which I have described elsewhere,[8] that I will only have to hint at the most important aspects here.

The party travelled on until evening and set up a night-camp with the fires covered in such a way that they were not noticeable from a distance. Early the next morning a tree was inscribed with zigzagging irregular lines and ovals of the usual native patterns from near the ground to as high up the trunk as the men could reach by standing on the shoulders of one another. The signs were carved into the bark with sharp sticks, stone splinters or axes. A gum tree, or especially a grey box, was preferred if available, because of its smooth bark.

Every man of the contingent participated in drawing on the tree in order to transmit as much magic as possible into it, until it was, so to speak, overloaded with harm. Another reason for the common participation in marking the tree was to strengthen the bond of unity between them so that no one felt any regrets or could give warning to the convicted man, so that he might be able to escape. While the work progressed, some of the prime sorcerers rubbed the signs with bullroarers, quartz crystals and human fat to enhance the effectiveness of the procedure.

When the marking of the tree is finished, the men dance or jump around it singing several times '*wure bunnungandha dumballadha*'. The purpose of the whole ceremony is to bewitch the victim so that he does not leave the resting place where he normally resides, but remains kept there by the magic until his pursuers reach it. At every camp place during the ensuing trip the very same procedure is repeated, and a fresh tree is marked every morning.

When they have reached their goal and discovered the place where the wanted tribe resides they get as close as they safely can and put up their camp at a somewhat distant spot where they are not likely to be observed. Two skilled men are now sent ahead as spies to undertake precise and careful observations of the enemy camp, to find out in which part of it the man they are seeking has his quarters, and in order to ascertain the numerical strength of the tribe, discover advantages, and so on.

While these spies are away on reconnaissance the remaining men mark a tree and clear the ground around it as usual. They paint their faces and chests white and make spots of the same colour on their upper arms. Furthermore, they erect around and over their small fire a shield of branches so it cannot be seen from a distance after the onset of darkness. This cover is made in the following way: some small trees are cut off and stuck into the ground with the cut end around the fire which is in the middle while the leafy ends lean against each other so that they form a pyramid or cone over the fire. Another leafy branch is then set on top with the end of the branch facing up.

As soon as the spies get a first look at the common camp of the enemy they hunch in a hole in the ground or hide behind bushes. Then they begin to quietly sing the words of a song called *guggarga* which is said to have the magic power of making smoke rise from the camp fire of the offender and thus show his whereabouts. While the men continue singing, they wait tensely until they see smoke come from any part of the camp. Then they creep closer to the camp towards the side indicated by the smoke until they can make out the man they are looking for and can locate the position of his camp fire. Should the real murderer not be present in the camp then the spies identify one of his elder brothers or his father; the respective person then has to endure the punishment instead of him.

After the messengers have identified the place of the convicted man, they return to their companions and report with the usual formalities about the state of the matter. After some refreshments have been distributed, some small pieces of wood are placed on the fire to give sufficient light so that the people can see what they are doing. All dance around the fire where the main sorcerers sit singing with quiet voices and executing some magic onto the enemy to destroy his chances of escape. After some time most get to sleep, but some of the older members keep watch continuously. A few hours before dawn everybody is woken and they move silently towards the enemy camp; the men hold small branches in front of themselves in order not to be discovered. The voice of the first bird greeting the new day is the sign for the attack. The attackers separate, one half marching on one side around the camp, the other taking the opposite direction, until they all unite at the opposite side of the camp in closest proximity to the prospective victim.

The details of the attacks are similar to those I described concerning the '*Pirrimbir* Expedition' to which I refer readers. When the victim falls, the executors secure pieces of his skin, flesh and fat, and sometimes the hands are cut off and taken away. When one of the friends of the man tries to interfere in order to protect him he is subjected to the same punishment.

Then the attackers retreat to their camp of the previous night, where they dance around the marked tree and spit in order to drive out the magic power it had acquired through their earlier magic. After this they take all the food and luggage they had left there and begin their trip home. When they return to their tribe a detailed report is given concerning the events of the expedition.

Amongst the tribes described here, the Magellanic Clouds are taken for two native companions,[9] with the bigger cloud representing the male and the smaller the female. When the stars have their lowest culmination and therefore cannot be seen easily in the densely forested areas, the natives superstitiously believe that the neighbouring tribe might organise a *Gurē* expedition to avenge some real or imagined grievance. During such times the young men exercise an unusual vigilance in observing the movements of their enemies.

ENDNOTES

[1] RHM 1903, 'Das Kumbainggeri, eine Eingeborenensprache von Neu-Süd-Wales', *Mitteilungen der Anthropologischen Gesellschaft*, vol. 33, pp. 321-8.

[2] RHM 1904, 'Die Sprache des Tyeddyuwurru-Stammes der Eingebornen von Victoria', *Mitteilungen der Anthropologischen Gesellschaft*, vol. 34, pp. 71-6.

[3] RHM 1904, 'Die Multyerra-Initiationszeremonie', *Mitteilungen der Anthropologischen Gesellschaft*, vol. 34, pp. 77-83. Reproduced this volume.

[4] I published a grammar and vocabulary of the Kurnū language in 'Languages of some Native Tribes of Queensland, New South Wales and Victoria', *Journal and Proceedings of the Royal Society of New South Wales*, vol. 36, 1902, pp. 154-79. [A more detailed description of the grammar was published as 'Langage des Kurnu, tribu d'Indigènes de la Nouvelle Galles du Sud' (1904). Reproduced this volume. Note—Editor.]

[5] RHM 1905, 'Sociology of some Australian Tribes', *Journal and Proceedings of the Royal Society of New South Wales*, vol. 39, p. 117.

[6] RHM 1904, 'Ethnological Notes on the Aboriginal Tribes of New South Wales and Victoria', *Journal and Proceedings of the Royal Society of New South Wales*, vol. 38, pp. 207-16.

[7] RHM 1904-5, 'Ethnological Notes on the Aboriginal Tribes of Queensland', *Queensland Geographical Journal*, vol. 20, pp. 49-75.

[8] See RHM 1904, 'Ethnological Notes on the Aboriginal Tribes of New South Wales and Victoria', *Journal and Proceedings of the Royal Society of New South Wales*, vol. 38, pp. 239-52.

[9] The native companion is *grus australasianus*, an Australian crane.

The Natives of Australia

R. H. Mathews

First published as 'Les Indigènes d'Australie' in *L'Anthropologie*, vol. 13, 1902, pp. 233-40. The article was written in English and translated into French by an unnamed translator. This version was retranslated into English by Mathilde de Hauteclocque.

The origin of Australia's races is a subject of high interest; I will also attempt in this paper to give a brief explanation of the way in which this large island was populated, as well as its neighbour, Van Diemen's Land. To solve this difficult problem we must turn to geography, botany, zoology and linguistics because, the Australian continent having no written history, all relative theory about its population must be in harmony with the facts revealed by these different sciences.

In times past, the physical geography of Australia was not what it is today. Geological investigations have shown that certain parts were alternatively submerged or above the water in succession. Africa and Asia were joined together in the past by a southern land, which extended east as far as Australia, Van Diemen's Land and Papua. This was Lemuria, now swallowed up by the Indian Ocean. Certain banks and shoals indicate its old site. Dr Blanford tried to show that many animals formerly followed this path to reach Africa and Sir J. D. Hooker, the botanical scholar, claims that an entire Indian flora can be found in tropical Australia.

The first human beings, spread across this immense territory, were of a Negroid type. They were not necessarily homogenous, as they must have mixed with the inhabitants of neighbouring lands, and their language had been somewhat modified. It is from this Negro race that the oldest islanders of Australia, Tasmania and Papua descended.

The primitive race spread south-easterly with ease, because the tropical countries that it crossed provided an abundant supply of food. However the migration was slow, the emigrants being few in number and the population movements being dispersed. Certain clans walked in one direction, others in a different direction and, perhaps, some tribes stayed put for a long time in privileged regions. Industry developed more or less, according to the conditions.

Some of the southerly reaches of this flood of emigrants reached the north and north-western coasts of the Australian continent and spread across the largest part of Australia as well as Tasmania, which was then joined to New Holland. These first occupants can be seen as the Aborigines of Australia. Other branches of the same migration reached New Guinea, New Caledonia, Melanesia and Polynesia, where not only fragments of the race can be found, but also traces of a common language, because a language can adopt foreign words without changing its fundamental character. Comparative philology and ethnology must always be studied at the same time. Moreover, according to their skeleton, the natives of Australia resemble the Negroes of Africa and the Melanesians, but have a look that is even more primitive.

The migrations continued for a long time, but it is impossible to be more specific about the duration. They followed one another at irregular intervals and ended up along the whole northern coast of New Holland. It is probable that the customs and the dialects of the last emigrants were slightly different from those of their predecessors. Each clan must have understood only a small number of individuals and the multiplicity of clans, that spread out over centuries across a continent as vast as Australia, explains the great variety of dialects spoken these days.

Later on, the primitive race was followed by hostile tribes of a higher character and a more advanced civilisation. Depressions and various geological disturbances had in the meantime changed the old configuration of the lands and the seas. The new emigrants must have followed a more northerly path than the first, as the connection between Australia, Asia and Africa via Lemuria had been submerged, but there was still an almost continual terrestrial route between India and the Australian continent via Ceylon, Nicobar, the Andaman Islands, the Malayan peninsula, Java, Borneo, Celebes and Timor.

For a long period, the second migration sent out isolated detachments to cross into Australia. When the two races came into contact to dispute the land, the advantage must have been with those newly arrived, who were better equipped for battle. The former inhabitants abandoned some of their customs, dialects and ceremonies, and assimilated those of the victors. The last invaders, however, did not reach Van Diemen's Land, which had become an island following the subsidence of a strip of land which became Bass Strait.

Although the philologists cannot establish a relationship between the Australian languages and those of the savages of southern India, it is not at all unreasonable to suggest that the Australians and the aborigines of southern India descend from a common stock. The Australians, thanks to their long isolation, have better retained the look of their Neanderthaloid ancestors; the later Indian ones have, on the contrary, noticeably evolved.

The Malay race never invaded any part of Australia. During historical times, the Malayans came to fish on the northern coast, but their relations with the natives were limited to the coast. If a few men married with Australian women and committed themselves to the inland of the country, they were not able to influence seriously either the appearance or the language.

*

The matrimonial customs of the Australian tribes are ruled by fixed laws, of a generally simple character. The communities are divided into two primary groups or clans, and the men of one group marry the women of the other. In some tribes, each clan is subdivided into two or (in the north) even four sections, and these sections intermarry, one with the other.

In some regions of Australia (South Australia, Western Australia, Victoria and New South Wales) marriage is of a very simple character. At irregular intervals, the old men assemble in council to appoint the women to the boys; the engaged couple take the name *tooar*. Great care is taken that the *tooar* are not closely related by ties of blood. The boys and the women thus allocated must speak neither to each other nor look at each other. If one of these women bears a daughter, she must give her, as soon as she is old enough, to the young boy to whom she is *tooar*. This one, in turn, when he has a sister, is supposed to give her to one of the woman's sons in exchange for his own wife. The children follow the line of the father and adopt his *totem*. By their appearance, their arms, their languages and their ceremonies, the natives in question are rather different from the other Australian tribes. But on the other hand, they greatly resemble the Tasmanians, which confirms the opinion advanced concerning their community of origin.

I am led to believe that the first inhabitants possessed the organisation that I have just described and that a part of their tribes escaped subjugation to the invaders, either because the invaders could not defeat them, or because they did not advance far enough towards the southwest to meet them. In the neighbouring regions, we find tribes divided into two intermarrying phratries, such as the Mattiri and the Karraru of Port Lincoln, the Krokitch and the Kamatch of Western Victoria, the Mukwarra and the Keelparra of the Barkunjee tribe, the Koolpirro and the Tinnawa of the Yowerawarrika tribe. I will give some details on this last tribe whose division into two phratries was first reported by me.

The natives told me several legends referring to former warriors and I noted that the bravest always belonged to the Koolpirro phratry. I concluded from this that the name Koolpirro must have applied to an old tribe of warriors, who, in times past, conquered the Tinnawa and that each of them possessed the *tooar* type of marriage laws. If we assume that this was so and that the Koolpirro, like the victors of today, were in the habit of killing the defeated males while sparing the women and the children of both sexes, they must have, whether they were already married or not, taken wives from the Tinnawa tribe. These Koolpirro already had children from their first wives; they therefore had to distinguish their offspring from their marriages with the strange women, which was easily done by calling them after their mothers, Tinnawa. On the other side, the boys who were spared, once they became adults, took wives from amongst the Koolpirro and their children took the name of their mother's phratry. In other words, the Koolpirro men married their sisters to the Tinnawa men in exchange for the sisters they received as wives. The children took—and still take—the name of their mother's phratry, from whom they adopt the *totem*.

Sometimes, two tribes, after being amalgamated like the Koolpirro and the Tinnawa, integrate with two other tribes amalgamated in the same way. The result is a community with four divisions who marry between themselves. That is what we see in the Miappe of Queensland,[1] where the marriages are made in the manner indicated in the following table.

Husband	Wife	Child
Jimmalingo	Marringo	Kooperungo
Bathingo	Kooperungo	Marringo
Marringo	Jimmalingo	Bathingo
Koopernago	Bathingo	Jimmalingo

Finally, two communities with four divisions each can unite in a way that gives birth to a confederation of eight subdivisions, as we notice among the Wombya of Northern Australia. These subdivisions intermarry while observing the rules which I indicated in 1898[2] and which can be summed up thus:

Husband	Wife	Child
Choolangie	Chingulum	Palyaringie
Cheenum	Chooralum	Bungaringie
Jamerum	Palyaringie	Chooralum
Yacomary	Bungaringie	Chingulum
Chingulum	Choolangie	Yacomary
Chooralum	Cheenum	Jamerum
Bungaringie	Yacomary	Cheenum
Palyaringie	Jamerum	Choolangie

On the south coast of South Australia, among certain tribes who have the *tooar* system, the children take their father's totem. Among the Yowerawarrika, who are the result of the fusion of two tribes, and among the Miappe who have four divisions, the totem is transmitted by the mother. In communities of eight divisions, it is, on the contrary, the father who transmits it. Moreover, this transmission is subject, according to the district, to variations.

*

In various papers I have published on the initiation ceremonies, I reported feigned quarrels between the fathers of the novices and the other men assembled outside the camp. I also said that human blood is occasionally sprinkled upon the trunks of the initiates; in other cases it is collected in vessels and swallowed. It also happens that a man is killed and served as a feast to the assistants. It is possible that these ceremonies originated from customs in use at the time of wars between tribes who later disappeared. If, as today, all the defeated adult males were killed, then it is reasonable to expect that the young captive males were brought up according to the customs of their captors. As a result of this, it would be necessary to remove them from the influence of their mothers who, naturally clinging to the customs of their ancestors, would have tried to instil them into their sons.

At the present time, among the Kamilaroi, this is how the *Bora* or initiation ceremony unfolds.[3] The neighbouring tribes gather together at a common meeting ground and the men of a distant tribe take charge of the novices of a tribe to whom they are more or less strangers. At dawn, that is to say at the time when the native tribes usually attack the enemy, all the novices are taken away from their mothers. The mothers are persuaded that an enemy has truly come into the camp and secretly taken the boys. They are prevented from watching what will happen and, to prevent them from seeing, they are hidden under bushes, grass or other coverings, from where they can hear the voice of the enemy and the sound of his footsteps.

During the *Bora* of the Kamilaroi, great sexual licence is given to the men of all the tribes who participate in the celebration. Usually a man is restricted to the women of a certain section, but at the time of initiation ceremonies he can have intercourse with women of different sections who are forbidden to him under normal circumstances. As soon as the novices and the men have disappeared from view, the elders of the strange tribes uncover the women and take them away to another camp where they remain as their prisoners.[4]

All these phases of the ceremony may be a symbol of what occurred in the past. When a tribe attacked another in the morning, a group of men may have taken charge of the women while the others took the young people away to bring them up in the traditions of the conquerors. This hypothesis is confirmed by the fact that, during their time in the bush, the novices see many things which are entirely new to them. They are taught a language, known only by the initiates, just as in times past they were taught the language of the conquerors, and they are given a new name which will remain unknown to their mothers and their sisters.

In the wars, as I have said, the women were always spared and taken as wives by the victorious party. The sexual licence to which I have referred had, without a doubt, its archetype in the libidinous orgies which took place when many strange women were captured, and during which each man indiscriminately used the women until exhausted. Even today, when a woman is allotted to a man, she must first have intercourse with a certain number of other men.

While the *Kooringal* [5] accompany the novices, two warriors, referred to by the name *Buddenbelar*, come out of the bush and each of them throws a boomerang towards the aggressors; then they withdraw hurriedly to fetch the *Beegay*,[6] whose participation signals the release of the novices. This is suggestive of a time when many small tribes were linked in more or less amicable relations, united against a common enemy. If one of these tribes were attacked, the men who escaped sought out the protection of their allies to punish the offenders. It is this that the contribution of the *Beegay* may symbolise, followed by the return of the novices to the camp.

*

I have tried to give a brief sketch of the probable origin of the Australians and to show, by examples borrowed from matrimonial customs still in use in different places, the different elements of their social organisation. I have also sought to link the origins of their initiation ceremonies to the battles of the past, which must resemble the current wars. Certain tribes, isolated during a long period, have obviously modified their usage, but among all of them, the initiation ceremonies must have had a common origin.

After studying these questions for a number of years, I have arrived at the conviction that neither promiscuity, nor what has been called *communal* or *group marriage* ever existed among the Australian tribes. I am equally certain that the division into clans was produced as shown above, and was not at all devised to prevent marriages between individuals of the same blood type.

ENDNOTES

[1] RHM 1898, 'Australian Divisional Systems', *Journal and Proceedings of the Royal Society of New South Wales*, vol. 32, p. 82.

[2] RHM 1898, 'Divisions of Australian Tribes', *Proceedings of the American Philosophical Society*, vol. 37, p. 152.

[3] RHM 1896, 'The Bora of the Kamilaroi Tribes', *Proceedings of the Royal Society of Victoria*, vol. 9 (new series), pp. 137-73.

[4] [Editor's note] In his other writings on initiation, Mathews never described the women as 'prisoners'. This is probably a misunderstanding on the part of the French translator. Women and children adjourned to a women's camp where they usually conducted their own ceremonies during the absence of the men and neophytes.

[5] [Editor's note] That this is the first appearance of the term *Kooringal* suggests that parts of the original paper were cut. In 1896 Mathews defined the *Kooringal* as 'the chosen band of athletes, who have the custody of the guardians and novices whilst the latter are going through the secret ceremonies in the bush'. See RHM, 'The Bora of the Kamilaroi Tribes', *Proceedings of the Royal Society of Victoria*, vol. 9 (new series), 1896, p. 151.

[6] [Editor's note] In 1896 Mathews defined the *Beegay* as 'a number of strange men who have arrived at the women's camp since the boys were taken away'. Eventually they are 'despatched to liberate them'. Ibid, p. 167.

Part 3: Mythology

Introduction

Martin Thomas

In an article on songs and songmakers, which R. H. Mathews must have read in his early days as an anthropologist, A. W. Howitt remarked that 'there is but little of the life of the Australian savage, either in peace or war, which is not in some measure connected with song'.[1] So it is not surprising that oral traditions were an important aspect of Mathews' cross-cultural research. His first contribution to the subject was a series of seven legends from various parts of New South Wales, published in 1898 as 'Folklore of the Australian Aborigines' by the anthropological magazine *Science of Man*.[2] He republished them as a short book the following year.[3] Two of these legends are reprinted in this volume. Over the next decade, Mathews published another dozen articles describing Aboriginal myths. In one of these, 'A Giant in a Cave—An Australian Legend' (reproduced this volume), the by-line is omitted. But the hand of Mathews is obvious, and offprints of the article appear in his own bound volumes of his collected works. Folklore study is the only strand of his research that was published entirely in English, so no translations appear in this section of the book. Evidence in Mathews' unpublished papers reveals that apart from a few legends from Western Australia that were documented by a correspondent,[4] the great bulk of his folklore research was done in person.

Mathews used the descriptor 'folklore' to describe Aboriginal stories. If this appears to trivialise them, that was not his intention. Folklore study was a serious branch of inquiry during Mathews' lifetime and it provided a framework for his documentation of oral traditions. While the influence of evolutionary anthropology on early Aboriginal studies has been extensively documented,[5] the impact of the long tradition of folklore research has received comparatively little attention. Although the term 'folk-lore' entered English as recently as 1846, the publication and analysis of vernacular beliefs, proverbs and stories had its roots in sixteenth-century Britain. Scholarly interest in folkloric culture blossomed in the nineteenth century, fuelled by concern that old ways and beliefs were disappearing with the changes wrought by the Industrial Revolution. The Folklore Society, formed in 1878, was dedicated to the study of traditional music, customs, folk art, fairy tales and other vernacular traditions.[6] The society published *Folk-Lore*, an internationally distributed journal, to which Mathews contributed five articles including some of the stories reprinted here.

R. H. Mathews documented the music and lyrics of this 'Song of the Breakers' on the South Coast of NSW. By permission of the National Library of Australia. (R.H. Mathews Papers, NLA6006/5/12).

The Folklore Society and kindred organisations in other parts of the world were initially concerned with the traditional life of Europeans. Eventually, however, the interests of many folklore scholars widened to include the study of so-called primitive cultures. It is by no means coincidental that Andrew Lang and E. S. Hartland, two of Mathews' few allies in British anthropology, played a significant role in directing folklore study towards Australian and other 'native' cultures. Hartland, a solicitor by profession, first published studies of fairytales and treatises on the oral lore of his home county of Gloucestershire. Lang, a Scotsman, was one of the most prolific writers in Britain. He published novels, poems, criticism, compendia of fairytales, and numerous works of anthropology. Lang followed the Australian scene closely, and corresponded with various ethnographic researchers including Catherine Eliza Somerville Stow (who published as K. Langloh Parker), Daisy Bates and R. H. Mathews. Lang wrote the preface for Parker's *Australian Legendary Tales* (1896), a collection of legends from western New South Wales. In its day, it was the most substantial book on Aboriginal mythology. Mathews read it closely, and it probably influenced his decision to research and publish on this aspect of Aboriginal culture.[7]

In 1898 Lang and Hartland debated each other about whether Australian Aborigines 'possessed the conception of a moral Being'.[8] This greatly stimulated Hartland's interest in Australia. The shared interest in folklore helps explain the rapport between Mathews and Hartland, evident in their friendly exchange of letters (see 'Correspondence', this volume). Writing of the mythology he had collected, Mathews suggested to Hartland that he could prepare a substantial book on the subject, 'a good sized volume, say 200 pages,' containing legends and songs.[9] But the plan never came to fruition.

As the articles reproduced here indicate, Mathews said little about the circumstances in which he heard the stories he documented. He also admitted to censoring parts of stories, owing to their 'obscene character'.[10] Consistent with the *Folk-Lore* style, he rephrased Aboriginal narratives in what to him was respectable English. It is interesting that this practice was not a problem for Hartland or for the British and American journals in which Mathews' versions of Aboriginal myth were published. But as we see in a letter from the German editor Moritz von Leonhardi, it was less acceptable in Europe. Responding to Mathews' transcription of an Aboriginal song, von Leonhardi complained:

> Are the words not translatable? It would be highly interesting to know the meaning. We are still lacking good texts in the original language with interlinear translation; of course the texts would have to have been recorded with the greatest precision. Such texts, though, would be more pertinent at the moment than grammars and vocabularies, which the scholar in the end—if the texts are only somewhat extensive—could

derive from them himself. How much there is still to do on the ethnography of Australia and how soon it will be forever too late![11]

Von Leonhardi was publisher of the Lutheran missionary-anthropologist Carl Strehlow who lived in the Central Australian settlement of Hermannsburg. Encouraged by von Leonhardi, Strehlow's documentation of myth is premised on just the sort of transcription and 'interlinear translation' promoted above.[12] But Strehlow translated into his mother-tongue, German, and not into English—and Strehlow's pioneering methodology remains under-recognised in the Anglophone world.

Von Leonhardi recognised, that 'the *ipissima verba* [actual words] of the person reporting often matters a lot'.[13] Mathews' rewording of legends tended to efface the idiom, the narrative strategies and the manner of performance. Many Aboriginal narratives belong to particular locations and are told in situ. But strangely, given his background in surveying, discussion of site is not a feature of Mathews' documentation. Occasionally he names individual storytellers, but never does he remark on the gestures and movements that accompanied the narratives. However, a comment in a notebook gives some insight into the qualities of the performances he observed.

> When telling a story the natives go into very full detail, giving an accurate description of everything that was done. If anyone's words are repeated, the intonation is changed.[14]

Mathews also acknowledged that story-telling was connected with the musical culture. He documented the lyrics of several Aboriginal songs and on a few occasions set them to music.[15] He pointed out that the

> songs or chants of the aborigines take a very prominent place in the customs and lore of the Tribes. These songs are essential factors in the great corroborees; they enter every part of the important and imposing ceremonies of initiation; they are found in the superstitions and folklore of the people.[16]

In his unpublished biographical notes, William Mathews made revealing comments about his father's interest in mythology. He discerned a correspondence between the ancient Hebrew stories at the heart of the Judeo-Christian tradition and those of Aboriginal Australia. William wrote:

> There were few people outside the ranks of the clergy who had so thoroughly digested the contents of the Bible as R. H. M. had done … [B]eing very much interested in folk lore and such things from an early age, he seemed to grasp the fundamental truths that underlay the stories related in the Bible, the writers of which had such a clear understanding of human nature, and, for the most part, recorded what they had to say

in such a simple and straightforward fashion … [I]n R. H. M.'s opinion, the Bible was largely a collection of the folk tales of an eastern people, for it seemed to him that these stories had their origin clearly stamped upon them, a factor which rendered them all the more interesting to him.[17]

So it is not surprising that notes from the Bible can be found among Mathews' papers.[18] There are also translations into Dharawal of excerpts from St Luke's Gospel, including the parable of the Prodigal Son.[19] These were drafted at the La Perouse settlement on Botany Bay, an area strongly influenced by missionaries. While Mathews also documented a Kamilaroi version of the death of Lazarus,[20] biblical translation was not a typical aspect of his cross-cultural research. His mission was to study Aboriginal beliefs, not proselytise his own. William describes his father as 'unusually tolerant of all forms of religious belief and ritual … and he was generally inclined to indulge his love of "leg-pulling" when anyone attempted to insist … that salvation could be reached by one road and by one road only'.[21] Mrs Emma Timbery, Mrs Golding, Mrs Robert Lock, Harry Mathews, and other Aboriginal teachers of Dharawal named in Mathews' notebook,[22] would have known Christian parables long before he visited in the 1890s. Finding common ground through storytelling was a valuable way of communicating language and other beliefs. Perhaps the Dharawal people narrated the story of the Prodigal Son in their language, knowing that Mathews would understand the basic narrative.

The complex dynamics of cross-cultural research and its attendant transformations are discernible in all the legends republished here. Mathews set out to 'collect' stories for possible publication, but we can assume that his storytellers had their agendas also. Stories are a form of education as well as entertainment, and Mathews' teachers undoubtedly used them to induct him into the culture. Readers of Aboriginal legends (or more often whitefellow renditions of them) sometimes complain that they sound like children's stories. This is not always so off-the-mark. While the long history of infantilising Aboriginal people should not be forgotten, we must bear in mind that outsiders are likely to first encounter the simpler aspects of Aboriginal culture, which has its own traditions of storytelling for children. Such tales, designed for the uninitiated (and thus not secret-sacred), would have been obvious choices for sharing with a researcher such as Mathews. They were simple and short and, as we know from the notebooks, told in English, which was often the second or third language of Mathews' Aboriginal teachers. So it would not be surprising if they veered towards simpler and shorter stories, if only for the ease of telling. Some of the legends reproduced here possibly fall into that category.

With this in mind, it is not surprising that the longer, more complex stories originate from areas close to Sydney where Mathews developed long-term relationships. The remarkable tale of Mirragañ and Gurangatch, recounted in 'Some Mythology of the Gundungurra Tribe, New South Wales' (1908), explains the creation of the southern Blue Mountains. A great fish (Gurangatch) carves out the rivers as he tries to escape a native cat or quoll (Mirragañ) who wants to eat him. Mathews made periodic visits to the Burragorang Valley where he met with Gundungurra people who resided for the most part on Aboriginal reserves. Mathews assembled a larger folio of Gundungurra traditions, perhaps intended for the book mentioned to Hartland.[23] But this work remained unpublished until 2003.[24] Despite the rather Victorian diction, the story of Mirragañ and Gurangatch is clearly rooted in the Blue Mountains topography, revealing a remarkable knowledge of the landscape and its fauna. As I have noted elsewhere, the story is a verbal map, sufficient in some parts for navigational purposes.[25]

It is interesting to compare Mathews' account of this story with the greatly vulgarised version published by A. W. Reed in his collection *Myths and Legends of Australia* (1965).[26] Reed used Mathews as his source, but dumbed the story down by eradicating place names and geographical detail, and taking other liberties with the text. The comparison emphasises the value of Mathews' perspective as a surveyor. His professional interest in cartography allowed him to appreciate the knowledge of terrain displayed in the story. These details survive, even if the original language is mostly lost. Similar traits are apparent in the Dharawal narrative titled 'The Hereafter', reprinted here. Concerned with the spirit's journey into the next world, the account starts at Coolangatta, an irregularly shaped massif near the mouth of the Shoalhaven River. The spirit of a deceased person ascends the mount and from there travels eastwards across the ocean, eventually arriving in the country of the afterlife. In some ways this account is even more remarkable than that of Mirragañ and Gurangatch, for Mathews describes the realm of the Hereafter with the same attention that he pays to the here and now.

The stories here are the residue of cultural brokerage between Mathews and his Aboriginal teachers. He also learnt about cultural exchange *within* Aboriginal society from his study of myth. Perhaps he was thinking about the quoll Mirragañ when he observed in 'Remarks on the Natives of Australia' (1906) (this volume) that through the retelling and circulation of stories 'ideas were exchanged between distant tribes, which never associated with each other'. Mathews himself would observe how *Mirragañ*, the great fisherman of the Blue Mountains, was also the name of a section of the Aboriginal fish traps at Brewarrina, 700 km away.[27] It is even possible that direct exchange occurred between the Blue Mountains and Brewarrina communities, even in ancient times. A story about a great flood, told by Ngemba people at Brewarrina to David Unaipon, the

Aboriginal writer and inventor, has an episode that occurs in the Blue Mountains.[28]

In the stories published here we can see for ourselves parallels between Gurangatch, the monster fish who creates rivers, valleys and cave systems, and the Rainbow Serpent, the protean creation hero known through much of Australia, especially in the north. In the article 'Australian Folk-Tales' (this volume) Mathews gives a short Kamilaroi version, related by Jimmy Nerang whom he met at Tallwood, northern New South Wales, in 1895. The 'serpent-like monster' is named Wahwee and through the mediation of clever men who meet with him in a den beneath a riverbank, he introduces new songs to the community. As I mentioned earlier in this volume, Mathews himself was associated with such clever men. He was given the nickname Birrarak, a term used in the Gippsland region of Victoria to describe people who communicated with the spirits of the deceased, from whom they learned dances and songs (see my general introduction to this volume).[29] With this information, and with the understanding that dances and stories circulate through economies of exchange, we might think about the role played by Mathews in communicating whitefellow understandings to the people with whom he worked. This is largely a matter for speculation, for Mathews was too secretive to document what stories he might have offered in exchange.

ENDNOTES

[1] Howitt, A. W. 1887, 'Notes on Songs and Songmakers of some Australian Tribes', *Journal of the Anthropological Institute*, vol. 16, p. 328.

[2] RHM 1898, 'Folklore of the Australian Aborigines', *Science of Man*, vol. 1 (new series).

[3] RHM 1899, *Folklore of the Australian Aborigines*, Hennessey, Harper and Company, Sydney.

[4] RHM 1909, 'Folklore Notes from Western Australia', *Folk-Lore*, vol. 20.

[5] See for example, Stocking, George W. Jr 1995, *After Tylor: British Social Anthropology 1888-1951*, University of Wisconsin Press, Madison; Mulvaney, D. J. and Calaby, J. H. 1985, *'So Much That is New': Baldwin Spencer, 1860-1929: A Biography*, Melbourne University Press, Carlton; Hiatt, L. R. 1996, *Arguments about Aborigines: Australia and the Evolution of Social Anthropology*, Cambridge University Press, Cambridge; and Wolfe, Patrick 1999, *Settler Colonialism and the Transformation of Anthropology: The Politics and Poetics of an Ethnographic Event*, Cassell, London.

[6] Dorson, Richard M. 1968, *The British Folklorists: A History*, University of Chicago Press, Chicago, ch. 1.

[7] In a footnote to the legend he published as 'The Hereafter' (reproduced this volume), Mathews says Parker 'deserves the thanks of all who are interested in the folklore of the Australian aborigines'.

[8] Dorson, *The British Folklorists*, p. 245.

[9] Mathews to Hartland, 9 April 1907, Letters to E. S. Hartland, National Library of Wales MS 16889C. Reproduced this volume.

[10] Mathews, *Folklore of the Australian Aborigines*, p. 6.

[11] Von Leonhardi to Mathews, 9 June 1908, Strehlow Research Centre (henceforth SRC) Manuscripts. Reproduced this volume. Trans. Christine Winter.

[12] Strehlow, C. 1907-20, *Die Aranda- und Loritja-Stamme in Zentral-Australien*, Joseph Baer & Co, Frankfurt am Main, vols I & II.

[13] Von Leonhardi to Mathews, 9 June 1908, SRC Manuscripts. Reproduced this volume. Trans. Christine Winter.

[14] 'General Notes re Aborigines [draft]', R. H. Mathews Papers, National Library of Australia (henceforth NLA) MS 8006/5/8.

[15] RHM 1901-02, 'The Thoorga Language', *Queensland Geographical Journal*, vol. 17, pp. 61-3 and RHM 1907, *Notes on the Aborigines of New South Wales*, Government Printer of New South Wales, Sydney, p. 35.

[16] Untitled draft, R. H. Mathews Papers, NLA MS 8006/5/12.

[17] Biographical and Historical Notes of the Mathews Family, R. H. Mathews Papers, NLA MS 8006/7/8.

[18] Notebook inscribed 'R. H. Mathews, Surveyor, Hassall Street, Parramatta', R. H. Mathews Papers, NLA MS 8006/3/1.

[19] Notebook with red cover, R. H. Mathews Papers, NLA MS 8006/3/6.

[20] Notebook No. 2, R. H. Mathews Papers, NLA MS 8006/3/5.

[21] Biographical and Historical Notes of the Mathews Family.

[22] Notebook No. 5, R. H. Mathews Papers, NLA MS 8006/3/5.

[23] 'Some Mythology of the Gundungurra Tribe', R. H. Mathews Papers, NLA MS 8006/5/10.

[24] RHM in Jim Smith (ed.) 2003, *Some Mythology and Folklore of the Gundungurra Tribe*, Den Fenella Press, Wentworth Falls, NSW.

[25] Thomas, Martin 2003, *The Artificial Horizon: Imagining the Blue Mountains*, Melbourne University Press, Carlton.

[26] Reed, A.W. 1965, *Aboriginal Legends of Australia*, Taplinger, New York, pp. 193-8.

[27] RHM 1903, 'The Aboriginal Fisheries at Brewarrina', *Journal and Proceedings of the Royal Society of New South Wales*, vol. 37.

[28] Unaipon, David 2001, 'The Flood and its Result' in Muecke, Stephen and Shoemaker, Adam (eds) 2001, *Legendary Tales of the Australian Aborigines*, Miegunyah, Carlton South, Vic.

[29] The tradition of learning songs through interactions with the dead still continues in northern Australia. See Marett, Allan 2005, *Songs, Dreamings, and Ghosts: The Wangga of North Australia*, Wesleyan University Press, Middletown, Connecticut.

Some Mythology of the Gundungurra Tribe, New South Wales

R. H. Mathews

First published in *Zeitschrift für Ethnologie*, vol. 40, 1908, pp. 203-06.
[1]

The territory of the Gundungurra tribe includes Burragorang, Katoomba, Picton, Berrima, Taralga and Goulburn, with the intervening country. The Bunan ceremony of initiation[2] described by me in 1896 applies to the Gundungurra, in common with the Thurrawal and Thoorga tribes. In 1901 I published an elementary grammar of the Gundungurra language.[3] In the present article I am submitting a legendary tale which I obtained personally from the remnants of the Gundungurra tribe now residing at Burragorang on the Wollondilly River.[4]

The natives of this tribe believe that in the far past times, which they call the *gun'-yung-ga'lung*, all the present animals were men, or at any rate had human attributes. These legendary personages are spoken of as the Burringilling, in contradistinction to the present race of people. It would appear, however, that the Burringilling folk were much cleverer than the people of the present time. They could make rivers and other geographical features, cleave rocks and perform many similar Herculean labours.

Gu-rang'-atch was one of the Burringilling, his form being partly fish and partly reptile. One of his camping places was a large, deep waterhole or lagoon at what is now the junction of the Wollondilly and Wingeecaribbee rivers; the waterhole and the country around it being called Mur-rau'-ral in the Gundungurra tongue. Gurangatch used to lie in the shallow water near the bank in the middle of the day to sun himself. One day Mir-ra'-gañ the tiger cat, a renowned fisherman, who searched only for the largest kinds of fish, happened to catch a glimpse of Gurangatch's eye which shone like a star through the water. Mirragañ tried to spear him but he escaped into the centre of the waterhole, which was of great depth. Mirragañ then went into the bush a little way off, and cut a lot of hickory bark, *millewa* in the native language, and stacked it in heaps under the water at different places around the lagoon,[5] in the hope of making Gurangatch sick, so that he would come to the surface. The poisoned water made Gurangatch very uncomfortable, but the solution was not strong enough to overcome such a large fish as he.

Seething with disappointment, Mirragañ went into the bush again to cut more hickory bark to increase the nauseating power of the water, but as soon as Gurangatch saw him going away he suspected what he was after and commenced tearing up the ground along the present valley of the Wollondilly, causing the water in the lagoon to flow after him and then he burrowed or tunneled under the ground for some distance at right angles, coming out again on a high rocky ridge on one side of the valley, where there is now a spring or water catchment, known to the white people as the 'Rocky Waterhole', but is called by the natives Bir'-rim-bun'-nung-a-lai, because it contains birrimbunnungs or sprats.[6] Gurangatch raised the head above this waterhole and shoved out his tongue which flashed like lightning. From this elevated point of observation he saw Mirragañ starting from Murraural along his trail.

Gurangatch then returned home along his burrow or tunnel to the Wollondilly where he had previously left off, and continued making a canal for himself. When he reached what is now the junction of the Guineacor river he turned to the left and made a few miles of the channel of that stream. Coming to a very rocky place which was hard to excavate, he changed his mind and turned back to the junction and resumed his former course. He had some difficulty in getting away from this spot and made a long, deep bend or loop in the Wollondilly which almost doubles back upon itself at that place. When Gurangatch got down to where Jock's Creek now embouchures with the Wollondilly, he turned up Jock's Creek excavating a watercourse for himself. Being a great magician he could make the water flow up hill as easily as downhill. On reaching the source of Jock's Creek, he burrowed under the range, coming up in the inside of Wam'-bee-ang caves, which are called Whambeyan by the white people, being a corruption of the aboriginal name.

We must now return to Mirragañ. When he came back to Murraural waterhole and saw how Gurangatch had escaped, he followed on down the river after him, going on and on till he overtook him at Wambeeang. Mirragañ did not care to go into any of the subterranean passages, therefore he went up on top of the rocks and dug a hole as deep as he could go and then prodded a long pole down as far as it would reach, for the purpose of frightening Gurangatch out of his retreat, much in the way we poke a kangaroo rat or other creature out of a hollow log. Not succeeding in his purpose with the first hole, he dug another and still another and shoved the long pole down each one as before. There are several weather worn 'pot holes' on top of the Whambeyan caves still, which are said to be those made by Mirragañ on that occasion.

When Gurangatch perceived that his enemy was continuing his relentless pursuit, he started off one morning at daylight through his tunnel or burrow and returned down Jock's Creek till he came out into the Wollondilly again. Some miles farther down was where Mirragañ's family resided. When they heard Gurangatch coming and the water roaring after him like a flood, they ran away up the side of the hill in great terror. By that time Mirragañ himself appeared on the scene and his wife began scolding him for having meddled with

Gurangatch and besought him to give up the pursuit, but he would not be dissuaded. He went on after Gurangatch and overtook him at what the white people call the 'Slippery Rock', but the native name is Wong'-ga-ree. There they fought for a long time, which made the rock smooth and slippery ever since.

Gurangatch at last got away and went on downwards, making the water flow after him. Every time that Mirragañ overtook him, he hit him with his big club or *boondee*, and Gurangatch struck Mirragañ heavily with his tail. This continued down to what is now the junction of Cox's river, where Gurangatch turned off to the left, digging out the present channel. He went on till he came to Billa'-goo'-la Creek, corrupted to 'Black Hollow' on our maps, up which he travelled some distance, but turned back, and resumed his course up the Cox to the junction of Ked-oom'-bar Creek, now called Katoomba by the Europeans. He excavated Kedoombar Creek as far as where Reedy Creek comes into it and turned up the latter a little way, where he formed a deep waterhole in which he rested for a while.

Gurangatch then journeyed back to the Cox, up which he worked his way for some distance and formed the waterhole Karrangatta. In order to dodge his enemy he burrowed under ground, coming out on Mee'-oo-wuñ mountain, now written Mou-in, where he made a deep hole or spring, which is even now a menace to the white man's cattle on account of its narrowness and great depth. Returning to Karrangatta waterhole, he made his way up to the junction of Koo-nang'-goor-wa, corrupted to Konangaroo, where he and Mirragañ had another fierce encounter. Gurangatch journeyed on up the Cox to the present junction therewith of Harry's Creek. He then excavated the valley of Harry's Creek till he came to Bin-noo'-mur, the present Jenolan caves, where he had the good fortune to meet with some of his relations.

Gurangatch was weary from his hard work and sore from all the blows he had received during his journey. He suspected that his enemy would still be in pursuit of him and therefore besought his friends to escort him out of his reach. They accordingly took him out of the caves and conducted him over the main range into a deep waterhole, called by the natives Joo-lun-doo.

While this was going on, Mirragañ had arrived close to Binnoomur, but was very tired and lay down on a little hill to rest himself. When he revived he searched about the caves and found tracks of where Gurangatch had been staying, and also the tracks of how he had been taken away to Joolundoo by his friends. Mirragañ was quite worn out by his prolonged encounter, and when he saw that his quarry had got among his relations, he thought that he also would go and obtain assistance. He then considered that it would be prudent, before he left the spot, to adopt some means of preventing Gurangatch from escaping back to his old haunts during his absence. He consequently set to work and built a precipitous wall of rock, Wan'-dak-ma-lai', corrupted by Europeans to Duckmulloy, along the side of the range between the caves and Joolundoo.[7]

Mirragañ then hurried away to his friends somewhere out westward. On reaching their camp they were eating roasted eels and offered him one. Although he was wary and hungry he answered, 'No, no, that is too small a thing for me to eat. I am chasing a great big fish and want you to come and help me.' He stated that this great fish was in an extremely deep waterhole and requested them to send the very best divers in the camp. They selected Billagoola the shag, Gool'-a-gwan-gwan the diver, Gundhareen the black duck and Goonarring the wood duck.

When Mirragañ returned to Joolundoo with this contingent, Gundhareen dived into the pool but returned after a while saying he was unable to get down to the bottom. Goonarring then made the attempt but without success. Goolagwangwan was the next to go down and after a considerable time brought a young or small Gurangatch to the surface, saying to Mirragañ, 'Is this what you have been after?' He replied contemptuously, 'No! that is too small; try again.' Goolagwangwan dived down the second time and brought up a larger fish, but Mirragañ would not look at it. Billagoola then took his turn at diving and when he got down a long way he observed several fish like those brought up by Goolagwangwan. They were trying to hide a very large fish by covering it with mud on the bottom of the pool. Billagoola tried to get hold of this monster, but its head was jammed into a crevice of the rock and its tail was fast in another crevice on the opposite side, so that he could not shift it. Being a very expert diver and a strong fellow withal, he pulled a huge piece of flesh off the back of Gurangatch and started up again. On reaching the surface, Mirragañ exclaimed with delight, 'That is a piece of the fish I was chasing.' When the meat was cooked Mirragañ and his friends had a great feast and returned to their respective homes.

Along the course of the Wollondilly, as well as along the Cox river, there are big waterholes here and there, which are said by the natives to be Gurangatch's resting places. The following are some of the holes in the Wollondilly:— Doogalool, Gungga'-look, Woonggaree, Goo-rit, Mullindee, Boonbaal, and Gurrabulla. In the Cox river there are:— Gaung-gaung, Junba, Billa'goola, Karrangatta, and several others. Many of the waterholes referred to are believed by the old natives to be inhabited to the present day by descendants of Gurangatch.

ENDNOTES

[1] Presented at the session of 19 October 1907.

[2] R. H. Mathews, 'The Būnān Ceremony of New South Wales', *American Anthropologist*, vol. 9, 1896.

[3] R. H. Mathews, 'The Gundungurra Language', *Proceedings of the American Philosophical Society*, vol. 40, 1901.

[4] [Editor's note] Now under Warragamba Dam

[5] There are some long, thin slabs of stone still lying in layers on the banks of Murraural waterhole which are said by the natives to be the sheets of hickory bark put there by Mirragañ to poison the water.

[6] The natives maintain that there must be a subterranean passage from Rocky Waterhole to the Wollondilly because sprats are found there as well as in the river.

[7] A precipitous sandstone escarpment, consisting of huge blocks of rock, layer upon layer, is still pointed out as the wall built by Mirragañ.

A Giant in a Cave—An Australian Legend

R. H. Mathews

First published in *American Antiquarian*, vol. 29, 1907, pp. 29-31.
1

Among the remote ancestors of the Girriwurru tribe there was a man of great stature, whose body was covered with hair. He dwelt in a cave in a rock on the bank of the Hopkins river, in the vicinity of Maroona. The natives aver that, in the olden days, if any person went to this place, during Murkupang's absence, the water in the river would surge up into the cave's mouth, and prevent intruders from going inside. During the day he used to go out hunting around about Mount William, Moorabool, Kirk's Mountain, and Mount Ararat.

Murkupang's mother-in-law resided near him, and one day she sent her two grandchildren to see him and ask him for some food, because in accordance with tribal custom she could not herself approach her son-in-law. As he had not been successful in the chase for the past day or two, he killed the children and devoured them. Fearing the retribution of his mother-in-law's friends, Murkupang left his habitation at daybreak next morning and journeyed down the Hopkins river to a place near Wickliffe, where he tried to make a cave in a rock by pulling loose pieces off with his hands, but did not succeed.

He next went on to Hexham, where the country opens out into plains, which enabled him to see in the distance Mount Shadwell, with its rocky sides. He accordingly bent his steps in that direction and on approaching the mountain he saw a suitable cave in one side of it, but it was up near the top where the ascent was difficult. Being a great conjuror or sorcerer, he commenced 'bouncing' or scolding the mountain, and commanded the portion containing the cave to come down nearer to the plain on which he was standing. He stamped his feet and made passes or signs with his hands, while he sang a magical song. Presently, in obedience to his incantations, a large portion, containing the cave, parted from the rest of the hill.

Murkupang turned around and ran away across the plain, shouting to the fragment of mountain to roll after him. After a while, when he thought he had reached a good camping place, he faced round again, stamping his feet and using other menaces, which caused the mountain fragment to stop. It then settled down and became what is now known throughout that part of the country as 'Flat-top Hill'. At the present day the aborigines point out a depression in one side of Mount Shadwell from which Flat-top Hill was disrupted. Markupang then selected a part of it which was sheltered from the weather by an overhanging rock—a sort of cave—and made his camp there.

In a few days' time his mother-in-law tracked him to his retreat. She had with her two young warriors, who were clever 'doctors' and had some knowledge of magic. When Murkupang went out hunting, these fighting men hid themselves a little distance from the cave's entrance—one on each side. Before taking up their positions they were smoked by the wily old mother-in-law, to repress or overpower the smell of their bodies. The men moreover covered themselves with stringy bark, softened by beating, so that they could roll it round and round their bodies to make them resemble the boles of trees. These precautions were taken to prevent Murkupang's dogs from scenting them.

While these treacherous proceedings were going on, Murkupang was away hunting as far as Ngurit or Black's mountain, where he filled his bag, *muka-muka*, with kangaroos which he caught, and started homeward. On nearing his cave, he dragged a dry tree after him to provide wood for cooking the game. On coming within sight, he observed the smoke of someone else's fire not far from his own, from which he concluded that his mother-in-law had found him out. He advanced cautiously, and 'sooled' his dogs to search around. He had eight dogs, comprising the soldier-bird or maina, magpie, black jay, crow, white cockatoo, eagle-hawk, and quail-hawk; some being very watchful and noisy, whilst others were very swift and voracious.

These dogs ran smelling everywhere about the camp, baying and uttering their various calls. Murkupang was so alarmed at this that he concluded he had better be generous to his mother-in-law, so he took one of the kangaroos out of his bag, and laying it on the ground, he called out to her to come and get it. He then continued his careful search about the camp, expecting to find some enemy, but his old mother-in-law had planned everything so well that he discovered nothing.

He now broke up the tree which he had carried home and made a good fire, with which he cooked a large kangaroo, and he and his dogs had a hearty evening meal. By and by he again went all round the camp, in the light of the blazing fire, jumping and assuming very obscene postures in the hope of making any hidden onlookers laugh, and so discover themselves, but there was not a sound audible in any direction. Feeling quite satisfied, he went into his cave and soon fell fast asleep, and so did all his dogs, being weary after a long day's hunting.

As before stated, the two warriors who were assisting the mother-in-law, had coiled stringy-bark around their bodies from head to foot, and being somewhat of magicians, they had then given themselves the appearance of real boles or high stumps of stringy-bark trees. There being plenty of other trees of that species growing in the locality, they were not noticed by Murkupang. After a while, upon receiving a sign from the old woman that all was quiet, the men divested themselves of their covering, and walking to the cave, stopped up the entrance with the stringy-bark. A fire was then applied to this inflammable material, which made a great flame and suffocated Murkupang and his dogs. His spirit flew out through the blaze and became a mopoke, called by the natives *mumgatch*, a bird which goes about at night. His dogs also emerged from the cave and assumed the forms of the birds whose names have been already mentioned.

ENDNOTES

[1] An abstract of this legend was published in 'The Native Tribes of Victoria: Their Languages and Customs', *Proceedings of the American Philosophical Society*, vol. 43, 1904, pp. 67-8.

Australian Folk-Tales

R. H. Mathews

First published in *Folk-Lore*, vol. 20 (1909), pp. 485-87.

The first of the following tales was told to me by an old blackfellow whom the white people called 'Jerry'. He spoke the Jirringañ language, a grammar of which I published in 1902,[1] with the habitat of the Jirringañ tribe. The story of the Wahwee is current among the Wiradjuri, Kamilaroi, Wailwan, and other tribes of New South Wales. It was related to me by an old Kamilaroi black-fellow, named 'Jimmy Nerang', whom I met at the Bora ceremony held at Tallwood in 1895.[2] The Rev. Wm. Ridley mentions the Wawi (my Wahwee) as a monster living in deep waterholes.[3] I gave a drawing of the Wahwee represented on the ground at the Burbung ceremonies of the Wiradjuri tribe in 1893.[4] (The two tales have, since their dispatch to *Folk-Lore*, been printed in the *Journal and Proceedings of the Royal Society of New South Wales*.)

1. *The Yarroma.*—Yar'-ro-mas are men of gigantic stature, with their body covered with hair, and having a large mouth which enables them to swallow a blackfellow alive. There are always two of these creatures together, and they stand back to back so that they can see in every direction. Their means of locomotion is by a series of long jumps, and every time their feet strike the ground they make a loud noise like the report of a gun or the cracking of a stock whip.

These men have large feet, shaped differently to those of a human being. When a Yarroma is heard in the vicinity, the people must keep silent, and rub their hands on their genitals. Some of the head-men or 'doctors' call out the name of some place a long way off, with the object of inducing the Yarroma to start away to that locality. If this *ruse* does not succeed, the head-men get sticks which have been lighted in the fire,—a fiery stick in each hand,—and strike them together so as to emit sparks, and the Yarroma then disappears into the ground, making a flash of light as he does so.

If a man is out in the bush alone, and is pursued by Yarromas, his only means of escape is to jump into a large waterhole, and swim about, because the monsters cannot wet their feet. They sharpen their teeth on the rocks in high mountains, and the natives aver that they know of rocks where marks of this grinding can still be seen.

On one occasion a blackfellow went under a fig-tree to pick up ripe figs which had fallen to the ground, when a Yarroma, who was hidden in a hollow at the base of the tree, rushed out and caught him and swallowed him head first. It happened that the victim was a man of unusual length, measuring more than a foot taller than the majority of his countrymen. Owing to this circumstance, the Yarroma was not able to gulp him down farther than the calves of his legs, leaving his ankles and feet protruding from the monster's mouth, which kept it open, and thus allowed a passage for the air to descend to the man's nostrils, which saved him from suffocation. The Yarroma, feeling a nausea something like what occurs when a fish bone or other substance gets stuck in one's throat, went to the bank of the river close by, and had a drink of water to moisten his oesophagus, thinking by this means to suck down the remainder of his prey and complete his repast. This was all to no purpose, however, and, becoming sick, the Yarroma vomited the man out on the dry land. The man was still alive, but he feigned to be dead, so that he might possibly get a chance of running into the water. The Yarroma then started off to get his comrade to come and help him to carry the dead man to their camp, so that they might cook and eat him. He wished, however, to make quite sure that the man was dead before he left him, so he walked a little distance and returned, but the man lay perfectly still. The Yarroma got a stalk of grass and tickled the man's feet, but the latter remained quiet; then the Yarroma tickled the man's nose with the grass, but the man did not move a muscle. Finally the Yarroma took a bull-dog ant, and made it sting him, but still the man never flinched. The Yarroma then, thinking the man was certainly dead, started off for help, and when he got a sufficient distance away, the man, seeing his opportunity, got up and ran into the water close by, and swam to the opposite side. His friends, who happened to come there just at that time, waved burning sticks in the air, and the Yarroma dived into the ground and vanished from their sight.

2. *The Wahwee.*—The Wahwee, a serpent-like monster, lives in deep waterholes, and burrows into the bank beneath the level of the water, where he makes his den. He has a wife and a son, but they camp in a different place. A 'doctor' or clever blackfellow can sometimes go and see a Wahwee, but on such occasions he must paint himself all over with red ochre. He then follows after the rainbow some day when there is a slight shower of rain, and the end of the rainbow rests over the waterhole in which is the Wahwee's abode. On reaching this waterhole, the man dives in under the bank, where he finds the Wahwee, who conducts him into the den, and sings him a song which he never heard before. He repeats this song many times in the presence of the Wahwee, until he has learnt it by heart, and then starts back to his own people. When they see him coming, painted and singing a new song, they know he has been with the Wahwee, and a few of the other head-men and clever fellows take him into the adjacent bush, where they strip pieces of bark off trees, on which they paint different devices in coloured clays. All the people of the tribe are then mustered, and these ornamented pieces of bark are taken to the corroboree ground, where everyone sings and dances. This is how new songs and corroborees are obtained.

ENDNOTES

[1] RHM 1902, 'The Aboriginal Languages of Victoria', *Journal and Proceedings of the Royal Society of New South Wales*, vol. 36.

[2] RHM 1896, 'The Bora of the Kamilaroi Tribes', *Proceedings of the Royal Society of Victoria*, vol. 9 (new series).

[3] Ridley, William 1875, *Kamilaroi, and other Australian Languages*, Thomas Richards, Government Printer, Sydney, p. 138.

[4] RHM 1896, 'The Būrbŭng of the Wiradthuri Tribes', *Journal of the Anthropological Institute*, vol. 25, p. 315.

The Wareengarry and Karambal

R. H. Mathews

First published as part of the article titled 'Folklore of the Australian Aborigines', *Science of Man*, vol. 1 (new series), 1898, p. 119.

On the Clarence River there once lived seven young women who were sisters, named Wareenggary; they were members of the Bunjellung tribe, and belonged to the Wirrakan division.[1] They were very clever, and had yamsticks, in the ends of which were inserted charms, which protected the girls from their enemies. Every day they went out hunting for carpet snakes, and always carried their yamsticks with them on these occasions. A young fellow named Karambal, of the same tribe, and of the division Womboong,[2] became enamoured of one of these young women, and followed within sight of them every day, but they did not favour his suit. He watched for an opportunity, and at length came suddenly upon one of the sisters who had strayed a little way from the rest, and had not her yamstick with her, and carried her off, taking her to his own camp. Her companions became very angry, and held a consultation as to what was best to be done to release their sister from Karambal, who was of the wrong division for her to marry, being in fact her tribal brother.

The eldest sister proposed sending a fierce storm of wind to blow up the trees by the roots, and tumble them upon Karambal and kill him. The other girls were afraid that their sister might also lose her life by the falling trees, and one of them made another proposal, that they should all go away to the west, where they knew the Winter lived, and bring the frost and chilly winds, and in this manner punish Karambal for what he had done. Accordingly, they went away and brought the Winter, and on the place where Karambal was camped with their sister they made the cold so exceptionally severe that he was almost perished with the frost. The girl whom he had captured did not feel this terrible cold, because her sisters had managed to send her, by a secret messenger, the charmed yamstick she formerly carried when out hunting with them. In a short time Karambal was glad enough to let Wareenggary return to her own people, who were very much rejoiced to get her back again amongst them. They then consulted amongst themselves, and determined to go away towards the east, in quest of the summer, so as to melt the frost and ice. They did not wish to impose any further hardship upon their tribe than was necessary, their only object being to rescue their sister from her captor.

After this trouble the Wareenggary resolved to leave the earth altogether, but before doing so they went into the mountains, and made springs at the heads of all the rivers, so that their people might always have plenty of water throughout their hunting grounds. The seven sisters then went up into the sky, where the constellation known as the Pleiades still represents their camp. They come into view every Summer, bringing pleasant warm weather for the benefit of their tribe, after which they go away gradually towards the west, where they disappear. They then send the Winter to warn their kinsmen not to carry off a woman of the wrong totemic division, but to select their wives in accordance with the tribal laws.

Soon after the departure of the Wareenggary from the earth the young man, Karambal, looked about for another sweetheart, and this time he was determined to comply with the marriage rules of his people. After a while he was smitten by the charms of a young woman who belonged to the Kooran[3] division, being that from which he could lawfully select a wife. She was, unfortunately, already united to another man, named Bullabogabun, a great warrior. Karambal succeeded in inducing her to leave her husband, and go away with him. When Bullabogabun discovered that his wife had eloped, he followed her tracks to the camp of Karambal. The latter, in order to escape the wrath of Bullabogabun, climbed up into a very large and tall pine tree growing near his camp, but his pursuer observed him hidden among the topmost branches. Bullabogabun then gathered all the wood he could find for some distance around, and piled it into an immense heap against the butt of the tree, and set fire to it. The fire raged with great fury, burning the pine tree into cinders. The flame reached high into the air, carrying Karambal with it, and deposited him in a part of the sky near the Wareenggary, where he became the star Aldebaran (Alpha Tauri), in order that he might follow the sisters continually, the same has he had done in his youth.

ENDNOTES

[1] See RHM 1897, 'The Totemic Divisions of Australian Tribes', *Journal and Proceedings of the Royal Society of New South Wales*, vol. 31, p. 169.

[2] Ibid.

[3] Ibid.

The Hereafter

R. H. Mathews

First published as part the article titled 'Folklore of the Australian Aborigines', *Science of Man*, vol. 1 (new series), 1898, pp. 142-43.

About three-quarters of a mile north-westerly from the Coolangatta homestead, the residence of the late Mr. Alexander Berry, is a remarkable rock on the eastern side of the Coolangatta mountain. This rock slopes easterly with an angle of about 30 degrees from the horizon, and on its face are six elongated depressions, caused by the weathering away of the softer portions of the stone. These places are suggestive of having been worn by the feet of many persons having used them, like the depressions worn in pavements by much traffic. This has given rise to a superstition among the aborigines that these marks were made in the rock by the feet of the spirits of many generations of natives sliding from the upper to the lower side of it. This belief is strengthened by the fact that the first two depressions are larger than the rest; the next pair on the left of them are somewhat smaller; and the last pair, farther to the left are smaller still. The aboriginal legend is that the larger marks were made by the feet of the men; the medium size by the women, and the smaller by the children. One of the old blackfellows, who was with me when I visited this place, stated that always after a death in the camp, this rock presented the appearance of having been recently used. If the deceased was a man, the large marks looked fresh; if a woman, the middle pair; and if a child, the smaller slides showed indications of someone having slipped along them.

It was from this rock that the shade of the native took its final departure from its present hunting grounds, and this was accomplished in the following manner: A very long stem of a cabbage-tree, imperceptible to human vision, reached from some unknown land across the sea to this rock. When a blackfellow died, his soul went in the night to the top of the rock, and, standing there for a few moments, looked out towards the sea, which is about two miles distant. Then he slid down the hollow grooves, one foot resting in each, and when he got to the lower side of the rock he could distinguish the end of the long pole, on to which he jumped, and walked away along it to the sea-coast, and onward across the expanse of water. The pole continued over the sea, and in following it along the traveller came to a place where flames of fire seemed to rise out of a depression in the water. If he had been a good tribesman he would be able to pass through the flames unscathed; but if he had been a bad man, who had broken the tribal laws, he might get scorched and fall into the sea, or perhaps he would get through it more or less singed.

After a while the end of the pole was reached at the other side of the sea. The traveller then continued on along a track through the bush, and after a time met a crow, who said: 'You once frightened me,' and thereupon threw a spear at him, but missed him, and the man kept on his way, the crow calling him bad names, and making a great noise. At another place he came to where a large native fig-tree was growing, and two men were there. One of these men was standing on the ground, and was some relative of the traveller; but the other man, who was up in the tree, was a vindictive person, and would kill him if he got the chance. He asks the traveller's friend to bring him under the tree, but in doing so the friend warns him to take care. The enemy up the fig-tree is gathering figs, and is squeezing them together around a quartz crystal, which has the effect of causing the lumps of figs to increase in size and weight. He then calls out to the traveller to stand out on a clear space, so that he can throw him the bundle of fruit. The pilgrim, however, suspects his evil intentions, and refuses to do this, but walks into a scrubby place under the tree, and being hungry, stoops down to pick up some of the figs which have fallen to the ground, having been shaken off by the wind. The enemy in the tree then throws the bundle of figs at him, which by this time has changed into a large stone, but he misses his mark, owing to the scrub and undergrowth obstructing his view.

The traveller now resumed his journey, and the track along which he was going passed through a narrow, rocky gorge, with scrub growing on either side, in which were some king parrots of gigantic size, who tried to bite him with their strong beaks, but he defended himself with his shield, and succeeded in getting through the pass. Upon this the parrots set up a great chattering, similar to that made by these birds in their haunts.

On proceeding farther he comes to a forest where there are plenty of trees but no under-scrub, and the grass is green. There are plenty of kangaroos and other native animals of various kinds. Presently he reaches a place where there are large numbers of black people of all ages, amongst whom are some young men playing ball in a clear place near the camp. There the traveller sees his relatives and all his friends who have died before him. He sits down a little way from the people, and when his relations see him, and conduct him into the camp, where they paint and dress him in the same way that he was accustomed to ornament his person in his own country. After that, great shouting and corroboreeing is indulged in, and he plays amongst the rest.

Presently, an old, dirty-looking blackfellow, with sores upon his body, comes near and calls out, 'Who came when that noise was made just now?' They answer him that it was only the young people playing about. This ugly old man cannot come into the camp because there is a watercourse dividing the boundary of his hunting grounds, beyond which he dare not pass. If he were to see the new arrival he might point a bone at him, or work him some other injury, by means of sorcery. This is why the people give him an evasive answer, on receiving which he returns to his own camp, which is a little distance farther on.

If the person who died had been greedy or quarrelsome, or had always been causing trouble in the tribe, he would meet with a different reception at the end of the journey. In order to describe this, it will be necessary to take the reader back to that part of the story where the crow threw the spear. If the traveller has been a troublesome fellow, the spear pierces him and the crow comes and picks mouthfuls of flesh out of him, and knocks him about; after which he pulls out the spear and starts the man on his journey again. When he reaches the place where the large fig-tree is growing, there is no friend there to warn him of danger, so he walks carelessly under the tree, and commences to pick up and eat the ripe figs which have fallen to the ground. The enemy up in the tree watches his opportunity, and throws the bundles of figs, which he has changed to stone by his jugglery, down upon the traveller, bruising him severely and stretching him almost lifeless on the ground. The man then comes down out of the tree, and shakes the traveller, and stands him on his feet and starts him on his way, bruised and bleeding from his wounds, and scarcely able to walk. When at last he reaches the forest of green trees and the camp of his countrymen, the people shout out to him that they don't want him there, and make signs to him to go on. The scabby old blackfellow before referred to then makes his appearance, and asks the usual question: 'Who came when that noise was made?' The people answer him that a stranger came; whereupon, the old man calls the traveller to him, and takes him away to this own camp. The wounds made by those clever, old wizards, the crow and the man in the fig-tree, never heal properly, and give the injured man a scabby and dirty appearance ever afterwards.

[As previously stated, the specimens of aboriginal folklore which I have placed before the readers of this journal are only a few out of a large number copied into my note books on this highly interesting subject during many years residence in the back country. I cannot conclude this article without expressing my appreciation of the labours of Mrs. K. L. Parker, who has recently written a small volume on 'Australian Legendary Tales' for the collection and publication of which she deserves the thanks of all who are interested in the folklore of the Australian aborigines.]

Part 4: Language

Introduction

Martin Thomas

The first language documented by R. H. Mathews was Gundungurra, the tongue of the Blue Mountains and Southern Highlands of New South Wales.[1] Published by the Royal Society in Sydney, the paper was co-authored with Mary Everitt, a Sydney school teacher, with whom Mathews intended to collaborate further, but disagreements developed between them and Mathews never again worked with another writer.[2] He was essentially a one-man operation. He maintained great enthusiasm for linguistic study after that initial publication in 1900. Language elicitation can be found in 36 of his 171 works of anthropology. They describe, in varying detail, some 53 Australian languages.

That he commenced with Gundungurra is intriguing. Mathews once said of his upbringing near Goulburn that 'black children were among my earliest playmates'.[3] According to the boundaries set out in his own writings, the people indigenous to that district would have spoken Gundungurra or the adjacent and related tongue, Ngunawal. His interest in Aboriginal language is important to understanding all aspects of his ethnographic research. When, as a young surveyor at Narran Lakes, he made notes of Aboriginal words in a field book (see the general introduction to this volume), he would have noticed the difference between this language and the one he had heard as a child. This may not seem particularly astounding, but we must remember that few white people at that time had any idea of the linguistic diversity of Aboriginal Australia.

The two linguistic articles published here, 'The Wailwan Language' (1903) and 'Language of the Kurnu Tribe, New South Wales' (1904), are translated from the French. As Mathews explains in the latter article, he had published a discussion of Kurnu in a paper dated 1902,[4] but unusual features of the grammar demanded further investigation. So he travelled by railway from his home in Sydney to western New South Wales. Kurnu, which linguists classify as a dialect of the Paakantyi language, was spoken along the Darling River north of Wilcannia.[5] The northern reaches of Kurnu territory are flanked on the eastern side by Wailwan country. Although described here as a language, Wailwan is technically the northernmost of two dialects spoken by Ngemba people.[6] It is likely that research on both Wailwan and Kurnu occurred concurrently. Mathews' diary records field trips to Brewarrina, Byrock and Bourke in the winters of both 1902 and 1903.[7] He went there on other occasions as well, and corresponded with several policemen in the area who advised him of the whereabouts of Aboriginal people whom they had come to know when distributing blankets and food rations. He discussed language and many other topics during his visits to these communities. The myths, kinship system and material culture of western New South Wales are all described at length in his writings. The short description of Djadjala (Mathews' Tyatyalla), appended to 'The Wailwan Language', resulted from separate fieldwork in Victoria.

Mathews tried as much as possible to carry out his linguistic research in person. As he writes in the Kurnu paper, 'I personally collected the following elements of the language in Kurnu territory, from reliable and intelligent elders of both sexes'. While words to this effect accompany most of his language elicitation, there are exceptions. A 210-word vocabulary of the Jingili language was prepared with the aid of a Northern Territory correspondent.[8] The Lutheran missionary Carl Strehlow supplied information for a paper on Luritja, the Central Australian tongue.[9] There are a few other examples.[10] Strehlow was a unique ally in such labour. His grasp of Aboriginal language was sufficient to allow him to translate parts of the New Testament into Arrernte and he was connected with the anthropological scene in Germany through his association with Moritz von Leonhardi (whose letters to Mathews appear in this volume). Scholars of Strehlow's calibre were of course rare in the backblocks of Australia, and since they had their own ambitions in terms of publishing, they were often cagey about sharing their findings. For the majority of Mathews' correspondents, who were not highly educated, the elicitation of detailed grammatical information was a considerable challenge. The consistent notation of Aboriginal words was also a problem. Although he met with only limited success, Mathews made some effort to tutor correspondents in this labour. He self-published a pamphlet titled *Thurrawal Grammar* (1901). In it a précis of Dharawal is presented as a model for grammatical research, followed by a section headed 'Directions for Obtaining Information'. It provides insight into the strategies used by Mathews in interview situations. He was intrigued by the fact that unlike English, Aboriginal languages have two forms of the pronoun 'we': one that includes the person being spoken to; and another that excludes him or her. Mathews suggests that the researcher first make a note of a common verb—he gives the example of 'to strike'. From there the various forms of the pronouns can be elicited by asking the speaker to say, 'I struck', 'Thou struck', 'He struck', etc.[11]

Mathews' unpublished notebooks in the National Library of Australia testify to the amount of linguistic research he did in person. They often name the individuals who taught him the language—a courtesy only seldom replicated in the published material. Notebooks indicate that in his study of Kurnu, Charlie Elliott, Melbourne Fanny, Eliza Knight and Melbourne Tommy were among his teachers.[12] He often found occasion to check or recheck his work, even after descriptions of the language had been published. Evidence of his method can be found in an offprint of 'Languages of some Native Tribes of Queensland, New South Wales and Victoria', the 1902 article in which his first description of

Kurnu appeared. Unlike the French text, the earlier article contains a vocabulary of 220 words. The list in the offprint is extensively corrected and a pencilled annotation reads: 'Checked with Melb.n Tommy & Charlie Elliott & Liza Knight.'[13]

A reluctance to name sources is apparent in much of Mathews' published work—not only his linguistic research. The fact that he had little trouble finding publishers is evidence that such lack of attribution was not a great problem for many of his peers. But standards were changing in the period in which Mathews worked. Anthropology was becoming more professional. A letter survives among Mathews' papers in which John L. Myres, honorary secretary of the Anthropological Institute, London, requests amendments to the paper 'Languages of the Kamilaroi and Other Aboriginal Tribes of New South Wales' (1903).[14] Myres informed him that

> all three referees have independently asked that precise and full particulars should be given in each case as to the circumstances (locality, date, collector, & c.) under which the information contained in these papers was collected.[15]

Mathews revised the paper to a standard that the journal deemed acceptable, but instead of naming informants he gave generalised statements about how he acquired the data: 'all my information had to be obtained orally from the natives by visiting them at their camping places'.[16] The evidence of the notebooks establishes beyond doubt the veracity of these claims. Mathews' reluctance to name his sources was partly a consequence of a research culture that honoured the researcher above the Aboriginal speaker, and was no doubt exacerbated by the fractious anthropological scene in Australia. Mathews resisted naming his Aboriginal sources lest his rivals should use this information to track them down.

Mathews' unpublished papers reveal an ongoing labour of checking and refinement, long after the publication of an article. They give many insights into the challenges he faced when recording language. Inevitably, he encountered differences in accent and pronunciation within language groups, and given that many speakers were conversant in a number of Aboriginal tongues, there may well have been confusion about what language he was documenting. The contact experience brought linguistic transformation; old words were lost or transformed and new terms were needed. All these factors presented challenges to the linguist who was also struggling with the problems of identifying sounds and working out how to transcribe them. He was obliged to revise his work not only because he sometimes met speakers who seemed more authoritative, but because his ear for Aboriginal language improved the more he listened. What his Aboriginal friends thought of his steely determination to describe grammar and produce word lists is not recorded. But it must have seemed strange and rather mechanical. Not surprisingly, the linguistic documentation in Mathews' notebooks often segues into accounts of legends or lists of totems. Campfire conversation did not conform to the neat categories suggested by the published writings. That men and women contributed to the Kurnu study is fairly typical of Mathews' work on linguistics. Language research was not usually gender-specific.[17] The significant contribution of women helps explain the amount of linguistic ground he covered. At places such as Bourke and Brewarrina, men were often absent labouring in the pastoral industry. Women and children predominated at the Aboriginal stations and reserves where Mathews tended to visit.

Readers of his linguistic publications will notice that a consistent template was used throughout. Of the two works reproduced here, 'The Wailwan Language' is the more substantial, and is generally typical of his work on language. First, the grammar is explained under headings that were replicated in every article. Then comes the vocabulary, first with the word in English and then its Wailwan equivalent. Words are grouped in categories which were loosely replicated in article after article: 'The Family', 'The Human Body', 'Natural Surroundings', 'Mammals', 'Birds', 'Fishes', 'Reptiles', 'Invertebrates', 'Adjectives' and 'Verbs'. The lack of a vocabulary in the Kurnu translation is due to his having published one in the earlier article, despite its limitations.[18]

Immediately noticeable, even in the longer Wailwan publication, is the brevity of this work: vocabulary is represented in 200 words. Admittedly, this is on the shorter end of the scale. Mathews often gave 300 words from a language and on one occasion 460.[19] Yet even this is a very partial representation, of limited use to a potential speaker. These days, Mathews' work is often consulted by Aboriginal people, sometimes in the hope of reconnecting with their heritage or revitalising the languages he recorded. Mathews, however, never anticipated such a readership, and was usually pessimistic about the future of Aboriginal culture. His methods were very much at odds with current expectations, so to understand his inscription and presentation of languages, we have to think about his motivations.

Indication of why he recorded language has appeared already in this volume. In 'The Natives of Australia' (1902) he expressed his views on Aboriginal migration.

> Some of the southerly reaches of this flood of emigrants reached the north and north-western coasts of the Australian continent and spread across the largest part of Australia as well as Tasmania, which was then joined to New Holland. These first occupants can be seen as the Aborigines of Australia. Other branches of the same migration reached New Guinea, New Caledonia, Melanesia and Polynesia, where not only fragments of the race can be found, but also traces of a common language, because a language can adopt foreign words without changing its

176   **R. H. MATHEWS.**

ENGLISH.	KURNU.	ENGLISH.	KURNU.
The Family.		Tongue,	dhurlunya
A man,	wimbadya	Chin,	wukka
Married man,	burrakulli	Back,	dhurnu
Small boy,	kŭtyungga	Arm,	wŭnye
Youth,	wilyarrungga	Hand,	murra
Novitiate,	kulta	Thigh,	mungga
Initiated man,	mŭnkamura	Calf of leg,	thiltya
Father,	ngambadya	Knee,	dhinggi
Elder brother,	kukkudya	Foot,	millinya
Younger „	bulludya	Blood,	muppurla
A woman,	burraka	Fat,	korai
Married woman,	yupparilla	Bone,	birna
Young girl,	karnkali	Penis,	wira
Marriageable girl,	kumbulla	Erection,	wandhadya
Child (neuter),	mundhanggura	Testicles,	mulu
Mother,	ngamugga	Vulva,	būlli
Mother-in-law,	gulirri	Nymphæ,	dhillin
Elder sister,	kunnittya	Hair on pudendæ,	murtubulki
Younger sister,	wŭrtuka	Copulation,	baingullana
The Human Body.		Masturbation,	burtaburtamŭntha
Head,	milpirri	Semen,	burdiñ
Forehead,	pikku	Urine,	kippurra
Hair of head,	bulki	Excrement,	kilkua
Beard,	wukkubulki	Venereal,	mikkali
Eye,	mainmurra	*Inanimate Nature.*	
Nose,	mindyumulu	Sun,	putyi
Neck (throat),	bunba	Heat of sun,	windhura
Ear,	yuri or munga	Moon,	dhintyanni
Mouth,	yulka	Stars,	buli or ngunyaga
Lips,	mimnai	Pleiades,	gumbalpirri
Teeth,	ngundi	Thunder,	butangutthu
Breast (female)	ngumma	Lightning,	birnde
Navel,	wirngu	Chain lightning,	nimuddheri
Belly,	mŭnda	Rain,	ngunburu

R. H. Mathews used this offprint of 'Languages of some Native Tribes of Queensland, New South Wales and Victoria' (1902) in later fieldwork. A vocabulary for Dhudhuroa (the language of the Mitta Mitta and Kiewa Rivers) has been pencilled alongside the printed documentation of Kurnu (a language spoken in western NSW). By permission of the National Library of Australia. (R.H. Mathews Papers, NLA MS8006/8.227).

fundamental character. Comparative philology and ethnology must always be studied at the same time.[20]

Other comments confirm this motivation. His study of Dharawal in 1901 was prefaced with the hope that the information would be valuable to philologists, 'enabling them to compare our aboriginal languages with each other, and also with those of the people of Polynesia and the East Indian Archipelago'.[21] The idea that language could be a scientific indicator of racial and geographical origins was quite acceptable in Mathews' period. The idea went out of vogue when it was recognised that the human race, and indeed the cosmos, are much older than was thought by the Victorians.[22] Working with this framework, Mathews never thought of glossing a language in such detail that someone would speak it. Instead, his research was a form of survey in which sets of uniform and quite restricted data were gathered from diverse language groups for comparative purposes.

So how did Mathews go about the complex task of documenting language? What models informed his process? One clue can be found in a comment made by his granddaughter-in-law Janet Mathews, who was familiar with his personal library. She claims that Mathews and his wife Mary returned from Europe in 1883 with 'a book containing the grammar of the Irish Gaelic language'.[23] This intriguing revelation is further evidence that Mathews was interested in matters linguistic long before he turned to anthropology in the early 1890s. It also hints at a further connection between his documentation of Aboriginal traditions and the influence of the folklore studies movement, which sought to investigate and preserve the folk culture of Europe, also thought to be endangered (see introduction to 'Part 3: Mythology', this volume).

The Gaelic grammar became part of Mathews' library, which occupied a room of his house in Parramatta. He also studied in the reading room of the Royal Society of New South Wales and at the Public Library in Sydney.[24] That is to say, he had access to a range of literature that guided him in the collection and presentation of linguistic data. This included manuals on anthropology, the best known of which was *Notes and Queries on Anthropology, for the use of Travellers and Residents in Uncivilized Lands*, issued by the Anthropological Institute in London. E. B. Tylor wrote the entry on language for the first edition of 1874 and Mathews seems to have heeded his stern counsel that the 'practice of judging of the affinities of a language by means of a short vocabulary of isolated words, without a guide to the grammatical structure, is to be condemned as loose and misleading'.[25] Mathews' approach to language was certainly more rigorous than the piecemeal collection of vocabulary, criticised by Tylor. His documentation of Aboriginal grammar was sufficiently impressive to win reserved praise from later, professional linguists including Arthur Capell and Diana Kelloway Eades.[26] His method was limited, however, by his dependence on European models. The linguist Harold Koch argues that the 'grammatical framework used by Mathews seems to be based primarily on the system of Traditional Grammar that emerged from Greek and Roman grammarians'.[27] Koch claims that this prevented him from discerning certain distinctive features of Aboriginal language. His discussion of case is an example. Explicated under the categories 'Genitive', 'Ablative', 'Dative', etc., it seems directly drawn from a Latin primer such as Mathews or his children would have used. Koch notes that a 'remarkable absence from Mathews' case inventory is the Locative, which modern studies have found to be universally present in Australian languages'.[28]

Mathews' offprints of his own articles, sometimes crammed with marginalia, confirm Koch's analysis. A publication on one language provided not only the schematic framework for future studies, but the very paper on which they were written. This seems to have been the case with the corrected Kurnu vocabulary, previously mentioned. That he travelled with offprints on his field trips and annotated them directly by the campfire is certainly suggested by their often dilapidated condition. Nearly all his vocabularies were based on a standard set of English words, and rather than rewrite it time and time again, Mathews simply inscribed a new vocabulary alongside the list of English terms printed in the earlier article. This is apparent in various offprints of 'Languages of some Native Tribes of Queensland, New South Wales and Victoria' (1902). In one, a vocabulary for Dhudhuroa (the language of the Mitta Mitta and Kiewa rivers, and part of the Murray valley) has been pencilled alongside the printed documentation of Kurnu.[29] Although pre-emptive, the method was convenient and in its own way logical, for it allowed him to see at a glance the affinities between his present study and languages he had previously documented.

The notation used by Mathews to capture the phonetics of Aboriginal language opens other intriguing issues. To what extent does his notation approximate the utterances he heard? The challenges of transcribing foreign languages were keenly felt in the period when Mathews began his research. Comparative linguistics was an emerging field. Since linguists everywhere were hampered by the fact that there was no system of notation applicable to all languages, a group of language teachers convened in Paris in 1886 to deal with the problem. They established the International Phonetic Association and two years later they issued the first version of the International Phonetic Alphabet (I.P.A.), a system modestly 'intended to provide a standardized, accurate and unique representation for every sound element in human language'.[30] If Mathews was aware of this new form of notation, he made no attempt to master it. Rather, as he mentions in the Wailwan paper (and many others), he used a simpler form of orthography recommended by the Royal Geographical Society in London.

Mathews' use of this system reveals how strongly his background as a surveyor influenced his anthropological methods. Through his surveying network he would have received notice of the Royal Geographical Society's system of orthography, which was never intended for the student of ethno-linguistics. The society's concern was consistency in nomenclature throughout the colonies, which would have a beneficial effect on imperial administration. First published in 1885,[31] the system was refined in 1892 in the hope it would 'reduce the confusion existing in British maps with regard to the spelling of geographical names, in consequence of the variety of systems of orthography used by travellers and others to represent the sound of native place-names in different parts of the world'.[32] In complete contrast to the I.P.A., which used special characters to reproduce unique phonetic values, the Royal Geographic Society employed English notation

> to provide a system which should be simple enough for any educated person to master with the minimum of trouble, and which at the same time would afford an approximation to the sound of a place-name such as a native might recognise. No attempt was made to represent the numberless delicate inflexions of sound and tone which belong to every language, often to different dialects of the same language. For it was felt not only that such a task would be impossible, but that an attempt to provide for such niceties would defeat the object.[33]

Undoubtedly, the simplicity of the system must have appealed to Mathews. It was based on a few cardinal rules: vowels should be pronounced as in Italian; consonants as per English. All letters must be pronounced. The acute accent was the only diacritic admissible.[34] As we see in the 'The Wailwan Language', Mathews was compelled to modify the system slightly. He used the Spanish ñ to express the *ny* sound common as a word ending in Australian languages. The placement of a macron above some vowels denoted a 'long sound' (*ā, ē, ū*). His manuscripts sometimes use other diacritics, but they appear only spasmodically in the printed versions. The typesetters in Austria were willing or able to reproduce a wider range of diacritics than those in Paris.

The changes that occurred in translating English descriptions of Aboriginal language into German and French epitomise the complications that beset Mathews' project from its inception. In this volume we have tried as much as possible to weed out the mistakes of the original translators, though it is easy to empathise with their bewilderment. A living language is always in a state of flux. That is true of both English and the Aboriginal tongues that Mathews tried to capture. His linguistic foray is a reminder that Aboriginal languages were already influencing the English of white Australians, many of whom would recognise the 'laughing jackass' by its Wailwan name, *kuguburra*. But Oscar Schmidt, translating in Paris, was understandably flummoxed. The bird became a *pie riante*, literally a 'laughing magpie'. The word 'clever man' posed similar problems. Schmidt translated it as *homme intelligent* (intelligent man), thus erasing most of its meaning.

When the context of Mathews' work on language is understood, any notion that his articles are literal representations of Aboriginal speech must be discarded. Like all his writings they are as much to do with the anthropologist and his culture as they are about the Aboriginal societies he visited. Certainly, they give tremendous insights into the thinking of Aboriginal people. Language is at the heart of how we interact with one another and the world around us. Through language we represent the past, negotiate the present and anticipate the future. Mathews' Kurnu paper is rewarding for anyone thinking about Aboriginal concepts of time. He outlines a grammatical system in which tense is marked by modification of the pronouns—a feature not found elsewhere in Australia. Typically, temporality in language is marked by modification of verbs. The Kurnu system seemed so unnatural to R. M. W. Dixon, the distinguished scholar of Australian languages, that he dismissed it as the concoction of 'a surveyor and amateur linguist' whose work 'must be treated with caution'.[35] But Stephen Wurm and Luise Hercus, who did linguistic fieldwork in the 1950s and 1960s with the last Paakantyi speakers, confirmed the veracity of Mathews' report.[36] This is testimony to the skill of his teachers and his own perception, which allowed him to overcome his lack of training and the limitations of grammatical models based on Latin and Greek.

In many ways, Mathews' linguistic project is defined by the technology available to him at the time. Phonographs were the only system of sound recording available for fieldwork in the early 1900s. The maximum duration of a recording was only a couple of minutes, and the wax cylinders on which they recorded were famously unstable.[37] So Mathews made do with pen and paper. This means that he alone controlled the recording of data. While his Aboriginal friends were clearly willing to share their language, it is likely that they tried to push his education in directions that were meaningful according to their own values and mores. There are hints of this in the notebooks, but they are always excised from the publications. R. H. Mathews' documentation is thus very different to the tapes recorded by Janet Mathews in the 1960s.[38] Working on occasions with descendants of people who taught her grandfather-in-law, she documented song and music on a portable electric recorder. At her suggestion, Jimmie Barker, a speaker of Muruwari and sound recordist par excellence, produced invaluable tapes in which he appraised offprints of Mathews' writings on his language and corrected various mistakes.[39] Aboriginal people became newly empowered by this type of technology.[40]

Janet's tapes give intimation of the sorts of dialogues and misunderstandings that R. H. must have experienced. They allow us to think about the strategies used by the speakers when Mathews came visiting. While researching this section of the book, I corresponded with the linguist Tamsin Donaldson who has studied the Ngemba dialects and other New South Wales languages. In collaboration with Bradley Steadman, a Brewarrina resident of Ngemba ancestry who is greatly interested in how his people were documented, she prepared a statement about the possible motivations of people who work with researchers. Donaldson and Steadman are convinced that speakers and singers are often untroubled by the conceptual limitations of the person asking the questions.

> When people sing songs for the tape recorder, they often first explain for the person with the microphone, sometimes in language and sometimes in English, that so and so 'gave me this song to sing behind'. This means that so and so had given them the song as an inheritance.

> When 'right through' [fluent] speakers of a language talk into the microphone they always make what they say part of a real conversation grounded in the reality of their own lives and the language they live them in, whatever the purpose of questions in English that they are being asked by the 'field worker' holding the microphone. If the question doesn't make sense to them in their own 'word-world' (the literal meaning of the language name Ngiyampaa) they will reframe it and answer it so that it does. And if the questioner is an outsider who is not able to 'take notice' and learn enough to become part of this conversation grounded in their here and now, they will speak past the questioner to another audience—the listeners of the future who are 'being given the language' to understand and 'talk behind'.[41]

ENDNOTES

[1] Mathews, R.H. and Everitt, M.M. 1900 'The Organisation, Language and Initiation Ceremonies of the Aborigines of the South-East Coast of N. S. Wales', *Journal and Proceedings of the Royal Society of New South Wales*, vol. 34.

[2] See letters from Everitt to A. G. Stephens in Organ, Michael (ed.) 1993, *Illawarra and South Coast Aborigines*, Report at MS 3303, Australian Institute of Aboriginal and Torres Strait Islander Studies, Canberra, pp. 194-200.

[3] RHM 1904, 'Ethnological Notes on the Aboriginal Tribes of New South Wales and Victoria', *Journal and Proceedings of the Royal Society of New South Wales*, vol. 38, p. 203.

[4] RHM 1902, 'Languages of some Native Tribes of Queensland, New South Wales and Victoria', *Journal and Proceedings of the Royal Society of New South Wales*, vol. 36.

[5] Hercus, L. A. 1982, *The Bagandji Language*, Research School of Pacific Studies, The Australian National University, Canberra, p. 7.

[6] Donaldson, Tamsin 1985, 'Hearing the First Australians' in Donaldson, Ian and Donaldson, Tamsin (eds), *Seeing the First Australians*, George Allen & Unwin, Sydney, p. 78.

[7] Diary 1893-1907, R. H. Mathews Papers, National Library of Australia (henceforth NLA) MS 8006/1/2. Entries for 20 June-12 July 1902 and 26 June–11 July 1903.

[8] RHM 1900-01, 'Ethnological Notes on the Aboriginal Tribes of the Northern Territory', *Queensland Geographical Journal*, vol. 16.

[9] RHM 1907, 'Languages of some Tribes of Western Australia', *Proceedings of the American Philosophical Society*, vol. 46.

[10] Egs RHM 1909-10, 'Notes on Some Tribes of Western Australia', *Queensland Geographical Journal*, vol. 25, and RHM 1907,'The Arran'da Language, Central Australia', *Proceedings of the American Philosophical Society*, vol. 46.

[11] RHM 1901, *Thurrawal Grammar: Part I*, self-published, Parramatta, unpaginated.

[12] Notebook with 'Criterion Hotel' on cover, R. H. Mathews Papers, NLA MS 8006/3/7, pp. 5 & 11.

[13] RHM, 'Languages of some Native Tribes of Queensland, New South Wales and Victoria', p. 175. Offprint at NLA MS 8006/8/231.

[14] RHM 1903, 'Languages of the Kamilaroi and Other Aboriginal Tribes of New South Wales', *Journal of the Anthropological Institute*, vol. 33.

[15] Myres to Mathews, 11 December 1902, R. H. Mathews Papers, NLA MS 8006/8/479. The author of the letter is significant. John Linton Myres was Wykeham Professor of Ancient History at Oxford and celebrated for 'introducing more systematic methods and promoting a definite progressive policy' at the Anthropological Institute in his roles as honorary secretary, editor of *MAN*, and as president. See Braunholtz, H.J and Firth, Raymond 1939, 'J. L. Myres: Past President of the Royal Anthropological Institute; Editor of "MAN"', *MAN*, vol. 39, no. 88.

[16] RHM, 'Languages of the Kamilaroi and Other Aboriginal Tribes', p. 275.

[17] A significant exception to this rule are what Mathews called the 'mystic' languages—spoken only at men's ceremonies. Mathews gave sketchy documentation of several of these languages.

[18] RHM, 'Languages of some Native Tribes of Queensland, New South Wales and Victoria', pp. 175-9.

[19] RHM 1901-02, 'The Thoorga Language', *Queensland Geographical Journal*, vol. 17.

[20] RHM 1902, 'Les Indigènes d'Australie, *L'Anthropologie*, vol. 13, p.234. Reproduced this volume.

[21] RHM 1901, 'The Thurrawal Language', *Journal and Proceedings of the Royal Society of New South Wales*, vol. 35, pp. 127-8.

[22] Research into genetics has brought new thinking about the value of correlating linguistic and genetic data when tracing the origins and movements of peoples. See Cavalli-Sforza, Luigi Luca 2000, *Genes, Peoples and Languages*, North Point Press, New York.

[23] Mathews, Janet 1994, *The Opal that Turned Into Fire*, Magabala Books, Broome, WA, p. 160.

[24] Thomas, Martin 2007, 'The Ethnomania of R. H. Mathews: Anthropology and the rage for collecting' in Poiner, Gretchen and Jack, Sybil (eds), *Limits of Location: Creating a Colony*, Sydney University Press, Sydney.

[25] Tylor, E.B. 1874, 'No. LXIX—Language' in British Association for the Advancement of Science, *Notes and Queries on Anthropology, for the use of Travellers and Residents in Uncivilized Lands*, Council of the Anthropological Institute, London, p. 114.

[26] Capell, A. 1971, 'History of research on Australian and Tasmanian languages' in Sebeok, T. (ed.), *Current Trends in Linguistics: Linguistics in Oceania*, vol. 8, Mouton, The Hague, p. 667 and Eades, Diana Kelloway 1976, *The Dharawal and Dhurga Languages of the New South Wales South Coast*, Australian Institute of Aboriginal Studies, Canberra, pp. 8-11.

[27] Koch, Harold (in press), 'R. H. Mathews' schema for the description of Australian languages' in McGregor, William (ed.), *Encountering Aboriginal languages: Studies in the history of Aboriginal linguistics*, Pacific Linguistics, Canberra, unpaginated.

[28] Ibid.

[29] RHM, 'The Aboriginal Languages of Queensland, New South Wales and Victoria', 1902. Copy at NLA MS 8006/8/227.

[30] 'International Phonetic Alphabet', *Wikpedia*, viewed 11 July 2006. <<http://en.wikipedia.org/wiki/International_Phonetic_Alphabet.>>

[31] Royal Geographical Society 1885, 'System of Orthography for Native Names of Places', *Proceedings of the Royal Geographical Society and Monthly Record of Geography*, vol. 7 (new series), no. 8.

[32] Duff, M. E. Grant 1892, 'Orthography of Geographic Names', *Proceedings of the Royal Geographical Society and Monthly Record of Geography*, vol. 14 (new series), no. 2, p. 116.

[33] Ibid, p. 117.

[34] Ibid, p. 118.

[35] Cited Wurm, S.A and Hercus, L. 1976, 'Tense-Marking in Gunu Pronouns' in Kirton, J.F., Sommer, B.A., Wurm, S.A., Hercus, L., Austin, P. and Ellis, R. (eds), *Papers in Australian Linguistics No. 10*, Research School of Pacific Studies, Canberra, p. 34.

[36] Ibid.

[37] Thomas, Martin 2007, 'The Rush to Record: Transmitting the Sound of Aboriginal Culture', *Journal of Australian Studies*, no. 91.

[38] Thomas, Martin 2003, '"To You Mrs Mathews": The Cross-Cultural Recording of Janet Mathews 1914-1992', *The Australasian Sound Archive*, vol. 29.

[39] Recordings by Jimmie Barker dated 1969, Australian Institute of Aboriginal and Torres Strait Islander Studies Archive Tapes A1706a and A 1581a. The paper discussed was RHM 1902-03, 'The Murawarri and other Australian Languages', *Queensland Geographical Journal*, vol. 18.

[40] The recordings resulted in the posthumous publication of Barker's life story. See Barker, Jimmie and Mathews, J. 1980, *The Two Worlds of Jimmie Barker: The Life of an Australian Aboriginal 1900-1972 as told to Janet Mathews*, Australian Institute of Aboriginal Studies, Canberra [1st pub. 1977].

[41] Tamsin Donaldson and Bradley Steadman, pers. comm., 7 July 2006.

The Wailwan Language

R. H. Mathews

First published as 'Le langage Wailwan' in *Bulletins et Mémoires de la Société d'Anthropologie de Paris*, 4 (5th series), 1903, pp. 69-81. The article was written in English and translated into French by Oscar Schmidt. This version was retranslated into English by Mathilde de Hauteclocque.[1]

The *Wailwan* language, one of the idioms of the natives of New South Wales, is spoken on both sides of the Barwon river, from Walgett as far as Brewarrina; it can be heard all the way back up the Castlereagh, Macquarie and Mara rivers up to about 70 miles to the south, where it meets the *Wiradyuri* and *Wongaibon* languages. To the east of Wailwan, *Kamilaroi* is spoken, and to the north, *Yualeai*.

The different parts of speech will first be dealt with, showing the declensions of the nouns and the adjectives, the modifications of the pronouns, the conjugation of the verbs, and then some brief lists of the adverbs and the prepositions. This will be followed by a vocabulary of some of the most important words of the everyday language. This paper does not claim to give a complete grammar, but merely an insight into the grammatical structure.

Perhaps this will interest philologists, allowing them to compare the different languages of the Australian natives with those of other primitive peoples.

Orthography

18 letters of the English alphabet are sounded, comprising thirteen consonants and five vowels, namely, *b, d, g, h, k, l, m, n, p, r, t, w, y,* and *a, e, i, o, u.*

The system of orthoepy recommended by the circular issued by the Royal Geographical Society, London, has been adhered to, except for the following modifications:

As much as possible, vowels have been left without special signs, but in a few cases the long sound of *a, e* and *u* is indicated as follows: *ā, ē, ū.* In some cases the short sounds of the *u* and *o* are notated *ŭ* and *ŏ.*

G is hard in all cases. *W* always commences a syllable or word.

Ng starting a word or a syllable has a peculiar nasal sound; at the end of a word it takes the sound of *ng,* as in the English word 'sing'.

The sound of the Spanish *ñ* is quite common; at the beginning of a word or syllable I have expressed it as *ny,* whereas when it is at the end of a word, it is the Spanish letter which has been used.

Y at the beginning of a word or syllable has its ordinary consonant value.

Dh is pronounced nearly as *th* as in the English word 'that', with an initial sound of *d* preceding it. *Nh* is also close to *th*, as in the word 'that', but adding an initial *n* sound.

T is interchangeable with *d*; *p* with *b*; and *g* with *k* in most words where these letters are employed.

Ty and *dy* at the *beginning* of a word or a syllable are pronounced rather like the English *y* or *ch*; so, *dya* or *tya* has nearly the same sound as *ja* or *cha*.

At the end of a word or syllable *ty* or *dy* are pronounced as *tch,* as in the English words 'pitch' or 'catch', but omitting the last whistling sound.

Nouns

The nouns are subject to variations according to number, gender and case.

Number. There are three numbers: singular, dual and plural. For example: *Mulyan*, an eaglehawk; *mulyangali*, a pair of eaglehawks; *mulyangalga,* many eaglehawks. Some nouns have a special plural form which is particular only to them, such as: *wiringamboi*, many women.

Gender. For human beings, this is expressed by different words, such as: *thur*, a man; *wiringa*, a woman; *wurru*, a child of either sex.

Among animals, the gender is indicated by the addition of a word which signifies 'male' or 'female', such as: *Kuragai mundava*, a male opossum; *Kurugai gunal*, a female opossom. *Baba* and *gunni,* the usual words for 'father' and 'mother', are also used for the same purpose, especially for birds.

Case

The nouns are declined with suffixes whose principals express the nominative, the causative, the instrumental, the genitive, the accusative, the dative and the ablative.

The *nominative* is the root of the noun, such as: *thur winyana*, 'the man is seated', and this root has no declension.

The *causative* represents the motive of an act expressed by a transitive verb and specified by a suffix such as: *Thuru murrawi gume*, 'a man hit a kangaroo' or *Mirrigu kuragai kutthe*, 'a dog bit an opossum'.

Genitive — Thuranggu bier, 'a man's boomerang'; *Wirnganggu kuni*, 'A woman's stick (yamstick)'.

One peculiarity of the genitive which is found in the Wailwan and in many of the Australian dialects, as well as on many islands of Melanesia and beyond, is the addition of a possessive suffix to a great number of nouns of which I give the following examples:

		My boomerang:	Bierdhi
	1st person	(boomerang of mine)	
Singular	2nd person	Your boomerang:	Biernu
	3rd person	His boomerang	Bierlugu

When it is a question of two or more objects:

Biergalidhi: My two boomerangs

Biergalgadhi: My many boomerangs, etc.

Instrumental — When it is an instrument or a weapon which represents the distant aim of the verb, it takes the same suffix as the causative. For example: *Thuru waru bume bieru*, 'a man hit a snake with a boomerang'.

Dative — The dative and the genitive are similar to each other, for example: *Nguranggu,* 'to a camp (*ngura*)'.

Ablative — *Ngurandyi*, 'from a camp'. The *accusative* is the same as the *nominative*.

In all the declensions mentioned above, the form of the suffix generally varies with the ending of the noun. They are therefore subject to certain euphonic rules which consist of connecting the suffix with various endings in such a way as to ensure an easy and pleasant pronunciation.

Adjectives

Adjectives follow the nouns they qualify, and take the same inflections: *Thur bitthe,* 'a tall man'; *Thuru betthegu murrawi gume*, 'a tall man hit a kangaroo'; *Thurgu bitthegu bier*, 'a tall man's boomerang'.

When the last letter of the noun affects a euphonic modification on the suffix, as indicated above, the causative and the genitive sometimes resemble each other as in the last two examples. In that case, ambiguity is avoided by the sense of the phrase.

The comparison is made by positive assertions, such as: *Nginya yedda, nginya wurrai,* 'this one is good, this one is bad'.

If an adjective is used as a predicate, it can be converted into a verb by adding the necessary suffixes and conjugated accordingly. For example: *Yeddadhu,* I am good (good me); *Yeddagedhu,* I was good; *Yeddagalagadhu,* I will be good; and so it follows for all persons, numbers and tenses.

Pronouns

Pronouns have person, number and case, but not gender. There are two forms in the first person of the dual and the plural, for the purpose of expressing the inclusion or exclusion of the person addressed.

Here is a list of the nominative, possessive and objective pronouns:

Singular

1st pers.:	I	*Ngadhu*	my	*Ngaddhi*	me	*Dhi*
2nd pers.:	you	*Ngindu*	your	*Nginya*	you	*Nu*
3rd pers.:	he	*Ngillu*	his	*Ngigula*	him	*Lugu*

Dual

1st pers.:	we incl	*Ngullu*	our incl	*Ngulligi*	to us, incl	*Ligi*
	— excl	*Ngullina*	— excl	*Ngullingina*	— excl	*Ligina*
2nd pers.:	you	*Ngindiwulu*	your	*Nginyanula*	to you	*Nula*
3rd pers.:	they	*Ngillibula*	his	*Ngigulagu*	to them	*Lugula*

Plural

1st pers.:	we incl	*Ngeane*	our incl	*Ngeanigi*	to us, incl	*Ngenaga*
	— excl	*Ngeaninna*	— excl	*Ngeanigina*	— excl	*Ngenagina*
2nd pers.:	you	*Ngindugal*	your	*Nginyuga*	to you	*Nugal*
3rd pers.:	they	*Ngillugula*	his	*Nguggagala*	to them	*Lugugal*

The compound forms of the pronouns are used above all as answers to a question. For example: 'Who is sitting over there?' can provoke the reply, '*Ngulligina*'; and to the question, 'Who is it?' one can answer, '*Ngeanigina*'. In everyday language, however, the natives prefer to use contractions, shown in the paragraph headed 'Verbs'.

There are also forms of objective pronouns which signify 'towards me', 'from me', 'with me', etc.

Interrogative pronouns — Who, *ngandi*? Who (did it), *nganduwa*? For whom, *ngangu*? What, *minyang*? Why, *minyangu*?

Demonstratives — This, *nginya*. That, *ngunna*. These are put after the nouns and are declined in their numbers, doubles and multiples.

Particular words are used to indicate the relative position of the object from the person who is speaking, while other particular words indicate this position in relation to the person being spoken to.

Often the third-person pronouns are used as demonstratives. Hence the great number and irregularity of these pronouns in the Australian languages.

The demonstrative pronouns also often acquire the sense of the definite article, as for example: *Kuragai nginya*, which can mean either 'this possum' or 'the possum' according to the text. The adverbs 'here' and 'there' are generally identical to 'this one' and 'that one' and have on occasions the same sense as the definite article.

Verbs

The verbs have number, person, tense and everyday mood. Like the pronouns, they have inclusive and exclusive endings to express the dual or the plural in the first person.

Each tense has its own special ending, such as: *gumurra, guma, gumullaga,* the present, past and future of the verb 'to hit'. A contraction of the pronoun is added to the root of the verb to point out the number and the person.

Here, for example, is a summary of the conjugation of the verb *gumulli* 'to hit'.

Present indicative

Singular	1st person	I hit	*Gumurra-dhu*
	2nd person	you hit	*Gumurra-ndu*
	3rd person	he hits	*Gumurra-lu*
Dual	1st person	we (incl) hit	*Gumurra-li*
	1st person	we (excl) hit	*Gumurra-lina*
	2nd person	you hit	*Gumurra-ndula*
	3rd person	they hit	*Gumurra-lula*
Plural	1st person	we (incl) hit	*Gumurra-ne*
	1st person	we (excl) hit	*Gumurra-ninna*
	2nd person	you hit	*Gumurra-ndugal*
	3rd person	they hit	*Gumurra-lugal*

The past and future forms of verbs have endings that vary according to whether the action was of longer or shorter duration. These different endings stay the same for all persons, whether in the singular, dual or plural. By adding the necessary pronominal suffix, the verb acquires a special ending for each person and each number of all the tenses, as shown by the conjugation of the indicative present given above. I will therefore give examples only of the first person singular, past and future.

Past

	I hit, indeterminate	*Gume gadhu*
Singular	I hit, this morning	*Gume ngurranyedhu*
	I hit, yesterday	*Gume gumbirradhu*
	I hit, a long time ago	*Gume ngargambodhu*

Future

	I will hit, straight away	*Gumulla-galladhu*
Singular	I will hit, indeterminate	*Gumulla-gadhu*
	I will hit, tomorrow	*Gumulngurriagadhu*
	I will hit, soon	*Gumullagawandugagadhu*

Imperative

Singular:	*Gumullagu,*	hit someone
Dual:	*Gumullagulla*	hit two people
Plural:	*Gumullagugal*	hit everyone

Conditional

Gumullagayadhu, perhaps I will hit

Reflexive mood

The reflexive form of the verb describes the action that a subject performs directly on himself:

Present:	I hit myself	*Gumadyillingadhu*
Past:	I hit myself	*Gumadyillingedhu*
Future:	I will hit myself	*Gumadyillingadhu*

Reciprocal mood

This modification of the verb applies to cases where two or more people hit each other and, as a consequence, is limited to the dual and the plural.

Dual:	We (incl) hit each other	*Gumullanullali*
Plural:	We (incl) hit each other	*Gumullamillane*

It is understood that in all examples given, the other numbers, persons and tenses are subject to the same inflections.

The passive has no special form. As such, the sentence 'a dog was bitten by a snake' is expressed by 'a snake bit a dog'.

Adverbs

Here are some adverbs which, in conversation, are usually placed after the verb:

Yes, *ngaru*. No, *wail*. Here, *nginya*. There, *ngunna*. Over there, *gurar*. Presently, *dhulungurra*. Sometimes, *wanduga*. Long ago, *ngurgambo*. Tomorrow, *kumbirragali*. Yesterday, *kumbirra*. Always, *thugowai*. How, *widdyu*? When, *widdyuwaru*? Where, *wundha*? Why, *minyali*? Where are you, *wundhullandu*? Quickly, *burrai*.

Prepositions

In front of, *wirringa*. Behind, *wuggurwila*. To the left, *mirambil*. Between, *wongga*. Above, *ngunnawa*. Below, *ngunnadhur*. Outside, *ngullugal*.

Many of these prepositions are subject to inflections indicating the number and the person, as in the following example which relates to everything found on the left:

	1st person:	on my left	*Mirranggadhi*
Singular	2nd person	on your left	*Mirrangganu*
	3rd person	on his/her left	*Mirranggalugu*

and so on, for all the persons of the dual and the plural.

Wirringgadhi, in front of me. *Wuggurwiladhi,* behind me, & c., subject to the same inflections.

Interjections and exclamations

Yà! To draw attention. *Chùh*! signifies sh! *Nginyalanduna,* is equivalent to 'well done'.

Numbers

One, muggu. Two, bulagar.

Conclusion

The language, of which the preceding pages provide a general survey, is spoken over a vast region of the central part of New South Wales. Across an area 350 miles in width, starting at Albury on the Murray River, and heading 600 miles north, dialects of Wailwan can be found. Along this route are the hunting grounds of the Wiradyuri, Wongaibon, Wailwan, Kamilaroi, Yukumbil, Yualeai, Pikumbil and other tribes who speak dialects of this large language.

This whole article is the result of my own personal investigations among the native tribes, without the assistance from any other person. Only those familiar with the difficulties of collecting such data, amongst illiterate people, will realise the obstacles I had to overcome to establish the grammatical form of the language. Some errors and omissions are practically inevitable in the first publication of a work of this nature. That is why the I crave the indulgence of the reader for any faults in these pages.

The initiation ceremonies of the Wailwan, Wongaibon and Wiradyuri, known under the designation *Burbung,* were described in detail by me in other articles.[2]

The initiation ceremonies among the Kamilaroi, Yukumbil and other tribes are called *Bora*, and have also been described by me elsewhere.[3]

These tribes have a common social organisation with only slight modifications. Marriage is regulated by the division of the community into four sections called Murri, Kubbi, Ippai and Kumbo. I have described this in detail in other journals.[4]

Appendix

The Tyattyalla Language

Two months ago I wrote an article for the Royal Society of New South Wales on 'The Aboriginal Languages of Victoria', which filled approximately 35 pages of that Society's Journal.[5]

The dual is very widespread in the Australian languages, but in all of those from the western part of Victoria, as well as those from a certain area in South Australia, there exists a triple number, a fact which has not been reported in any other part of the continent. I thought that a condensed summary of the grammar of the *Tyattyalla* language, as it is spoken on the banks of the Wimmera River, might interest members of your Society interested in linguistics.

Nouns

As in number, the nouns have the singular, the dual and the plural. The cases are declined similarly to the Wailwan, except that in Tyattyalla, the possessor and the thing possessed both assume a suffix, although it differs for each word. Here are a few examples: *Wutyu*, a man; *gattim-gattim*, a boomerang. But 'a man's boomerang' is expressed as: *Wutyuga gattim-gattimuk*. To give the sentence greater euphony, the grammar allows that the thing possessed can be uttered first. In that case, the suffixes are transposed. So, instead of saying: *Laiura lahrnuk,* a woman's camp, a more euphonic turn of phrase is used by saying, *Lahrga laiurk. Laiur* is 'a woman' and *Lahr* is 'a camp'. The variations of the suffixes taken by the declined noun vary according to the last letters in the same way as in the Wailwan language, described above.

Adjectives

These follow the nouns which they affect and are subject to the same rules of declension.

Pronouns

Here, I give only the nominal pronouns.

	Singular		Dual
I	Yurwek	We, incl.	Yurwal
You	Yurwin	We, excl.	Yurwalluk
He	Yuruk	They	Yurwengurrak

	Triple		Plural
We, incl.	Yurwengurrakullik	We, incl.	Yurwengurrak
We, excl.	Yurwendakullik	We, excl.	Yurwendak
You	Yurwuddakullik	You	Yurwuddak
They	Yurwennakullik	They	Yurwennak

It is apparent, from the above table, that the triple is formed by the addition of a special ending to the plural form.

Verbs

With the conjugation of the verbs, the triple number is, made by the addition of *kullik* to the suffix of the plural, as occurs with the pronouns. In all other cases, the verb is subject to the same variations as in the Wailwan language.

Adverbs

These are the everyday adverbs of affirmation, negation, time, place, etc. Some of them can be declined for number and person:

Singular:	Where are you?	*Windyar*
Dual:	Where are you?	*Windyawul*
Triple:	Where are you?	*Windyatkullik*
Plural:	Where are you?	*Windaty*

There are also special forms of declension for the past and the future and for all numbers and persons.

Prepositions

Like the nouns and the adverbs, some prepositions have declensions:

	1st person:	Behind me	*Walmengek*
Singular	2nd — :	Behind you	*Walmengin*
	3rd — :	Behind him	*Walmenguk*

It is the same for the double and triple numbers and for the plural.

Interjections and exclamations

These are not numerous but, as with the prepositions, nouns and other parts of speech, they can be declined.

Singular:	Stop!	*Tyarrigi!*
Dual:	Stop!	*Tyarriyiwal!*
Triple:	Stop!	*Tyarriyuatkullik!*
Plural:	Stop!	*Tyarriyuat!*

Numbers

One, *kainp*. Two, *bulaty*.

Vocabulary

The vocabulary contains 200 words of the Wailwan language, gathered by me in the camps of the natives. Words of the same type are grouped together under different headings: the family, the human body, natural surroundings, animals, adjectives and verbs.

I have arranged these findings in alphabetical order.

The Family

Men, collectively	*Maii*	Husband and wife	*Nguan*
A man	*Thur*	Children of both sexes	*Wurra*
Clever man	*Wirringan*	Father	*Bubba*
Chief	*Dhurrungal*	Mother	*Gunni*
Boy	*Murrakunga*	Older brother	*Kukka*
Woman	*Wiringga*	Younger brother	*Kullumi*
Girl	*Mariyungga*	Older sister	*Gatthi*
Maiden	*Kumadhilia*	Younger sister	*Giddyurai*
Young woman	*Nikimikai*		

The Human Body

Head	*Wulla*	Hand	*Murra*
Forehead	*Ngulu*	Fingers	*Wurria*
Beard	*Kir*	Thumb	*Gunendyir*
Moustache	*Muludyin*	Hip	*Dhurra*
Eye	*Mil*	Knee	*Bundai*
Nose	*Muru*	Calf	*Kaia*
Back of the neck	*Nan*	Shin	*Piyu*
Throat	*Nugi*	Foot	*Dhinna*
Ear	*Kuringgera*	Blood	*Goai*
Mouth	*Ngundal*	Fat	*Gudhal*
Lips	*Willi*	Skin	*Yulai*
Tongue	*Thulle*	Anus	*Nge*
Teeth	*Wira*	Penis	*Mundai*
Chest	*Wirri*	Testicles	*Buru*
Breast (female)	*Ngummu*	Sexual desire	*Girinya*
Navel	*Gindyur*	Vagina	*Munne*
Stomach	*Buri*	Nymphae	*Wugga*
Backbone	*Nirrimirri*	Copulation	*Gunggamulli*
Arm	*Nuru*	Semen	*Buddhe*
Forearm	*Pi*	Masturbation	*Wirringraimuddha*
Armpit	*Kilkilburi*	Urine	*Kil*
Elbow	*Ngunuga*	Excrement	*Guna*

Natural Surroundings

Sun	*Dhuni*	Fire	*Wi*
Moon	*Giwa*	Smoke	*Budhu*
Stars	*Girrila*	Honey	*Wurrungunna*
Planet Venus	*Ngindigindiwa*	Grass	*Gurun*
Sky	*Gununggulla*	Leaves of trees	*Gira*
Rain	*Ngiddyunna*	Camp	*Ngura*
Hail	*Mugorai*	Eggs	*Kubbo*
Water	*Kulle*	Shadow	*Kual*
Ground	*Thagun*	Echo	*Wurrungun*
Stones	*Kurrul*	Food (meat)	*Dhingga*
Light	*Ngullan*	Bird's nest	*Mudhi*
Darkness	*Bullowi*		

Mammals

Dog	*Mirri*	Kangaroo rat	*Bilba*
Kangaroo	*Murrawi*	Pademelon	*Wiru*
Porcupine	*Thigarila*	Bandicoot	*Guru*
Wild dog	*Yugi*	Bat	*Wibullabulla*
Opossum	*Kuragai*		

Birds

Emu	*Nguri*	Crow	*Waru*
Diver	*Duguru*	Swan	*Burrima*
Black duck	*Budunba*	Laughing jackass	*Kuguburra*
Teal duck	*Dharawaiya*	White cockatoo	*Murai*
Wood duck	*Kunambi*	Curlew	*Kawila*
Whistling duck	*Thipaiyu*	Pigeon (bronze wing)	*Yamur*
Musk duck	*Wukkabuddhal*	Squatter pigeon	*Munumbi*
Eaglehawk	*Mulyan*	Willy Wagtail	*Diridyiri*
Ibis	*Willidubai*	Swallow	*Millimaru*
Pelican	*Wirea*	Crow	*Waru*

Fish

Eel	*Kuddu*	Bream	*Bunngulla*
Prawn	*Dhunul*	Silver bream	*Birunge*
Catfish	*Dhungur*	Crayfish	*Wingga*
Yellow belly	*Biddhan*		

Reptiles

Ground iguana	*Duli*	Carpet snake	*Yubba*
Tree iguana	*Gugar*	Death adder	*Murrai*
Black snake	*Yugai*	Turtle	*Munggalia*

Invertebrates

Spider	*Gillidya*	Mosquito	*Kummogin*
Common fly	*Burimul*	Centipede	*Yerrir*

Adjectives

Dead	*Buga*	Quick	*Burrai*
Large	*Bitthe*	Jealous	*Kurugur*
Small	*Buttyu*	Sick	*Girrumbia*
Long	*Kungal*	Strong	*Kurgirri*
Short	*Ngurdhu*	Heavy	*Murdil*
Good	*Yudda*	Angry	*Kulgigara*
Bad	*Wurrai*	Tired	*Iri*
Hungry	*Yerringin*	Hot	*Kirru*
Red	*Girawil*	Cold	*Gunundai*
White	*Bunggoba*	Young	*Dhullungaimba*
Black	*Bulwi*	Old	*Bugaia*
Green	*Gidyungidyun*		

Verbs

Eat	*Dharridyanna*	Sing	*Wuggaimulli*
Drink	*Nurrunnha*	Cry	*Yungani*
Sleep	*Yuanna*	Dance	*Wuggagiri*
Sit	*Winya*	Sneeze	*Thigar*
Go	*Yunna*	Cough	*Gunungguna*
Speak	*Ngea*	Steal	*Munnamulli*
Say	*Dhumbulludha*	Bite	*Kutthulli*
Run	*Bunnhagunna*	Blow (with breath)	*Bumbilli*
Bring	*Thai-gaga*	Build	*Womma*
Take	*Ngullugal-gaga*	Kill	*Gumaibugagu*
Carry	*Wumburra*	Chop	*Kugga*
Break	*Gumma*	Catch	*Mummulli*
Beat	*Guma*	Climb up	*Walgagiri*
Fall	*Dhuane*	Die	*Gurinya*
See	*Nganhi*	Fly	*Wurrannha*
Hear	*Winnungulli*	Jump	*Baranhi*
Grow	*Yurunnha*	Laugh	*Gindani*
Whistle	*Wilwa*	Scratch	*Wirmuggiri*
Get up	*Wurraga*	Pinch	*Nimmulli*
Be standing	*Warrana*	Rub	*Muma*
Spit	*Ngundyar*	Smell	*Budhe*
Throw	*Gurarwa*	Pretend	*Bir*
Give	*Ngunhi*		

ENDNOTES

[1] [Editor's note] An offprint of this article, containing pencilled corrections in Mathews' hand, is located at National Library of Australia MS 8006/8/495. These amendments have been incorporated into the text.

[2] RHM 1896, 'The Būrbŭng of the Wiradthuri Tribes', *Journal of the Anthropological Institute*, vol. 25, pp. 295-318; RHM 1897, 'The Būrbŭng of the Wiradthuri Tribes (Part II)', *Journal of the Anthropological Institute*, vol. 25, pp. 272-85; RHM 1897, 'The Burbung, or Initiation Ceremonies of the Murrumbidgee Tribes', *Journal and Proceedings of the Royal Society of New South Wales*, vol. 31, pp. 111-53.

[3] RHM 1896, 'The Bora of the Kamilaroi Tribes', *Proceedings of the Royal Society of Victoria*, vol. 9 (new series), pp. 137-73; RHM, 'The Bora, or, Initiation Ceremonies of the Kamilaroi Tribe (Part II)', *Journal of the Anthropological Institute*, vol. 25, pp. 318-39.

[4] RHM 1897, 'The Totemic Divisions of Australian Tribes', *Journal and Proceedings of the Royal Society of New South Wales*, vol. 31, pp. 154-76.

[5] [Editor's note] RHM 1902, 'The Aboriginal Languages of Victoria', *Journal and Proceedings of the Royal Society of New South Wales*, vol. 36, pp.71-106.

Language of the Kūrnū Tribe, New South Wales

R. H. Mathews

First published as 'Langage des Kurnu, tribu d'Indigènes de la Nouvelle Galles du Sud' in *Bulletins et Mémoires de la Société d'Anthropologie de Paris*, 5 (5th series) (1904), pp. 132-38. The article was written in English and translated into French by Oscar Schmidt. This version was retranslated into English by Mathilde de Hauteclocque.[1]

In a previous article addressed to the society, I dealt with the language of the Wailwan, one of the native tribes of New South Wales.[2] Here, I will attempt to show the grammatical structure of the language of the Kūrnū tribe, who occupy a large territory along the Darling river.

The grammar of the Kūrnū language is one of the most interesting, because it possesses characteristics that I have not observed in any other of the native idioms in New South Wales. Thus, for example, it can be seen in the table of pronouns that their form is modified to express the present, the past and the future. It will also be seen that the pronouns governed by transitive verbs differ from those used with intransitive verbs. Although the present, past and future tense can be expressed within the verb itself, the pronoun suffix can also express tense.

In 1902 I communicated to the Royal Society of New South Wales[3] a summary of Kūrnū grammar, but I omitted the verbs and other details because I did not then understand the difficulties presented by the pronouns and the more uncommon variations they are subjected to in conjunction with the verbs. Since that first, succinct report, a journey to this tribe allowed me to collect much new data.

Kūrnū grammar

The territory of the native tribes who speak the Kūrnū language begins on the Darling, between Tilpa and Louth, and extends on both sides of the river, up to Bourke, and a little beyond. It also extends along the Warrego river as far as Ford's Bridge. Dialects of Kūrnū are spoken all along the Darling downstream from Tilpa, via Wilcannia and Menindie, as far as Wentworth, that is to say for a distance of about 350 miles. The Kūrnū language, with a few dialectal variations, also extends further beyond the Darling River, as far as the Tarowoto lake and the Barrier Ranges and back to the Paroo River, following it as far as the

Queensland border. I personally collected the following elements of the language in Kūrnū territory, from reliable and intelligent elders of both sexes.

Orthography

The system of spelling used in this article is the same as that in my previous paper on the Wailwan language, already published by the Anthropological Society.

Articles

The demonstrative pronouns in their various forms replace the definite article. The equivalent of the English adverb 'here', as well as its variations, is often treated as a demonstrative pronoun in the native language. These natives do not seem to have the abstract idea of a man, an emu or other similar subjects, but speak always of a particular man or animal and, as a consequence, make use of a demonstrative, such as: 'this man', 'the emu over there' and so on. If they want to specify that they do not have just one object in view, they do it by using the plural which can be considered a replacement for our indefinite article.

Nouns

Nouns have number, gender and case.

Number — There are three numbers: the singular, the dual and the plural. The dual and the plural are formed by adding the number 'two' or 'several' to the singular: *Thurlta,* a kangaroo; *Thurltapakula,* a couple of kangaroos; *Thurlta gutthalagu,* several kangaroos.

Gender — For human beings, gender is defined by the use of different words: *Wimbadya,* a man; *Kambukka,* a woman; *Kurtyungga,* a boy; *Karnkali,* a girl; *Mundhanggura,* a child of either sex.

The gender of animals is shown by the use of words which indicate male or female: *Thurlta dhuladya,* a male kangaroo; *Thurlta ngammugga,* a female kangaroo.

Certain male animals have a name that distinguishes them, without the sex being specified and certain females are also recognisable by a special word. In these cases, it is unnecessary to give the name of the animal.

Case — The principal cases are: nominative, causative, instrumental, accusative, genitive, dative and ablative.

Nominative — When the action described stays with the subject, the noun is not declined. Example: *Wimbadya ningganunna,* the man is seated.

Causative — When the given action can be transferred to an object, in the accusative, the subject takes a case-suffix: *Wimbadyawa waku burtatyi,* the man a snake killed. *Kulliwa yerrandyi dhuttatyi,* a dog an opossum bit.

Instrumental — In many Australian languages, the grammar of which I have previously studied, the suffix is the same for the instrumental and the causative, but in Kūrnū it is the genitive suffix which is applied in the instrumental case. Examples: *Kumbukkawa wimbadya bulkatyi kurnkarna,* a woman beat a man with a yam stick. *Wimbadyawa thurlta bundatyi karpukkarna,* a man pierced a kangaroo with a spear. *Kutyunggawa thapura wurtatyi mulkarna,* the boy caught a cod with a net. *Bulkawutthuru wangulu wunnarna,* he killed a wallaby with a boomerang.

Genitive — *Wimbadyarna wunna,* a man's boomerang. *Kumbukkarna kurnka,* a woman's yam stick. *Kullirna gurni,* a dog's tail.

Accusative — Is the same as the nominative.

Dative — *Yuppira,* a camp. *Yuppiramirra,* to a camp.

Ablative — *Yuppirandu,* of a camp/from a camp.

Adjectives

Adjectives follow the nouns which they qualify and take the same inflections for number and case: *Wimbadya wurta,* a man large. *Wimbadyawa wurtawa wunna ngartatyi,* a tall man threw a boomerang. *Wimbadyrna wurtana wunna,* a tall man's boomerang.

The suffix is often omitted from one of the words and applied either to the substantive or only to the adjective to indicate the number and the case of it, usage being governed by the euphony of the sentence.

Comparison of adjectives is expressed by two positive statements, such as: *Ithu gundyalka, ithugaru dhulugalla,* this one is good, the other is bad.

Pronouns

Kūrnū pronouns have several special inflections which are not found in other Australian languages described by me. An entire series of pronouns applies only to transitive verbs, while another series is used only with intransitive verbs. Moreover, these pronouns change as much for the transitive verbs as for the intransitive verbs, according to whether they relate to the present, the past or the future. There are two forms for the first person, according to whether a dual or plural is intended.

Here is a table of nominative pronouns, used with transitive verbs, in each of the three tenses. Apart from their use as pronouns, they express, at the same time, the different forms of the auxiliary verb 'to be'; for example, *ngutthu* which not only signifies 'I' but also 'I am'.

		Present	Past	Future
	I	*Ngutthu*	*Wutthu*	*Gutthu*
Singular	You	*Ng'irndhu*	*Wirndu*	*Girndu*
	He	*Ngutthera*	*Wutthera*	*Gutthera*
	We, incl.	*Ngulli*	*Wulli*	*Gulli*
Dual	We, excl.	*Nguttherangulli*	*Wuttherawulli*	*Guttheragulli*
	You	*Ngupa*	*Wupa*	*Gupa*
	They	*Nguttherangulu*	*Wuttherawulu*	*Gutteragulu*
	We, incl.	*Nginna*	*Winna*	*Ginna*
Plural	We, excl.	*Dhūndinginna*	*Dhūndiwinna*	*Dhūndiginna*
	You	*Ngurta*	*Wurta*	*Gurta*
	They	*Ngutthē*	*Wutthē*	*Gutthē*

The pronouns that are used with intransitive verbs differ from the preceding ones, in the first and second person, in the present, past and future, as the following table shows:

		Present	Past	Future
	I	*Nguppa*	*Wuppa*	*Guppa*
Singular	You	*Ngimba*	*Wimba*	*Gimba*
	He	*Ngutthera*	*Wutthera*	*Gutthera*

As intransitive and transitive verbs are conjugated identically in the dual and plural there is no need to repeat the forms here.

The possessive pronouns are as follows:

	1st person	mine	*Ngari*
Singular	2nd person	your	*Ngoma*
	3rd person	his	*Githuna*
	1st person	our (incl)	*Ngullina*
		our (excl)	*Wuttherangullina*
Dual	2nd person	your	*Ngupunna*
	3rd person	their	*Wutthawuna*
	1st person	our (incl)	*Nginnunna*
		our (excl)	*Dhūndinginnunna*
Plural	2nd person	your	*Ngurtunna*
	3rd person	their	*Wutthina*

The following are the accusative forms of the singular pronouns:

	1st person	me	*Ngunnha*
Singular	2nd person	you	*Ngūmma*
	3rd person	him	*Ginnunna*

There are other modifications of pronouns, signifying 'to me', 'away from me' etc. as in the following examples.

	1ˢᵗ person	to me	*Ngunnhari*
Singular	3ʳᵈ person	to him	*Gitthunari*
Dual	1ˢᵗ person	to us, incl	*Ngullinari*
Plural	1ˢᵗ person	to us, incl	*Nginnanari*
Singular	1ˢᵗ person	of me	*Ngunnarndu*
	3ʳᵈ person	of him	*Wutthunardu*
Dual	1ˢᵗ person	of us, incl	*Ngullinarndu*
		of us, incl	*Nginnanarndu*
with me, near me			*Ngariri*

In each of the above examples the same inflections can be applied to all persons in the singular, dual or plural.

Interrogatives — Who (in the singular) *windyaka*. Who (dual) *windyula*. Who (plural) *windyiwindyi*. What, *minnha*. What for, *minnhamundi*.

Demonstratives — The demonstratives are numerous and varied and indicate the position, the distance, the direction, the size, the number, the person, the possession etc. All pronouns in the third person are, in fact, demonstratives, which explains their irregularity and the absence of their etymological connections.

Here are some examples of these demonstratives: This one, *ithu*. This other one, *ithugari*. These two, *ithuwutu*. All these, *ithangirnga*. That, *githu*. That other one, *wutthagari*. That one over there, *wurradyalanaga*. That one behind me, *dhurnangurrina*. That one (above me), *buringunna*. That one (below me), *kukuruna*. On this side (of the person who is being spoken to), *yaumirri*. On the other side (of the person being spoken to), *wurramungamirri*. That big one there, *wurtuwurri*. Belonging to this one, *ithuna*. Belonging to these two, *ithuwuna*. Belonging to all these ones, *ithinna*.

Many of these demonstratives are modified to adapt them to the accompanying transitive or intransitive verbs and also to adapt them with the tense, as is the case with pronouns.

Verbs

Verbs have three numbers and three persons and have a variant 'inclusive' or 'exclusive' in the first person of the dual and plural forms.

Each tense has its own distinct form, but the tense can also be indicated by pronouns suffixed to the verb. Here, for example, is a summarised conjugation of the verb *bulka*, to strike or to kill.

Present Indicative

	1st person	I strike	*Bulkangunna-ngutthu*
Singular	2nd person	You strike	*Bulkangunna-ngirndhu*
	3rd person	He strikes	*Bulkangunna-ngutthera*

I do not consider it necessary to give examples for the dual and the plural; the variations of number and person can be expressed by applying in each case the special pronoun that can be found in the table of nominative pronouns given on an earlier page of this article.

Past

	1st person	I struck	*Bulkangga-wutthu*
Singular	2nd person	you struck	*Bulkangga-wirndu*
	3rd person	He struck	*Bulkangga-wutthera*

Future

	1st person	I will strike	*Bulkara-gutthu*
Singular	2nd person	You will strike	*Bulkara-girndu*
	3rd person	He will strike	*Bulkara-gutthera*

Imperative

Strike, *bulkalla*. The negative or prohibitive form is expressed thus: *killa bulkalla*, do not strike.

Conditional

Should I strike? *Killamura bulkaragutthu*.

Reflexive

The reflexive form of the verb describes the action of the subject directed towards himself.

	1st person	I strike myself	*Bulkamuldhanguppa*
Singular	2nd person	You strike yourself	*Bulkamuldhangga-wuppa*
	3rd person	he strikes himself	*Bulhamuldhara-guppa*

Imperative

Strike yourself. *Bulkamuldha*.

Reciprocal

One form of the verb serves to express the communal and reciprocal action of two or more persons; this form is obviously restricted to the dual or plural.

We (dual inclusive) hit each other, *Bulkkamilla-ngulli*. We were hit by each other, *Bulkamillangga-wulli*. We will hit each other, *Bulkamillara-gulli*. In the preceding examples all forms of 'person' and 'number' can be indicated by pronouns.

The conjugation of an intransitive verb can only change according to the pronouns that are added to it as shown by the following example, *ngingga* to sit:

Indicative

Present	1ˢᵗ person	I sit	*Nginggangunna-nguppa*
Past	1ˢᵗ person	I sat	*Nginggangga-wuppa*
Future	1ˢᵗ person	I will sit	*Nginggara-guppa*

And so it follows for the other 'persons' and 'numbers' the appropriate pronouns being used as shown in the preceding tables.

Verbs, whether transitive or intransitive, have forms that indicate whether the action described is immediate, imminent or distant, either in the past or in the future; these forms also express continuity or repetition of the action. Numerous other modifications of the verbs serve to highlight a whole series of nuances of meaning. I will refrain from entering into a discussion of these for the moment.

The passive has no special form and the sentence 'a boy was punished by his father' would be expressed by the paraphrase 'a father punished his son'.

Adverbs

Yes, *ngi*. No, *ngattha*. Here, *kungara*. There, *wurra*. Over there, *wurtityallinnaga*. Today, *kailpomainka*. Yesterday, *yillana*. Tomorrow, *wambinna*. By and by *gunni*. In the future, *gundigundyi*. First, *mirraga*.

Where are you, *windyarra ngimba*. Where are you going, *windaywurradhani ngimba*. How many, *ngulthurra*. How or why, *nunguna*.

Prepositions

In front of, *mirrika*. Behind, *ngunda*. Between, *bukkula*. Beside, *gungo*. At the bottom, *baikakika*. At the top, *wunggalu*. Inside, *ngungguru*. Other side, *murlaka*. This side (of the river), *wurrangurraga*. Behind me, *dhurna-ngariri*. Behind you, *dhurna-ngumari*. Behind him, *dhurna-gitthunari*.

ENDNOTES

[1] [Editor's note] Offprints of these articles, containing pencilled corrections in Mathews' hand, are located at National Library of Australia MS 8006/8/199 and 8006/8/200. Another is in the possession of Mathews' descendants. These amendments have been incorporated into the text.

[2] [Editor's note] R. H. Mathews, 'Le langage Wailwan', *Bulletins et Mémoires de la Société d'Anthropologie de Paris*, vol. 4 (5th Series), no. 1, 1903. Reproduced this volume.

[3] RHM 1902, 'Languages of some Native Tribes of Queensland, New South Wales and Victoria', *Journal and Proceedings of the Royal Society of New South Wales*, vol. 36, pp. 154-57.

Part 5: Ceremony

Introduction

Martin Thomas

R. H. Mathews recognised that ceremonial life was integral to the social cohesion of Aboriginal communities. The practice of initiation, he explained, 'tends to strengthen the civil authority of the elders of the tribe and enables them to administer the laws in a more effectual manner'. Strengthened through ritual, Aboriginal law possesses 'all the force of divine precepts … or the might of divine authority'.[1] Mathews' interest in ritualistic practices dates from the beginning of his career as an ethnographer. His first publication in 1893, a paper on rock art, was quickly followed by a description of a Bora ceremony, held by Kamilaroi people at Gundabloui in 1894.[2] He returned to the subject of Kamilaroi initiation in his last paper, 'Description of Two Bora Grounds of the Kamilaroi Tribe' (1917), published the year before his death.[3]

In the intervening years, Mathews wrote extensively on ceremonial life, mostly in southeast Australia. His more limited descriptions of ceremonies in South Australia and the Northern Territory were written with the aid of correspondents. Of his 171 anthropological publications, 50 are partly or wholly concerned with ceremony. The majority consist of a detailed description of the initiation ritual practised by a particular community.[4] As early as 1897, Mathews could claim to have documented the initiations of about three quarters of the land mass of New South Wales.[5] His publications continued well beyond that date, and, had he collected all his writings on the subject, they would have made a substantial book.

It should be emphasised that the subject here is *ceremony* and not corroboree (with which it is sometimes conflated). Mathews recognised this distinction, as we see in the 'The Mŭltyerra Initiation Ceremony', translated here. Explaining how people filled the time as they assembled from disparate locations, he stated that 'corroborees were held nearly every fine night during which the different contingents took it in turns to provide the evening entertainment'. Corroboree is, as Mathews realised, a form of campfire entertainment, typically involving music and dance, and accessible to all. Ceremony, in contrast, concerns the sacred, ritualistic life of the community and in a secret-sacred society, participation is often restricted according to gender and seniority.

Mathews' first paper on the Bora at Gundabloui opens with a brief literature review—evidence of the time he spent in libraries, scouring historical sources for descriptions of ritual.[6] From the earliest days of British settlement in Australia, a few Europeans witnessed secret-sacred rituals or received information about them. Mathews mentions the well-known observations in *An Account of the English Colony in New South Wales* (1804) by the First Fleet chronicler David Collins. He also consulted John Henderson's *Observations on the Colonies of New South Wales and Van Diemen's Land* (1832) and various works by Rev William Ridley including *Kamilaroi and Other Australian Languages* (1875), a book he cited frequently in his work on New South Wales. Equally, or perhaps more, important, although not mentioned in the survey of literature, were several writings on initiation, dating from the 1880s, by Mathews' eventual rival, A. W. Howitt. In a valuable study of Howitt's methods and exposition, the archaeologist and historian D. J. Mulvaney gives an account of Howitt's role in opening up the sacred-secret life of Aboriginal people to the scientific gaze.[7]

Mulvaney argues that in contrast to the often brief and sometimes casual observations of earlier writers, Howitt produced detailed narratives of ceremony from an 'inside' perspective. Mathews certainly read this work in *Journal of the Anthropological Institute*, and it is likely that the narrative structure of Howitt's paper 'The Jeraeil, or Initiation Ceremonies of the Kurnai Tribe' (1885) influenced his deliberations about how a long and complex ceremony is best described.[8] But there are many differences between the two writers; among them Mathews' surveying background which led him to measure and map the ceremonial grounds (usually forest clearings connected by pathways). Many of his initiation papers contain detailed maps of the sites. He also prepared line drawings that illustrate the sacred motifs often carved into tree trunks or cut into the ground. Indeed, Howitt's relative deficiency in mapping ceremonial sites, and his vagueness about locations, may have played a role in the drastic falling out between the two men. In 'The Būrbŭng of the Wiradthuri Tribes' (1896), one of Mathews' early contributions to *Journal of the Anthropological Institute*, he took the liberty of including maps that detailed the locations of ceremonies described by Howitt in his articles 'On some Australian Ceremonies of Initiation' and 'The Jeraeil, or Initiation Ceremonies of the Kurnai Tribe', published in the *Journal* some 10 years earlier.[9] There is no suggestion of malice on Mathews' part; in the article he refers to Howitt as his 'friend and co-worker'—a description almost surreal in light of their later feuding.[10] But Howitt drew scant comfort from the knowledge that Mathews was taking an interest in his 'own' areas of southern New South Wales and Victoria, let alone adding postscripts to his work. Describing the incident to Baldwin Spencer, he wrote: '[s]ince I saw you I have found that our "friend" Mathews described the Bora ground & the proceedings therein … At any rate his description (Journ. Anth. Inst. 1896) relates to the very same locality'.[11]

At the beginning of this volume I cited the testimony of Mathews' friend W. J. Enright who described the readiness with which Mathews was accepted as an initiated man by the Aboriginal community at Port Stephens. Mathews was highly respectful of ceremonial traditions, and it is likely that differences in attitude to secret-sacred matters worsened the relationship between him and Howitt, which became overtly hostile in 1898 (see the general introduction to this volume). Unlike Mathews, who in his many writings on this subject endeavoured to describe ceremonies in fairly objective terms, Howitt's paper on the Jeraeil reveals a sort of role play in which the anthropologist casts himself as a ceremonial leader. In saying this, it should be acknowledged that the Kurnai people of Gippsland had reportedly not held a major Jeraeil since the 1850s. The event witnessed by Howitt in 1884 was something of a staged revival, performed at his request.[12] Even so, there is quite a degree of fantasy with which Howitt portrays himself as 'tribal elder', to use Mulvaney's phrase. Not just an observer, he portrays himself as the instigator of the proceedings: '[t]hus, in calling together the Jeraeil which I describe in this paper, I sent out my messengers to the headman of the Brabra clan in August, and the Jeraeil was held at the end of January following.'[13]

Even in the long and extravagant tradition of whitefellows claiming positions of 'high degree' in Aboriginal knowledge systems, Howitt's approach was ethically dubious. Mulvaney reveals that he used various ruses, including the manufacture of a bullroarer, to create the impression that Aboriginal men in other parts of the country had inducted him into their sacred rites.[14] It seems that some of the Kurnai had serious misgivings about the way secret information had been divulged to Howitt.[15] It is possible that some of these rumblings reached Mathews, who had many connections with the Aboriginal communities of the New South Wales South Coast and through them the culturally connected areas of eastern Victoria. As mentioned earlier, there is oral testimony from this part of the country that Mathews himself went through the rites of initiation, but he made no claims to this effect (see the general introduction to this volume). Whatever the truth of the claim, it is easy to see how Howitt's self-casting as ceremonial ringleader would have rankled with Mathews. The latter took a very different path in investigating ceremony, and in terms of the territory and number of communities covered, he went much further.

*

Although extensive, Mathews' study of ceremonial life was strictly demarcated. Not only did he focus almost exclusively on male initiation, but he dealt predominantly with its initial rites. Anthropologists such as Elkin have shown how the first stage of initiation is only a part of a greater educational process with many degrees of induction.[16] Thus preoccupied, Mathews said little about other aspects of ritual. Mourning rites, for example, are enormously important throughout Australia, and Mathews himself knew something about the subject, as we see in his work on material culture. He wrote five papers, all fairly similar, that describe the manufacture and use of 'kopai balls' and 'widow's caps'—gypsum artefacts associated with burial rites and mourning along the

Darling River and its tributaries.[17] He also wrote descriptive papers about the shaped and incised stones, often referred to as 'cylcons' or cylindro-conical stones. These artefacts apparently served ceremonial or medicinal purposes, with an importance similar to that of the *tjurunga* in Central Australia. Mathews recorded evidence for their use in increase ceremonies in western New South Wales. One of these papers suggests a possible reason for his failure to explore such matters further. Information was provided by Harry Perry, a Nawalgu man, who stated that the stones 'were used in incantations for producing an abundant supply of *nardoo* and other seed bearing plants, as well as for an increase in game and fish'.[18] Although 'an old aboriginal' (who had died at the time of writing), Perry had never seen an increase ceremony performed. The account he gave to Mathews was told to him by his father.

Harry Perry's experience was part of a broader pattern. With the incursion of white people and their hard-footed livestock, yam beds were compacted and destroyed. Native grasses disappeared with the introduction of exotic species. The artefacts associated with both ritual and sustenance (if the two categories are really separable) were distributed through the traditional territories. This made them extremely vulnerable. Even the heavy grindstones, used for milling the spore cases of *nardoo* and the seeds of native grasses, were trampled and broken by cattle. So the fragile objects made from gypsum and left upon graves had no chance of survival. The rise of antiquarianism brought its own dangers, as Aboriginal artefacts and bodily remains became fetishised by collectors. It is worth mentioning that apart from the small number of bullroarers discussed below, Mathews did not amass a collection of artefacts. At least none is mentioned in an inventory of his possessions, drawn up after his death.[19] The objects described in his writings on material culture were borrowed from collectors such as E. J. Suttor, a grazier from Tilpa on the Darling River, who picked them up by the cartload.[20] The removal or destruction of sacred objects played its own part in contributing to the despair felt by Aboriginal people at the loss of life, tradition and territory. Old ways were abandoned, sometimes by necessity and sometimes for strategic purpose. Given the importance in Aboriginal culture of being laid to rest in one's ancestral country, burial in a Christian cemetery might have seemed a safer prospect than a traditional entombment where the bones could be easily robbed.[21]

This complex historical situation was the context for Mathews' documentation of initiatory practices. In the case of southeast Australia, his writings on the subject constitute the most important documentary evidence concerning such rituals. Like any body of evidence, the documentation presents problems of interpretation. Are these writings a reflection of what Mathews *chose* to document, or were the older men particularly keen to discuss this aspect of their culture with a trustworthy outsider? Could it be that Aboriginal people made special efforts to maintain these traditions when other rites had fallen into abeyance? Perhaps all these questions can be answered in the affirmative. The tradition of 'man-making' was enormously important, and if we read Mathews carefully we get some intimation of the factors that allowed it to endure; among them the unique requirements of location. Although the actual rituals were secret-sacred, they involved a great coming together of entire communities, often from a wide catchment. People from Cobar, for example, travelled 200 km to reach one of the events described by Mathews.[22] As 'The Mŭltyerra Initiation Ceremony' makes clear, there was a festival atmosphere as the different mobs arrived. It is important to bear in mind the diverse aspects of ceremony, ranging in mood from the highly serious to the carnivalesque. This diversity, combined with the affirmation of kinship ties, and the aesthetic quality of the performances, helps explain the determination to keep initiations going when other rituals had perished, just as it explains the readiness of older people to supply Mathews with detailed descriptions of initiations in areas where they were no longer practised.

Outsiders have come to think of initiation as a painful 'ordeal', but this is a gross over-simplification. During recent research in western Arnhem Land, I discussed film footage of the Wubarr ceremony (a genre of initiation not performed since the 1970s) with older men who had participated in the rite.[23] So intense was the affection for the ceremony and the wonderful memories prompted by the film, that one man spoke of it in terms of endearment normally reserved for a lover. Although Mathews' investigations were confined to men's ceremonies (a reflection, of course, of his gender) men, women and children were all brought together by these events. Entertainment occurred every evening, and in some communities a degree of sexual liberty was permitted. When all the tribes had assembled, the neophytes were ceremonially taken from their mothers. They were led by the men to the place of the ceremony proper. Although strictly out of bounds to non-initiates, it was never far from the main encampment where women and children remained. Where topography permitted, as it usually did in coastal regions, rugged and forested sites—less attractive to settlers—were invariably chosen. This in itself might explain why some continued as long as they did, even when the bulk of a community's ancestral territory had been seized by Europeans.

Colonisation affected the initiation rituals in a variety of ways. We know from Mathews' reportage that sometimes rituals were adapted so people could make sense of their historical situation. At one Bora site visited by Mathews the motifs cut into the ceremonial ground included a train complete with carriages, windows, wheels and rails; a bullock attached to a colossal chain; and the four aces from a deck of cards.[24] Not all settlers in the 1890s and early 1900s were opposed to Aboriginal ceremony. Many depended on Aboriginal labour and some were prepared to indulge their employees with periods of vacation for the pursuit of traditional business. Some graziers provided food,[25] and for a time there was the possibility of government largesse. Mathews notes that the New South Wales Aborigines' Protection Board supplied rations for the 98 people who attended a Wiradjuri initiation in 1893.[26] The Bora at Gundabloui received similar support the following year.[27] Mathews later wrote:

> It should be explained that during recent years, when the blacks can obtain food from the white people, a Bora lasts much longer than in the old, wild times, when a native's life was one long struggle for subsistence. For example, the Bora that took place at Gundabloui, in 1894, lasted about three months, because the Aborigines' Protection Board supplied rations to the aged blacks and the children, besides which the manager of Gundabloui station, close by, gave them an allowance of beef all the time. The natives who held the Bora at Tallwood, in 1895, were likewise supplied with food by the white residents of the district, and consequently the meeting was prolonged for some months. I myself contributed liberally to the commissariat of the blacks who came to the Tallwood Bora. A severe drought was prevailing throughout the district at the time, and some of the old natives confided to me that they would make the Bora last as long as they could get provisions from the Europeans.[28]

Mathews' admission that he and other whites prolonged the Tallwood ceremony raises further questions about the impact of observers on the display of traditional culture. In this case, which occurred during a time of drought and limited employment, prolonging the ceremony was a strategy for survival. Mathews' observation also points to the double standards at work in the competitive world of Australian anthropology. The same year that he wrote this, he chastised W. Baldwin Spencer for providing Arrernte people at Alice Springs with food and other inducements to 'rehearse all their old ceremonies'. Mathews complained that this had misled some English commentators into thinking 'that the Arunta natives possess a higher degree of culture than other Australian savages'.[29]

Initiations might have endured longer than other forms of ceremony, but their future was far from certain. The writings translated here describe initiations from western New South Wales, northeast Victoria and southern Queensland. Mathews was not a witness to any of these ceremonies. Rather, as he writes of the Queensland ritual, the information was 'obtained by me direct from the mouths of old natives of the region indicated, who had themselves passed through all the stages of the Bundandaba ceremony'. In fact, Mathews attended very few of the ceremonies he documented, not always from want of trying. Flooding prevented him from reaching the 1893 Wiradjuri initiation; the late arrival of several contingents forced him to depart before the commencement of the

Tallwood Bora in 1895. However, these setbacks did not prevent him from writing about the ceremonies. He walked the sacred grounds with senior men who narrated a chronology of the ritual. Sometimes they acted out parts of it for him. Marked trees, ground drawings and other features of the site were carefully documented. While the limitations of this method are self-evident, it had some advantages. Mathews gained a clear idea of events that occurred in darkness, and he was often in a position to describe the activities that occurred in the women's camp while the men and neophytes were absent. The names of many Aboriginal women are listed in Mathews' field books, so it is possible that he spoke to women about these matters. The descriptions are sufficiently detailed to suggest that female informants were his source. The fact that Mathews was approaching 60 when he began this work might have affected his success in gaining information. With old age it seems that the rules of secrecy between men and women were loosened. Confidences were sometimes shared between husbands and wives on ceremonial matters.[30]

Mathews' general conviction that Aboriginal traditions were rapidly disappearing was confirmed by much of his work on ceremonies. By the turn of the century the tradition was very much in decline. In *Invasion to Embassy* (1996), a study of land and Aboriginal politics, Heather Goodall describes the brutal impact of government policy on Aboriginal life in New South Wales.[31] In the early twentieth century, cajoled by settlers who wanted a greater distance between themselves and the Aboriginal population, the Aborigines' Protection Board began to relocate large segments of the Indigenous population to institutions known as Aboriginal stations. It was a far cry from supporting Aboriginal ceremony through provision of rations. All aspects of traditional culture suffered from this uprooting and amalgamation of disparate groups. The effect on community life was devastating, since many children were sent to institutions or apprenticed to settlers, far from their families. Mathews' writings on initiation were increasingly informed by older men who took him to ceremonial grounds now overgrown, recalling events that had occurred decades earlier.

Jimmie Barker (1900-75), the Muruwari man whose autobiographical tape recordings were collected and written up by Janet Mathews (granddaughter-in-law of R. H.), related how he missed out on initiation by just a few years. Prior to being sent to the Brewarrina Aboriginal Station, Barker lived with his mother's people near the Culgoa River. He was only 11 when two senior men raised the possibility of his initiation. 'The normal age for going through the *bora* was 14 and Mother refused them firmly, saying that she considered I was too young.'[32] The implication here is that the elders proposed a premature initiation because they feared the ceremony would not occur again—as seems to have been the case. R. H. Mathews, however, published an account of it in 'Initiation Ceremonies of the Murawarri and Other Aboriginal

Tribes of Queensland' (1906-07).[33] While ceremonies in so many areas declined, memories of them were retained and there are numerous examples of twentieth-century revival, even in areas long-settled by whites. Writing of the North Coast of New South Wales in the 1930s, Elkin described a deliberate 'return' to tradition as a means of dealing with the exigencies of poverty and colonial dispossession.

> This is not merely a matter of the continuing influence of native culture, but a conscious retaking, re-establishing and re-using of those elements in the tribal past which are not lost and which can serve to build up cohesion, to provide comfort, to express difference and even defiance, and restore prestige in what is obviously an outcast, depressed and underprivileged condition.[34]

Elkin was convinced that regimes of secrecy were an understandable response to the racial segregation experienced by these communities.

> The real content and some of the form of the tribal ceremonies of an earlier day has been recaptured. There is one interesting difference. Then, the ritually uninitiated could not approach. Now the white man is for the most part on the outside, and wants to be; while to the acculturated Aborigines, these meetings are an expression of his solidarity against white society into which he is not admitted.[35]

Obviously, there is much more that could be said about so important a subject, documented at such length. Mathews' writings on initiation are essential reading for understanding the influence of Baiame, the great creation hero of southeast Australia, who was honoured in many of the rituals. And they tell us much about the degree to which he was trusted by Aboriginal elders. Unlike Howitt, who made his own bullroarer in a bid for status as an initiate, Mathews was entrusted with bullroarers as gifts from both Kamilaroi and Wiradjuri people. These sacred instruments were at the heart of the rituals he described.[36]

The three articles reproduced here are all translated from the German. They are evidence of the international interest in the subject. Mathews' writings on Australian ceremony, like those of his rivals Spencer and Howitt, were studied closely by Europeans and cited, for example, by his Parisian friend Arnold van Gennep, in his classic study *Les Rites de Passage* (*The Rites of Passage*) (1909). Only one of these three articles, the description of the Birdhawal initiation from Victoria, had an English-language version—and it was abridged.[37] The description of the Bundandaba ritual from Queensland has a special place in Mathews' writings on ceremony, which were almost exclusively concerned with the initiatory rites that followed the removal of the adolescent boy from his mother. As already noted, this was only the first stage of a process that occurred incrementally over a number of years. The Bundandaba, as Mathews explains, is a *secondary* ritual, performed after the Toara ceremony, which he had described in 1900.[38]

Even after the lapse of 100 years, the translation and republication of these articles pose ethical quandaries, given that the descendant communities have strong feelings about the material. To ensure that publication would not violate contemporary values about the status of secret-sacred knowledge, the texts were sent to relevant community organisations and in some cases individuals. No objections were expressed, although members of the Kurnu community in western New South Wales requested that a few sections from 'The Mŭltyerra Initiation Ceremony' be edited out because it was felt that they might not be understood by non-Aboriginal people, and could be used to ridicule or stigmatise Aboriginal customs. The process of discussing the articles with descendants of people who worked with Mathews brought many insights. One of the men consulted told me how he discussed the matter in a general way with several senior women, although he did not go into the detail of the ceremony. 'I explained to them that it was a man's initiation ceremonial paper, but there are things we could pull out to help teach the young girls too, because a lot of it is about discipline and respect. They all agreed.'[39] Mindful of its educational value and its potential to strengthen the contemporary culture, many Aboriginal people see enduring value in Mathews' research.

ENDNOTES

[1] Red notebook, R. H. Mathews Papers, National Library of Australia (henceforth NLA) MS 8006/3/11, p. 55.

[2] RHM 1894, 'Aboriginal Bora held at Gundabloui in 1894', *Journal and Proceedings of the Royal Society of New South Wales*, vol. 28.

[3] RHM 1917, 'Description of Two Bora Grounds of the Kamilaroi Tribe', *Journal and Proceedings of the Royal Society of New South Wales*, vol. 51.

[4] The term 'community' appears often in Mathews' writings on ceremony. He would probably have concurred with Howitt's definition of the term: 'the aggregate of all those tribes which meet at the same initiation ceremonies'. Howitt, A. W. 1884, 'On some Australian Ceremonies of Initiation', *Journal of the Anthropological Institute*, vol. 13, p. 437.

[5] RHM 1897, 'The Burbung, or Initiation Ceremonies of the Murrumbidgee Tribes', *Journal and Proceedings of the Royal Society of New South Wales*, vol. 31, p. 114.

[6] RHM, 'Aboriginal Bora held at Gundabloui in 1894', pp. 99-105.

[7] Mulvaney, D. J. 1970, 'The Anthropologist as Tribal Elder', *Mankind*, vol. 7, no. 3.

[8] Howitt, A.W. 'On some Australian Ceremonies of Initiation' and Howitt, A.W. 1885, 'The Jeraeil, or Initiation Ceremonies of the Kurnai Tribe', *Journal of the Anthropological Institute*, vol. 14.

[9] RHM 1896, 'The Bŭrbŭng of the Wiradthuri Tribes', *Journal of the Anthropological Institute*, vol. 25, pp. 316-18.

[10] Ibid, p. 313.

[11] Howitt to Spencer, 12 September 1898, Sir Baldwin Spencer Manuscripts, Pitt Rivers Museum, MS Box 1/Howitt 8.

[12] Mulvaney, 'The Anthropologist as Tribal Elder', p. 213.

[13] Howitt, 'The Jeraeil', p. 302 (note).

[14] Mulvaney, 'The Anthropologist as Tribal Elder', pp. 209-10.

[15] Ibid, p. 214.

[16] Elkin, A.P. 1994, *Aboriginal Men of High Degree*, Inner Traditions, Rochester, Vermont [1st pub. 1946].

[17] See for example RHM 1909, 'Some Burial Customs of the Australian Aborigines', *Proceedings of the American Philosophical Society*, vol. 48.

[18] RHM 1909, 'Ceremonial Stones used by the Australian Aborigines', *Proceedings of the American Philosophical Society*, vol. 48, p. 7. See also McCarthy, F. D., Bramell, E. and Noone, H.V.V., 1946, *The Stone Implements of Australia*, Australian Museum, Sydney, pp. 66-69.

[19] Estate of Robert Hamilton Mathews 1918 (probate document), Probate Division, Supreme Court of NSW, No. 87417 Ser. 4.

[20] See RHM, 'Ceremonial Stones used by the Australian Aborigines', p. 2.

[21] See Griffiths, Tom 1996, *Hunters and Collectors: The Antiquarian Imagination in Australia*, Cambridge University Press, Cambridge.

[22] RHM, 'The Būrbŭng of the Wiradthuri Tribes', p. 298.

[23] Thomas, Martin 2007, 'Taking Them Back: Archival media in Arnhem Land today', *Cultural Studies Review*, vol. 13, no. 2.

[24] RHM 1896, 'The Bora of the Kamilaroi Tribes', *Proceedings of the Royal Society of Victoria*, vol. 9 (new series), p. 146.

[25] In his first publication on ceremony, he noted that a pastoralist provided beef rations to participants. RHM, 'Aboriginal Bora held at Gundabloui in 1894', p. 114.

[26] RHM, 'The Būrbŭng of the Wiradthuri Tribes', p. 299.

[27] RHM, 'Aboriginal Bora held at Gundabloui in 1894', p. 108.

[28] RHM 1907, *Notes on the Aborigines of New South Wales*, Government Printer of New South Wales, Sydney, pp. 18-19. Mathews described the Tallwood ceremony in 'The Bora, or Initiation Ceremonies of the Kamilaroi Tribe', *Journal of the Anthropological Institute*, vol. 24, 1895.

[29] RHM 1907, 'Notes on the Arranda Tribe', *Journal and Proceedings of the Royal Society of New South Wales*, vol. 41, pp. 157-8. Mathews employed Spencer's spelling 'Arunta' in this part of the text.

[30] Barker, Jimmie and Mathews, Janet 1980, *The Two Worlds of Jimmie Barker: The Life of an Australian Aboriginal 1900-1972 as told to Janet Mathews*, Australian Institute of Aboriginal Studies, Canberra [1st pub. 1977], pp. 50-1.

[31] Goodall, Heather 1996, *Invasion to Embassy: Land in Aboriginal Politics in New South Wales, 1770-1972*, Allen & Unwin, St Leonards.

[32] Barker and Mathews, *The Two Worlds of Jimmie Barker*, p. 50.

[33] RHM 1906-07, 'Initiation Ceremonies of the Murawarri and Other Aboriginal Tribes of Queensland', *Queensland Geographical Journal*, vol. 22.

[34] Elkin, A. P. 1951, 'Reaction and Interaction: A Food Gathering People and European Settlement in Australia', *American Anthropologist*, vol. 53 (new series), no. 2, p. 176.

[35] Ibid, p. 177.

[36] RHM 1897, 'Bullroarers used by the Australian Aborigines', *Journal of the Anthropological Institute*, vol. 27.

[37] RHM 1916-18, 'Initiation Ceremony of the Birdhawal Tribe', *Queensland Geographical Journal*, vol. 32-3.

[38] RHM 1900, 'The Toara Ceremony of the Dippil Tribes of Queensland', *American Anthropologist*, vol. 2 (new series).

[39] Pers. comm., 5 December 2006. The correspondent does not wish to be identified.

The Mŭltyerra Initiation Ceremony

R. H. Mathews

First published as 'Die Mŭltyerra-Initiationszeremonie' in *Mitteilungen der Anthropologischen Gesellschaft*, vol. 34 (1904) pp. 77-83. The article was written in English and translated into German by an unnamed translator. This version was retranslated into English by Christine Winter. At the request of members of the Kurnu community, a few parts of the text have been edited.

The following pages offer a brief account of the initiation ceremonies carried out by the Kūrnū, a native tribe of New South Wales. This tribe inhabits lands on both banks of the Darling river from Bourke downstream to near Tilpa, as well as north and southwards into the hinterland of the Darling extending over large stretches of country.

The custom of induction in force among the Kūrnū is known by the name of *Mŭltyerra*, and as a description of it has not been attempted by any previous author, it is hoped that the following details will be sufficiently extensive to allow a comparison with similar ceremonies in other parts of New South Wales. The details described here I have myself learned from intelligent old natives of the Kūrnū tribe, whose veracity I could trust. In addition, I tested this information by obtaining a description of the ceremony from people from different parts of the tribal area and found that their information matched very well.

When the number of boys who are old enough for initiation is deemed sufficient, the head man, whose task it is to call the community together, sends messengers to all neighbouring tribes. The head man does not undertake this step of his own accord, but after considerable deliberation with the elders of his people. Two Messengers, the *buruki,* went together, accompanied by a young man, who had been admitted to the previous Mŭltyerra. These men carried a *mŭltyi* with them as signs of their standing,[1] consisting of a piece of wallaby skin cut into small strips, which were tied together at one end, while the others were loose. Some feathers were attached to the tied end of the *mŭltyi* fastened to it with a string. The messengers were also equipped with a *wilpabulka* or man's belt and a bullroarer, *yantamakaddya.* Upon the arrival of the messengers at the camp of a tribe that they had been instructed to summon, the procedure was more or less the same as that I have described in my reports about the initiation ceremonies of the Kamilaroi, Wirradyuri, Darkinyung and other tribes, and can therefore be summarised as follows. The bearers of the message on approaching the boundaries of the camp of the foreign tribe sat down in view of the dwellings of the single men and made friendly signs. Some of the old men then walked over to them and led them to the special meeting place of the initiated men where they were brought before all the chiefs and warriors. After a while they then brought forth the *mŭltyi, wilpabulka, yantamakaddya* and other things entrusted to them and recited the oral message concerning the time and place of the Mŭltyerra.

In the course of several days the invitation is sent on to the next tribe. This is done either by the same messengers or by the head man they had visited. When the latter course is chosen, the head man selects suitable men from his own tribe to act as messengers, to whom he then hands over the *mŭltyi*, bullroarer and other emblems received. These men now move on to the next tribe and the process is repeated until the whole community is invited. It is important to point out that every chief, when making his invitation, selects messengers who belong to his own phratry,[2] and sends them to other men of the same phratry among the invited tribes. The men are also often from the same totem as their chief.

While the messengers are away making the invitations, the men of the host tribe are busy preparing the common meeting place. The location chosen is a place with fairly even ground close to water where firewood is obtainable. It is also chosen in a part of the tribal hunting grounds where sufficient game exists to provide a supply of food for the people being hosted for the duration of the ceremonies. The people of the place itself are the first to set up the dwellings, and the other invited tribes camp around it, each situated in the direction of the region from where it has come.

In the vicinity of this main camp a round space called the *mŭltyeragara*, about 25 or 30 yards (22.9-27.4 m) in diameter, is cleared of all wood and grass and the surface made flat. A small footpath, formed by removing the ground and by throwing loose soil onto one side, leads from the *mŭltyeragara* to another similarly cleaned place, called the *bŭlkinya* about 15 or 20 chains (300-400 m) distant, or sufficiently far away to be out of sight of the main camp. Inside the *bŭlkinya* a few small hills called *kunya* are formed by laying several pieces of wood on the surface of the ground and covering them with loose soil.

The messengers stay with the tribe to which they were sent until the time comes to depart for the appointed meeting place. All men, women and children were then gathered and the journey to the *mŭltyeragara* started. As soon as the common camp place was approached, a stopover was made and the women, children and old people stayed there with the luggage. The men then march in single file in sinuous lines toward the *mŭltyeragara* where the people from the place itself and all the other tribes which had arrived earlier, had gathered already. As soon as the newcomers had reached the *mŭltyeragara* they marched around inside it until the last man was inside the cleared space. The novices brought by this tribe for initiation were in the middle of this human throng.

After they had come to a halt they all turned their faces toward the direction of the land they had come from, and the chiefs called the names of their main fighting places, water holes, hills, totem animals, and so forth. The names of shady trees, flowering and fruit-bearing trees and bushes were mentioned. Likewise the men called out the names of the genitalia of both sexes. While the men announced this they aimed their boomerangs at their own land and stomped the ground with their feet.

After this reception had ended the novices brought by this contingent were led by their guardians[3] to a part of the camp which was set apart for the accommodation of the novices belonging to all tribes present. This place is called the *wilyarunga*, and the novices accompanied by their guardians are accommodated on that side which is closest to their homeland. In the meantime the women and children, who had been left behind with the luggage, approached in the company of some young men and settled down on their own side of the common camp place.

One or two weeks and, in some cases, a much longer time passes between the arrival of the first tribe and the last contingent invited from the surrounding districts so that the early arrivals had to wait a good time in the main camp. During this time corroborees were held nearly every fine night during which the different contingents took it in turns to provide the evening entertainment. Every native camp is kept free of refuse; when the people want to meet the call of nature, they make a hole in the ground and cover the defecation with soil.

As soon as seems appropriate after the arrival of all tribes whose participation in the ceremonies is expected, the chiefs assemble and after deliberations amongst themselves nominate the day on which the novices are to be taken for initiation. The *thŭnthurra* or mob of men who have to undertake the ceremonies in the bush is chosen. The location where the women have to erect a new camp and await the return of the novices is also nominated. The part of the tribal area into which the novices are to be brought while they undergo the initiation test is considered and decided.

On the day following the meeting, a big yard called the *gūlpi* is created with branches close to the *mŭltyeragara*. This yard has approximately the shape of a horseshoe, open at one side. At nightfall all the women and children of the camp are gathered in the *gūlpi* and remain there for the entire night. During the evening some men who camp on the *bŭlkinya* let the bullroarers sound.

The next morning, at the break of dawn, the novices are woken and lifted to the shoulders of their overseers, by whom they are carried from the *mŭltyeragara* to the *gūlpi,* where they are set down on green leaves thickly strewn on the ground. The boys of each tribe are placed in one group at the side of the *gūlpi* which is closest to their land. The old men then take some nardoo and grind it into flour between two stones and spread it on small trough-shaped pieces of bark which serve as plates. Every novice is then handed one of these pieces of bark with its contents and instructed to eat the nardoo dough. After the boys have enjoyed this food, each is given a small drink of water, after which they take another sip, with which they rinse their mouth, and spit it out. This procedure is to clean the mouth and assist the later extraction of a tooth. Every novice is then painted in his tribe's usual way and clothed with a belt and other things which are the prerogative of a native man.

All women are gathered in the *gūlpi* and covered with branches, blankets and grass. They are told that this is done to hide them from the gaze of the evil being who will come to the boys, but the real reason is to prevent them from seeing any of the following events.

When these preparations are finished the men in the immediate proximity begin to let the *yantamakaddya* sound, and some men come along the path from the *bŭlkinya* and run around the *mŭltyeragara* beating the ground with a piece of bark they hold in their hand. These pieces of bark are about the length of a man's arm and about four inches wide at the widest point, but taper off towards the end held with the hand. All men standing around the *mŭltyeragara* and the *gūlpi* cheer and bang their weapons together. During this combined noise of the bullroarers, the shouting and the hitting of the ground, the guardians, the *ngutthaddya*, grab the novices by the arm and lead them away. Their heads are lowered onto their chests, and they are prohibited from looking at anything.

All boys have to march away to a clear patch of ground close to the *bŭlkinya*, and each of the novices has one of the upper middle incisors knocked out in the following way: one man lies with his whole length face down on the ground. The guardian supported by some strong men grabs the boy and throws him down lengthwise with his face up onto the back of the man lying on the ground. An old man who is used to this work, then sits astride the chest of the boy, who is kept in his position by the other men. The surgeon then grabs the face of the boy and opening his mouth pushes the gums back with his thumbnail and then knocks out the tooth with a strike of the thin sharp end of his *nulla-nulla*. Then he takes the tooth with his fingers and holds it up, visible to all.

After all the novices have been operated on, they and their guardians are led away into the bush by the *thŭnthurra* who are responsible for all events, and towards evening they reach some suitable camp places where a yard is made out of branches in which the boys sleep in the company of their overseers. During this night, as well as during the time they are kept in the bush by the *thŭnthurra*, the novices are fed with young possums, widgeons, teals, nardoo, yams, and other vegetable foods.

Between the camp place of the men and the yard in which the boys are kept is a place cleared of all loose debris and lit with one or more fires to give enough lighting. After the boys have taken supper they are brought out of their yard and sat down facing the fire while the *thŭnthurra* perform various pantomimes and traditional songs. The performances consist mainly of imitations of animals with which the audience is familiar, or with scenes from everyday life; and like the ceremonies of other primitive peoples they are amply accompanied by obscene gestures. Some of the animals chosen are the totems of the people present, while others are connected with myths and superstitions prevalent among the people.

During the day the men go hunting to provide the whole community with food, but the novices stay in the camp under the supervision of some overseers. Some days may be spent in one camp, or every night a new camp place may be reached, especially when game is sparse. In the latter case the novices of course have to accompany the other men.

Among the numerous burlesques to instruct and entertain the novices are the following. Some of these performances occur at night-time by the glow of the campfire, while others are performed during the afternoon.

The novices are brought to a place where one of the *thŭnthurra* is lying on the ground, apparently in the final death throes. Some men walk around him, imitating crows and occasionally making a peck with their mouth towards the 'nobler part',[4] which makes the dying man moan. Now and then one of the 'crows' pecks at the penis of the man.

At another time the men hop around and act like the birds known as 'native companions'.[5] Sometimes a few men impersonate kangaroos jumping busily, pursued by the *thŭnthurra* who throw spears and clubs after them.

One of the games at the camp fire at night consists of two or three men each taking a dry piece of a stick and, after lighting one end, sticking the other between the thighs as close to the buttocks as possible. The burning end of the stick is behind, and when the men jump or walk around they seem to have glowing tails.

One afternoon the *thŭnthurra* erect a *gurli*—a hut built from green branches and bark. After twilight some of the old men pretend that it will rain and suggest that the boys are to be brought into the *gurli* as shelter. This is done immediately and a hearty fire is lit to keep them warm. Soon the men pretend to fight and a group of them surrounds the *gurli*, lifting burning pieces of wood, coals and ash from the fire, and throwing them into the building, at which some of the hot projectiles fall onto the boys. After a while the uproar abates and the novices are brought from the *gurli* back into the camp, and everybody retires for a night's rest.

On another day the novices are brought to a place where some old or middle-aged men lie on the ground, their bodies painted with a mixture of burned grass and fat and wearing fanciful ornaments in their hair. One of the overseers pretends that he can see a star in the light part of the sky and asks the boys to look in that direction. He points with his finger and says *burli, burli, burli* (star, star, star). After the novices have gazed for a while without finding the star they are allowed to cast their eyes down. In the meantime the painted men have stood up and started to swing bullroarers. As the lightness of the sky has momentarily blinded the eyes of the boys while they were peering for the star in vain, they are unable to see very clearly and therefore the scene in front of them seems to be the more supernatural and intimidating. Some armed warriors now step in front of the novices and warn them that if they ever convey one of the ceremonies they have seen in the bush to an uninitiated person or woman, they will be killed. Each novice is warned by a man who does not belong to his own tribe.

I must now lead the reader back to the *mŭltyeragara* and *gulpi* where the women and children were left behind, covered with branches etc., as described above. Shortly after the guardians, boys and others were out of sight, the cover was taken off by some men who stayed behind to supervise the women. Then they packed their things and moved to another location, some miles away, where they pitched a new camp with every tribe choosing its accommodation on that side of the camp place which was situated in the direction of its homeland. This same camp may be inhabited during the whole time the novices are away, or the women can change it every few nights to another location in accordance with the movements of the *thŭnthurra*. A patch of ground, called *butthuwullu*, close to each of these camp places, is cleaned, and every evening the mothers and sisters of the novices go to it to attend to traditional singing during the time of the absence of the boys.

The time spent by the novices in the bush, during which they undergo the initiation ceremonies, is about two to three weeks depending on the weather and other circumstances. Every day and evening different performances take place, but the overall character of the events is the same. When the instruction of the novices is completed the chiefs send messengers to the women with the information that the boys will be brought back to them the following evening. At twilight the *thŭnthurra*, overseers and novices approach the women's camp. Some of the men at the back of the procession let bullroarers sound to bestow upon the ceremonies the appropriate solemnity. The boys are allowed to go to the *butthuwullu* where they are sat down with downcast heads. The mother of each novice now approaches and touches him gently with a piece of bark she holds in her hand. All mothers then retreat from the *butthuwullu* to their own camp. The novices are brought to a place prepared for them a little distance away from the accommodation of the men.

It should be noted that the bullroarers used during the leading away of the novices from *gulpi*, while similarly shaped, have different names to those used at the return of the boys to the *butthuwullu*. The first ones are called *yantamakaddya*; the latter *wambinggulli*. In addition there is a smaller bullroarer called *nyugara* used in connection with the *wambinggulli* when the boys are being brought back to the *butthuwullu*.

After a few weeks the novices are again taken close to the women's camp and they have to stand in thick smoke made by burning green bushes, placed on the fire for this purpose.

Now the initiation ceremonies have ended, the tribes present as guests prepare to start their return trip and a few days later most of them are on their way back, each tribe taking its novices with them. The boys are placed for a considerable time under the control of the elders and have to observe certain rules which are set out by the old men. It is also necessary that they participate in one or more further Mūltyerra ceremonies until they are fully familiar with the different parts of the ceremony and can be admitted to full membership as men of the tribe.

ENDNOTES

[1] [Editor's note] Germ. *Wuerde*—dignity, laureateship, honorableness, portliness.

[2] [Editor's note] *Phratry* was Mathews' usual term for 'moiety'. The observation reveals how the moiety system applied across diverse communities.

[3] [Editor's note] The German term *Waechter*, meaning custodian, overseer or guard, makes limited sense in this context. We have used 'guardian', assuming that the German translator mistranslated *guardian* as *guard*.

[4] [Editor's note] Germ. *ein edler Teil*—a euphemism for bottom.

[5] [Editor's note] Brolga or *Grus rubicunda*.

Initiation Ceremony of the Birdhawal Tribe

R. H. Mathews

First published as 'Initiationszeremonie des Birdhawal-Stammes' in *Mitteilungen der Anthropologischen Gesellschaft*, vol. 38 (1908), pp. 17-24. The article was written in English and translated into German by an unnamed translator. This version was retranslated into English by Christine Winter with reference to Mathews' original English draft in the National Library of Australia (NLA MS 8006/5/5).

The ceremony of initiation described in the following pages, known as the *Dyer-ra-yal*, was in operation among the Birdhawal tribe, whose hunting grounds were situated in the northeast corner of the state of Victoria. The boundaries of their territory, which overlapped the New South Wales border, are fully set out in my paper on the 'Birdhawal Language', now in the course of publication elsewhere.[1] In the present article I shall deal only with the most important portions of the ceremony, and my description of even these will be curtailed as much as possible, in order to keep the paper within moderate limits. It is hoped, however, that the details will be found sufficiently comprehensive for the purpose of comparison with similar rites in other parts of Australia.

The Dyerrayal has some interesting points of resemblance to the initiation ceremonies in vogue on the Macleay, Bellinger, Clarence and some other northern rivers of New South Wales. For example, the candidates for initiation are taken away from the main encampment in the evening, and the mothers and other women are permitted to witness their departure and even accompany them up to a certain stage.

In my description of the *Murrawin* ceremony[2] the men take charge of the novices in the evening, in sight of all the women. Next day the women are permitted to see the boys prior to their departure into the bush. At the *Walloonggurra* ceremony[3] the novices are removed from the main camp about dusk, in full view of the women. The men again meet the women next morning before finally going away with the novices.

Another point of resemblance between the Dyerrayal, Murrawin, and Walloonggurra ceremonies is that bundles of small sticks or pieces of bark are thrown during the proceedings connected with the separation of the novices from their mothers. In some cases green twigs are cast over the heads of the women and boys; in other instances the women throw bundles of sticks at the men, as in the Murrawin; in other cases the men throw small pieces of bark over the heads of the women, as in the Walloonggurra ceremony.

In contradistinction to the practices just related of taking charge of the novices in the evening and allowing the women to be spectators of their departure, there are many tribes in New South Wales and Victoria who take charge of the novices in the early morning and place coverings over the women to prevent their observing any part of the proceedings. For examples, see my 'Bunan Ceremony',[4] 'Bora of the Kamilaroi',[5] 'Burbung of the Wiradjuri',[6] 'Wonggoa Ceremony',[7] and others.

There are other tribes who, although the boys are removed from the camp in the morning, allow the women to witness the proceedings. Examples are given in my 'Wandarral Ceremony',[8] 'Toara Ceremony of Queensland',[9] 'Dolgarrity Ceremony of Victoria',[10] 'Nguttan Ceremony',[11] and others.

In regard to the launching of missiles, such as small sticks, pieces of bark, or green leaves, over the heads of the men, women or boys, this is practised at some period during the course of nearly all the inaugural ceremonies, but in many of them the projectiles are thrown when the graduates are brought back to the main camp after having been away in the forests with the old men. In some cases the missiles consist of burning sticks or bark taken from the camp fire. Moreover, in a few of the initiation ceremonies the men fling small sticks at the marked trees while exhibiting them to the novitiates.[12]

The time occupied in connection with the initiation ceremony of the Birdhawal tribes was kept within the shortest possible limits. When the messengers were sent to gather the neighbouring tribes, the date of the arrival of the contingents at the main camp was so arranged that they would all turn up within a day or two of each other, if practicable. When all the participating mobs had arrived, the business of the meeting was promptly proceeded with; and when the novices were taken away from their mothers, the duration of their sojourn in the bush with the elders and the *Kuringal* [13] was no longer than was absolutely required. The necessity for all reasonable expedition is obvious when we remember that the life of all Australian savages is one continual struggle for existence, and hence the extra demand on the game and vegetable products due to the 'invasion' of the visiting tribes is quite a serious and momentous matter.

It will not be out of place to mention here that the remarks in the last paragraph apply to the meetings for initiation purposes in all Australian tribes. In their native state, before they could rely upon getting supplies from the white people, it was unusual for the aborigines to remain in one camp more than a few days; their stay for a longer time depending upon the productiveness of the locality. As soon as the natural food supply was exhausted they were compelled to move to a fresh camping ground. With a large temporary increase in the number of the people, incidental to these ceremonies, the difficulties of obtaining food were correspondingly increased. The various parts of the inaugural rites were consequently disposed of as speedily as practicable, in order to let the visiting tribes disperse and return to their hunting grounds.

We will now give a short account of the details of the ceremonies as carried out by the Birdhawal tribe and their allied groups.

The mustering of the people to attend the *Dyer-ra-yal* was accompanied by substantially the same routine as that in vogue among their neighbours. While the messengers were away gathering the different tribes, the men who remained at home selected a suitable place for the meeting and erected their camp there. Around this camp at a given point the new arrivals took up their quarters facing the direction from which they had come. As far as the nature of the ground permitted they occupied exactly the same relative position to each other in the camp as they did when at home in their respective hunting grounds. The locality selected for this general camp was an area of moderately level ground in the proximity of water where firewood was easily obtained. It was also chosen in a portion of the tribal hunting grounds where game and other food were sufficiently abundant to afford a supply of food for the people attending the ceremonies. On the arrival of a contingent of men and their families who had been invited, they approached the main camp and assembled on a clear space prepared for this purpose, and their headmen called out the names of remarkable mountains, waterholes, camping places and other characteristics of their country, pointing their weapons in that direction. Each contingent would have one or more novices to be initiated.

When all the visitors who were expected to join in the ceremony had arrived at the main camping ground, all the headmen present assembled at the *wurradhang* or private meeting place of the initiated men, and after consultation among themselves they determined the day for the commencement of the principal function of the meeting. The guardians or preceptors of the novices, and also the men who controlled the entire proceedings, were selected at this meeting, or, if there was an adjournment, at the next such meeting. These men were called collectively the *Ku-ring-al*, some of them being taken from each of the tribes present.

About the middle of the appointed day the novices brought by each contingent were gathered up at a convenient place within the confines of the camp and the body of each boy was painted in accordance with the custom of his people and his hair ornamented with feathers. This work was entrusted to the mothers and sisters of the boys, accompanied by several of the elder women. The young girls who were the possible wives of the youths also took part in the painting, and so did some of the men who were appointed guardians, to see that everything was carried out according to ancient custom. The guardian or sponsor of a boy at these ceremonies was called *bul-lu-wrung*; he was one of the brothers, actual or titular, of the women from among whom the novice could, when old enough, obtain a wife in accordance with the tribal laws. An indispensable qualification for the duty of a guardian was that the man must have passed through the inaugural rites of his people.

The afternoon was far advanced before the decoration of the novices was completed. They were then placed sitting down in groups, the boys of each contingent sitting together, while their mothers and the elder women droned some chants similar to the *bobbarubwar* songs[14] of the Kamilaroi women at the Bora ceremonies. Late in the afternoon the women and novices were directed to proceed to a location a short distance out of sight of the camp, accompanied by some of the guardians to show them where to go. This place, if not naturally clear, was prepared by removing the undergrowth and accumulations of small broken timber from its surface, which was then levelled and made smooth. The novices were placed sitting down in the same order as they had been sitting at the camp, with their heads bent forward. They were seated on green boughs or pieces of bark spread out on the ground for the purpose. The mother of each youth stuck her yamstick into the ground beside him, to the top of which a bunch of green twigs was tied. The novices were now called *dhūr-tu-ngurriñ.*

Presently the men constituting the *kuringal* were seen approaching in Indian file in a sort of jog, forming a winding line, having their bodies painted and grotesquely ornamented. Each man had a narrow piece of bark in one hand, with which he struck the ground at intervals of a few paces, uttering grunt-like exclamations. The women beat their folded rugs with their open hands, uttering in a low tone. The men came up in front of the boys, about half a dozen paces from them, and formed a curved line, the concave side of which was towards the boys and the women. They then crouched down and one of the outside men hit the ground in front of him with his piece of bark; each of the other men followed in succession, terminating at the other end of the line.[15] This was repeated backward and forward along the row of men several times, after which all hands returned to their respective camps, the men going by a slightly different way to that taken by the women and novices. The novices belonging to each contingent went with their mothers to their own respective camps.

The following day the men went away some 300 to 400 metres from the main encampment and erected a bough yard,[16] approximately in the shape of a horseshoe, being open at one end. The enclosure varied in size according to the number of novices and guardians to be accommodated. The convex end was generally towards that quarter of the compass from which the wind was blowing. Leaves of such trees that grew in the locality were thickly strewn on the floor, which had previously been made level. Having finished their work the men all returned to the main camp.

In the afternoon of that day, about an hour before sunset, the women, novices and guardians repaired to the place where the beating of the ground with bark took place the day before, whither the men of the *kuringal* detachment shortly afterwards followed them and went through a similar performance. At its conclusion the men withdrew, leaving the women and their companions there. In a little while the men reappeared, walking leisurely in a sinuous line, the headman in the lead. Every man carried in his hands a few small green twigs, from which the leaves had been stripped, known as *deddeluñ*. These twigs had been broken or cut from the extremities of growing bushes, and were about 45 cm long, varying in thickness from that of a goose quill to that of a lead pencil. As the men appeared the novices were raised to their feet and placed standing in a line, with their faces toward the land of their nativity. The women stood in two or three parallel rows a few yards from them.

When the men came up close they formed a circle around the novices and commenced throwing the *deddeluñ* over their heads. Some of the men brought an extra supply of twigs which they handed to the mothers, sisters-in-law, and sisters of the novices. The women then took part in casting twigs into the air above the boys' heads. This performance lasted but a few minutes until all the twigs had been thrown, after which the young women gathered them up off the ground. Each novice was then held up on the shoulders of the men who had charge of him, and while in that position he raised his arms and gave a heaving or vibratory motion to his chest by spasmodically drawing his breath in and liberating it again, swaying his body at the same time. Each boy was elevated in succession and handfuls of leaves were cast at him by all the people present, amidst congratulatory shouts. The whole party, male and female, then started away to the semicircular enclosure described above, the men carrying the novices being in the centre, and the women in the rear carrying the *deddeluñ* which had been gathered off the ground.

On arrival at the bough yard, the *dhurtungurriñ* were placed lying down, face upward, on the leafy bed which had been prepared for them and were covered over with bushy twigs and leaves.[17] One or more fires were lit not far from their feet to keep them warm. The boys were told that they must not turn over, nor in any way change the position in which they had been laid. They were forbidden to scratch their heads or any other part of their bodies. If they wanted to attend to any necessities of nature, they must do it where they were lying.[18] They were not allowed to speak; if a boy wanted anything he must make a sign to the guardian who had charge of him.[19] The same women who had been connected with the ceremonies from the first took up their position at the outside or convex end of the bough fence and made fires there at which they sat down to rest themselves.

After a short time the elder women, accompanied by the others, got up and commenced walking round the enclosure, the men joining in the procession at the rear. The women carried in each hand a few of the twigs which had been cast over the novices, as already stated, which they beat together as a sort of accompaniment to a monotonous chant, which was supposed to act as a lullaby in putting the novices to sleep. The meaning of the song was unintelligible even to the singers themselves. This marching round and round the enclosure, and the beating together of the *deddeluñ*, was kept up all night. Soon after daylight next morning the humming sound of *Turndun*, the name of a bullroarer, was heard in the near distance, upon which the women were directed to lay down the twigs in a heap on the ground alongside the bough fence, and to depart to the main encampment. All the women and children then went away to a fresh camping place, the location of which had been decided by the old men.

When the women were out of sight, the head men and magicians proceeded to remove the leafy covering from the novices and wake them up. They were all placed in a sitting posture, but still remained silent. Each boy was now dressed in the full regalia of a man of his tribe, comprising a brow-band, waist-girdle, apron and other articles. A rug or other covering was then cast over each novitiate's head in such a way that he could not see anything that was going on around him. All this having been satisfactorily completed, the *bulluwrung* or guardian who had been assigned to each novice assumed charge of him. A firebrand was now applied to the bough yard and the whole structure. The leafy bed and the *deddelun* were completely consumed. The whole party then started away to another camp several miles distant, where the boys were placed sitting on leaves spread on the ground, cross-legged, with their heads bowed upon their breasts. Their guardians remained constantly with them and the novices were not allowed to converse either among themselves or with their guardians. If a boy wanted anything he made a sign to his guardian, who then asked him what it was and the novice told him in a whisper.

The men of the *kuringal* went out hunting and returned a short time before sunset, each bringing game and other food obtained. This was cooked, and a limited allowance of the best parts given to the novices. A few days might be spent at this camp, or a fresh camping place might be reached every night, depending upon the food supply.[20] If the party shifted to a different camp every night, the novices were taken out hunting with the men during the day. They marched along with the covering on their heads, in the custody of the *bulluwrung*, and on arriving at the locality which had been agreed upon as the camping ground for the night, a windbreak of boughs was made for the novitiates if the night were cold, some of the guardians remaining constantly with them.

At these camping places in the bush, different burlesques were performed every night by the light of the camp fires, such as pretending to dig a wombat[21] out of its burrow, frightening opossums out of a tree,[22] and the like, for the instruction and amusement of the neophytes. As the representations were similar in character to others described by me in the initiation ceremonies of many other Australian tribes, it is not considered necessary to give further details here.[23]

In the afternoon of the last day of their stay in the bush, the boys were sat down, with the covering still upon their heads. A number of the *kuringal*, who had painted their bodies with powdered charcoal and grease, with grotesque decorations on their bodies and in their hair, now assembled on a clear space, in a curved line, some 20 yards in front of where the novices were, and commenced swinging the bullroarer *Turndun*. The guardians helped the boys to their feet and, removing the covering from their heads, directed them to pay special attention. An old man then approached each novice and rubbed the instrument on his breast and some other portions of his body and invited him to take particular notice of it. Each boy was cautioned by a man belonging to a tribe other than his own that if ever he betrayed anything he had seen or been taught in the bush, he would be killed. From this time onward, the novices' heads were left uncovered and they were free to look around them and converse if first spoken to by their seniors.

The day being now far advanced, all hands proceeded to the women's camp, which might be a mile or two distant or perhaps farther, where they were all passed through the customary smoke ordeal. A short time after dark, some of the men and novices went into the bush adjacent to the *burrikin* or camp of the women and swung the longer and smaller bullroarer. After that everybody retired for the night, the neophytes being conducted to a place prepared for them close to the men's quarters. During the next day all the visiting tribes departed on their homeward journey, each tribe taking with them the graduates belonging to a neighbouring tribe, this matter being arranged by the old men. During this term of probation the scarring of the youths' bodies was carried out and they were further instructed in the songs, dances and folklore of the people.

It was incumbent upon each neophyte to participate in one or more additional inaugural gatherings before he was fully qualified to take his place as a man of the tribe. The reason for this is evident when we remember that at the first Dyerrayal a novice attended, he was prevented from seeing the whole of the ceremony in consequence of being covered over and having to keep his eyes down cast during some of the most important parts of it. In some cases a boy was not more than 12 or 14 years of age when he was first initiated, which was further grounds for delay in admitting him to the full status of manhood.

During the case of instruction that commenced from the time the novices were separated from their mothers until they were finally recognised as men, they were taught what kinds of food they might catch and eat, as well as what foods were taboo to them. The food rules governing the eating of flesh were explained by the old men, but there were certain occasions when the boys were conducted to a place where the women were assembled. The mothers and female relatives of the graduates gave them vegetable food, which conferred upon them the freedom to eat a particular vegetable from that time onward. On another day the boys were brought up and the women gave them water in a native vessel, after which they could drink water from any stream in the tribal territory. Compare this with my description of the *Keeparra* ceremony[24] and the 'Burbung of the New England Tribes',[25] where the women gave the neophytes a drink of water out of a *koolamin*.[26]

It should be stated that the bullroarer that was sounded on the morning the boys were taken possession of by the *kuringal*, was not the same instrument that was exhibited to the novitiates in the bush; the latter being somewhat larger and giving a louder sound. There was also a much smaller bullroarer used at the conclusion of the assemblage, in conjunction with the larger one, within hearing of the women and children. Compare with my 'Mŭltyerra-Initiationszeremonie'.[27]

In 1896 I described the *Bunan* Ceremony of the Thoorga and other tribes.[28] In 1885 A. W. Howitt had given a short report about the initiation ceremonies of the Kurnai tribe, whose border lies to the west of the Birdhawal.[29] In 1896 I published an improved report about the Kurnai ceremonies, accompanied by a map of the different camps and other localities.[30] The present article completes the details of all initiation rites exercised by the coastal tribes beginning in Sydney, New South Wales, to Port Phillip in Victoria; and it is of special satisfaction to me to see this work published by the Anthropological Society in Vienna. The remarks and suggestions of your members will be enormously important to me.

The foregoing description of the Dyerrayal ceremony is compiled from notes, which I myself have written down in the course of some personal meetings with survivors of the Birdhawal tribe at their places of residence. I have published a grammar and vocabulary of the Birdhawal language[31] elsewhere, as well as a grammar and vocabulary of the Kurnai dialect,[32] to which I refer the reader.

ENDNOTES

[1] See R.HM 1907, 'Language of the Birdhawal Tribe in Gippsland, Victoria', *Proceedings of the American Philosophical Society*, vol. 46, pp. 346-59.

[2] RHM 1900-01, 'The Murrawin Ceremony', *Queensland Geographical Journal*, vol. 16, p. 37.

[3] Ibid, pp. 67-8.

[4] RHM 1896, 'The Būnān Ceremony of New South Wales', *American Anthropologist*, vol. 9, p. 336.

[5] RHM 1896, 'The Bora of the Kamilaroi Tribes', *Proceedings of the Royal Society of Victoria*, vol. 9 (new series), p. 154.

[6] RHM 1896, 'The Būrbŭng of the Wiradthuri Tribes', *Journal of the Anthropological Institute*, vol. 25, p. 308.

[7] RHM 1904, 'Ethnological Notes on the Aboriginal Tribes of New South Wales and Victoria', *Journal and Proceedings of the Royal Society of New South Wales*, vol. 38, p. 310.

[8] RHM 1897, 'The Wandarral of the Richmond and Clarence River Tribes', *Proceedings of the Royal Society of Victoria*, vol. 10 (new series), p. 33.

[9] RHM 1900, 'The Toara Ceremony of the Dippil Tribes of Queensland', *American Anthropologist*, vol. 2 (new series), p. 142.

[10] RHM, 'Ethnological Notes on the Aboriginal Tribes of New South Wales and Victoria', p. 330.

[11] RHM 1898, 'Initiation Ceremonies of Australian Tribes', *Proceedings of the American Philosophical Society*, vol. 37, p. 69.

[12] RHM 1897, 'The Keeparra Ceremony of Initiation', *Journal of the Anthropological Institute*, vol. 26, p. 330.

[13] In 1896 Mathews defined *Kooringal* as 'the chosen band of athletes, who have the custody of the guardians and novices whilst the latter are going through the secret ceremonies in the bush'. See RHM 1896, 'The Bora of the Kamilaroi Tribes', *Proceedings of the Royal Society of Victoria*, vol. 9 (new series), p. 151. This is consistent with the explanation given later in the text.

[14] RHM, 'The Bora of the Kamilaroi Tribes', p. 153.

[15] RHM, 'The Būnān Ceremony of New South Wales', p. 338.

[16] RHM, 'Ethnological Notes on the Aboriginal Tribes of New South Wales and Victoria', p. 313.

[17] RHM, 'The Murrawin Ceremony', *Queensland Geographical Journal*, vol. 16, 1900, p. 37.

[18] RHM 1899-1900, 'The Walloonggurra Ceremony', *Proceedings and Transactions of the Queensland Branch of the Royal Geographical Society of Australasia*, vol. 15, p. 68.

[19] RHM, 'The Keeparra Ceremony of Initiation', pp. 330-1.

[20] Every time the men moved their camp from one place to another, the women and children also shifted their quarters, but kept several miles away from the men. Messengers were in daily communication between the *kuringal* camp and that of the women, in order that the men might know exactly where the women and children were located. A few men remained constantly with the women to check that the instructions of the *kuringal* in regard to their movements were carried out.

[21] A marsupial, *phascolomys*, which lives in burrows similar to that of rabbits. Note—German translator.

[22] RHM, 'Ethnological Notes on the Aboriginal Tribes of New South Wales and Victoria', p. 319.

[23] See for example *Mitteilungen*, vol. 34, p. 81. Note—German translator.

[24] RHM, 'The Keeparra Ceremony of Initiation', pp. 336-9.

[25] RHM 1896, 'The Burbung of the New England tribes, New South Wales', *Proceedings of the Royal Society of Victoria*, vol. 9 (new series), pp. 133-4.

[26] *Koolamin* is the name used by the natives of Port Jackson (New South Wales) for a small trough made of bark or wood. The word has, like many native terms, entered into Australian English.

[27] RHM 1904, 'Die Mŭltyerra-Initiationszeremonie', *Mitteilungen der Anthropologischen Gesellschaft*, vol. 34, p. 82. Reproduced this volume.

[28] RHM, 'The Būnān Ceremony of New South Wales', pp. 327-44, with plate.

[29] Howitt, A. W. 1885, 'The Jeraeil, or Initiation Ceremonies of the Kurnai Tribe', *Journal of the Anthropological Institute*, vol. 14, pp. 301-25.

[30] RHM, 'The Būrbŭng of the Wiradthuri Tribes', pp. 317-18, with plate.

[31] RHM 1907, 'Language of the Birdhawal Tribe in Gippsland, Victoria', *Proceedings of the American Philosophical Society*, vol. 46.

[32] RHM 1902, 'The Aboriginal Languages of Victoria', *Journal and Proceedings of the Royal Society of New South Wales*, vol. 36, pp. 92-106.

The Bundandaba Ceremony of Initiation in Queensland

R. H. Mathews

First published as 'Die Bundandaba-Zeremonie in Queensland' in *Mitteilungen der Anthropologischen Gesellschaft*, vol. 40 (1910), pp. 44-7. The article was written in English and translated into German by an unnamed translator. This version was retranslated into English by Christine Winter with reference to Mathews' original English draft in the National Library of Australia (NLA MS 8006/5/4).

The *Bundandaba* ceremony of initiation was practised by the aboriginal tribes who inhabited a part of southern Queensland, situated along the coast from the boundary of New South Wales northerly to the vicinity of Port Curtis, extending inland to comprise a zone from 150 to 200 miles wide. This area contains the country drained by the Burnett, Mary, Brisbane and other rivers, as well as the valley of the Dawson and upper portions of the Condamine River.

The native inhabitants of the tract of country approximately outlined had two forms of initiatory rites. The preliminary rite was called *Toara*, and the final rite Bundandaba. A brief description of the Toara ceremony was published by me in 1900,[1] but no account of the Bundandaba has ever appeared in print. I shall therefore give a short report of the principal parts of the latter, obtained by me direct from the mouths of old natives of the region indicated, who had themselves passed through all the stages of the Bundandaba ceremony. Every novitiate who graduated by means of the Toara was required to undergo the further ordeal of the Bundandaba before he is qualified to take his place as a full man of the tribe.

About six months or a year after the Toara ceremony, preparations are made for putting the candidate through the final rites. The whole community need not be summoned, it being sufficient to invite the initiated men of one or more of the surrounding tribes. This is done by means of messengers in the usual way, appointing the time and place of meeting. The local mob—that is the tribe who sent the invitation—in due time repairs to the agreed place, but no circle or ornamental ground is required. The people who have been invited also journey to the appointed rendezvous, and meet each other before they present themselves to the hosts. The messengers have so arranged matters that the different mobs get within a few miles of each other on the same day.

The visitors are conducted by the messenger to a common camping ground, each mob locating itself on the side nearest the place they have come from. That evening some of the principal men of each contingent set off to the hosts' camp, which they make a point of reaching an hour or two after dark. On coming into sight of the camp fires they sit down and tap their boomerangs or other weapons together, accompanying this with singing. The men in the local camp give a shout of welcome, but remain where they are. The strangers do not approach any nearer and in a short time they clap their hands as a signal that they are going away.

Next morning the fathers, uncles, and other relatives of the novitiates gather them out of the camp and, after appointing a guardian for each, they go over and find the place where the strangers were sitting the night before. They now bend the heads of the novices down and proceed along the men's tracks for a couple of miles or so, where they come to a row of men lying on the ground side by side, their feet being towards the men who are approaching. The head man of the Barrang section is standing at one end of the prostrate row and at the other end a Balgoin man is standing. These men represent the Kappaian cycle, which will be explained at the end of this paper.[2] A guardian takes a novice who is a Barrang by the arm and they both go up in front of one of the erect figures—a Barrang man—but owing to the novice's head being bowed upon his breast, he sees nothing at first. The guardian slightly raises the boy's head saying, 'Look at the man's feet!' The guardian moves his head a little higher and he sees up to the man's waist. He pulls the youth's head up quite straight, and then he observes the whole man in front of him, who is standing quite still. The guardian then gives the youth a piece of stick, picked up off the ground, and tells him to throw it at the Barrang man's chest. He does so and the man pretends to fall back dead.

Another guardian takes a Balgoin novice and leads him to the other side of the row, where the Balgoin head man is standing. He raises the youth's head until he sees successively the feet, waist and entire figure. The guardian then gives him a piece of stick, which he throws as directed, and the Balgoin man falls on his back, apparently dead. The guardian then says to the two novices in question, 'You have killed those two great men, you are bad boys and will perhaps marry wrong women.' The row of men now rise to their feet, jumping and singing before the novices, whose heads have been straightened up.

The combined contingent of *koorbeengoor*[3] and strangers now go away through the bush to hunt for food. The novitiates are brought along by their guardians, and at midday are laid down on the ground, where they must remain silent. Late in the afternoon a camping place is reached where the youths are put into a bough enclosure and fed. At night by the camp fires the *koorbeengoor* perform an obscene dance as follows: a man stands in a slightly stooping posture with his hands clutching his genitalia; another man in the same attitude stands behind him at the distance of about a couple of feet, and so on, until perhaps a score of men are all standing in a line one behind the other. The first man, followed by the others in single file, tramps along in front of the camp fires, moving his loins as in the act of copulating. The novices have been sat down, so that they can have a good view of these men filing past between them and the light of the fires, every man going through the same gestures. When they have gone past into the darkness on one side, they turn round and come back in the same order on the other side. This dance, which is called *toongbirraman*, is kept up for half an hour or more, after which all the party goes to sleep.

Next morning after breakfast the youths are brought out of their yard again and the *toongbirraman* is repeated for a short time. All hands now leave the camp, hunting as they go, until midday, when a halt is made to cook such game as may have been caught. In the meantime, the novices are treated to another exhibition of the *toongbirraman* dance. They go forward to a new camp, hunting until near sundown, and that night the men play at wrestling. Before commencing, the two combatants rub ashes from the camp fire on their hands to enable them to grasp each other's greasy skins. They do not use their feet to trip one another like white men do in this exercise. At first there is only one pair of wrestlers at a time, but towards the finish several couples may join in. After the wrestling one or more pairs of men may engage in fighting with clubs and shields. The evening's program terminates with singing and beating time.

Next morning the *toongbirraman* is again enacted, after which the novices are made to lie down and are covered with rugs or bushes. Presently they hear the sound of the Bundandaba or smaller bullroarer coming nearer and nearer. The guardians say, 'Here they come! They will eat you!' and help the boys to their feet. Within about 20 yards, two head men, a Bunda and a Dyerwain, representing the Deawai cycle, stand swinging the implement. It is tied to the end of a string about three feet long which is fastened to the thin end of a pliable rod that serves as a handle, and it is used in the same way as the *Moonibear* amongst the Wirraidyuri tribes.[4] The Bundandaba is rubbed on the penis, navel, and under the arms of each novice, and he is cautioned never to divulge this secret to any person who has not passed through the necessary ceremonies. A bundle of Bundandabas, equal in number to the novices, is now produced, and an instruction given to each, again warning him to keep it out of reach of the uninitiated.

It may be explained here that if the two old men, Barrang and Balgoin, supposed to have been killed by the novices, had instead belonged to the Bunda and Dyerwain sections, then in that case the two old men who exhibited the Bundandaba would have been Barrang and Balgoin. In other words, if the men of the Kappaian cycle discharge the first function, then the men of the Deawai cycle must exhibit the bullroarer, and vice versa.

This important business being over, the novitiates are greased and dressed, after which they are marched away to the *Bunyunggan* or women's camp, with the same ceremonial I described in my article of 1900 on the Toara. During the afternoon, the *koombeengoor*, novices and guardians go to meet a strange mob of men, who have come to act the part of *poopoon*[5] and there is a sham fight, in which the novices, as newly admitted men, are entitled to participate.

It often happened that the *poopoon* mob had some junior recruits of their own, admitted at a Bundandaba held in another tribe's territory. In such a case the two lots of fresh men were opposed to each other, while the elder warriors looked on and applauded. When the novices finished, the men of maturer years engaged in the contest. If a man or a youth were killed in these encounters, by accident or design, the body was eaten; the same course was followed in the event of more than one casualty.

This finished the Bundandaba and the visitors dispersed to their own homes, as already particularised in regard to the Toara. If the novices are old enough, they are now entitled to claim their promised wives, but this matter is regulated by the old men. The candidate for a spouse must have acquired a man's voice and have a sufficiently developed beard before his claim will be recognised.

In the foregoing pages I have dealt only with the most important portions of the *bundadaba* and my descriptions are much abridged, in order to keep the paper within reasonable limits. It is hoped, however, that the account is sufficiently full to enable a comparison with ceremonies of a similar character in different parts of Australia.

Mention has incidentally been made of the social divisions, *De-a-wai* and *Kap-pai-an* during the progress of the rites, and it will therefore be necessary to give a brief explanation of them. The people are collectively divided into two primary cycles[6] or groups, Deawai and Kappaian; the former is again divided into two sections[7] called Dyerwain and Bunda, and the latter into two called Barrang and Balgoin. The feminine of the cycles and sections are made by the suffix *gan*. The following table will make the matter clearer:

Cycle	Wife	Husband	Son	Daughter
Deawai	Dyerwaingan	Balgoin	Bunda	Bundagan
	Bundagan	Barrang	Dyerwain	Dyerwaingan
Kappaian	Barrangan	Bunda	Balgoin	Balgoingan
	Balgoingan	Dyerwain	Barrang	Barrangan

Each cycle has perpetual succession through its women; eg. Dyerwaingan has a daughter Bundagan, and in the next generation Bundagan has a daughter Dyerwaigan, and so on alternately for ever. Moreover, as the totems, *moorang*, descend through the women it necessarily follows that they must belong to both sections of the cycle. A man may have more than one *moorang* or totem, but he inherits them all from his mother and his mother's mother.

The above table shows the normal or usual marriages, but there are variations. Taking Balgoin, the first name in the 'Husband' column, we observe that he marries Dyerwaigan as his normal or No. 1 wife; or he takes a Bundagan of a certain lineage as his No. 2 spouse; or he mates with Balgoingan as No. 3; or with Barrangan as No. 4 wife. The section name, and the cycle of his children, would depend entirely, in every case, upon their mother, quite irrespective of their father's section name or cycle.

Among the natives of Burnett, Mary and Dawson rivers, the common bat, *deering*, was the friend of all the men, while a small owl or night hawk, *boorookapkap*, was the friend of the women. T. Petrie reports that the blacks of Brisbane river believe that the bat, there called *billing*, made all their menfolk, and that the *wamankan*, or night hawk, made the women.[8] In 1834, Rev L. E. Threlkeld reported that the tribe at Lake Macquarie, New South Wales, had a belief that a certain small bird was the first maker of women, and that the bat was venerated on the same grounds by the men.[9] J. Dawson in 1881, describing the customs and beliefs of the Aborigines of western Victoria, states that the common bat belongs to the men, and the fern owl to the women.[10]

ENDNOTES

[1] RHM 1900, 'The Toara Ceremony of the Dippil Tribes of Queensland', *American Anthropologist*, vol. 2 (new series), pp. 139-44.

[2] [Editor's note] As the table shows, Mathews refers to the two primary kinship groups as 'cycles', although more often he called them 'phratries'. The common contemporary term is 'moiety'.

[3] *Koorbeengoor* is the native name for the group of men who, during the initiation ceremony, had to look after the novices. The orthography of the English original was kept. Note—German translator.

[4] RHM 1896, 'The Būrbŭng of the Wiradthuri Tribes', *Journal of the Anthropological Institute*, vol. 25, p. 298, plate 26, fig. 39. [*Moonibear* was the name of a bullroarer. Note—Editor]

[5] *Poopoon* is the name for men who have come to participate in a sham fight.

[6] *Phratry*. Note—German translator.

[7] Clan, class. Note—German translator. [In English Mathews most often used the term 'section' to describe the subdivisions of what he referred to at different times as a 'phratry', 'cycle' or 'moiety'. Other authors referred to them as 'clans' or 'classes'. Hence the original translator's explanation. Note—Editor.]

[8] Petrie, Constance C. 1904, *Reminiscences of Early Queensland*, Brisbane, p. 62.

[9] 'An Australian Language, p. 49.' [L. E. Threlkeld's *An Australian Language as Spoken by the Awabakal* was not published until 1892. Mathews is possibly referring to Threlkeld's *An Australian Grammar* of 1834. Note—Editor.]

[10] 'Aborigines of Victoria', p. 52-3. [Mathews is apparently referring to James Dawson's *Australian Aborigines: The languages and customs of several tribes of Aborigines in the western district of Victoria* of 1871. Note—Editor.]

Part 6: Correspondence

Introduction

Martin Thomas

The contents of this volume are testimony to the highly globalised anthropological scene of the turn-of-the-century era. With his friendships in Aboriginal communities, his rural correspondents and his international network of publishing contacts, R. H. Mathews channelled the flow of information from the Australian backblocks to the major imperial centres. The postal system was as fundamental to him as the internet is to a researcher today. That he would have envied the instantaneity we take for granted is suggested when he grumbles to E. S. Hartland that his letters to Britain take a month to arrive. The system was fairly slow, but measures were put in place to allow scientific knowledge to flow as efficiently as possible. The Smithsonian Institution in Washington ran an International Exchange Service, specifically designed to distribute research publications between governments and societies throughout the world. Mathews' correspondence with his editor at the American Philosophical Society reveals that he made generous use of this scheme.[1]

Many books could be made from correspondence in the R. H. Mathews Papers, National Library of Australia. But as I noted in the general introduction to this volume, his failure to keep copies of the many letters he wrote means that his own voice is largely missing. Also absent from the National Library collection are most of the letters he received from overseas anthropologists. His diary indicates that he wrote to many luminaries in the social sciences. His British correspondents included Ernest Crawley, Alfred C. Haddon, Andrew Lang, W. H. R. Rivers, Northcote W. Thomas and Sir E. B. Tylor—all major figures at the time.[2] It is rather a mystery that letters from none of these men survive in Mathews' papers. Given the care he took in ordering and preserving other paperwork, it is hard to believe that he disposed of letters from leaders in his field of study. It seems more likely that these documents were set aside for 'safekeeping', perhaps by Mathews' son William, who took great interest in his father's legacy. Their present whereabouts is unknown. It is unlikely that they were among the great bulk of Mathews' papers that A. P. Elkin borrowed from the family in the 1950s. Had he seen letters from the likes of Lang and Tylor, he would surely have said so in his trilogy of articles, 'R. H. Mathews: His Contribution to Aboriginal Studies' (1975-6).[3] Nor is it likely that Elkin ever read the letters Mathews received from Baron Moritz von Leonhardi, reproduced here. Von Leonhardi was the editor and confidante of the Lutheran missionary, Pastor Carl Strehlow, who also corresponded with Mathews. Janet Mathews (granddaughter-in-law of R. H.) gave the letters to the linguist Luise Hercus who in turn gave them to Carl's son, the linguist T. G. H. Strehlow. They can now be found in the collection of the Strehlow Research Centre, Alice Springs.

It would be fascinating to reconstruct the dialogue between Mathews and von Leonhardi (1856-1910). But the baron's villa in Frankfurt, where his manuscripts and ethnographic collections were held, was destroyed during World War II.[4] The one extant letter from Mathews to von Leonhardi is published here, copied from the Australian Institute of Aboriginal and Torres Strait Islander Studies, Canberra. Its existence in Australia is explained by its date—1911. Mathews was unaware that von Leonhardi had died the previous year until his letter was returned to sender. Some of Mathews' correspondence does survive in British and American institutions. Via Britain's National Registry of Archives, an on-line search tool, I was led to the papers of the folklorist E. S. Hartland, another correspondent mentioned in Mathews' diary. The eight letters Mathews wrote to him over an 18-month period in 1907-08 are part of a large collection of Hartland manuscripts, held by the National Library of Wales.

Edwin Sidney Hartland (1848-1927) was a solicitor from Gloucester in the south of England. His abiding interest in folk narratives led him to the Folk-Lore Society, of which he became president. His contributions to the society's journal *Folk-Lore* began in the 1880s and in 1890 he published *English Fairy and Other Folk Tales*. This was followed by *The Science of Fairy Tales, An Enquiry into the Fairy Mythology* (1891), which the historian of folklore study Richard M. Dorson regards as a 'masterly treatise'.[5] Dorson describes how Hartland's work gradually shifted 'from folk narrative to primitive institutions'—a transition echoed more broadly in British intellectual life. The consequence of this was a period of sustained dialogue between folklorists and anthropologists. Hartland, for example, believed that folklore study could be sharpened by the scientific methods of ethnology. Interpreting data collected by colonial observers, he led a vigorous debate about whether 'primitives' were cognisant of the connection between sexual intercourse and conception. In this he made a major impact on early twentieth-century anthropology.[6]

Hartland communicated with Mathews and other Australians including Catherine Eliza Somerville Stow (who published as K. Langloh Parker) and A. W. Howitt. (Their letters can also be found in the National Library of Wales.) He reviewed Mathews' *Ethnological Notes on the Aboriginal Tribes of New South Wales and Victoria* (1905) in 1906.[7] This was probably the impetus for their correspondence, for the first evidence of communication with Hartland appears in Mathews' diary of July that year.[8] Although their correspondence seems to have lasted only 18 months, a confidence quickly developed. These eight letters give valuable insights into how Mathews presented himself as an anthropological correspondent, a role to which he was well accustomed, but of which so little evidence survives.

*

The correspondence from von Leonhardi, translated from the German, provides another perspective on Mathews' international project. It is pertinent to this collection for several reasons. Firstly, it reveals that Mathews' language skills were sufficient for him to read von Leonhardi's quite technical German, although insufficient for him to *write* in that language. Mathews' sole surviving letter to von Leonhardi is in English, and is presumably representative of the others. Secondly, the correspondence gives an indication of the highly detailed scrutiny that Australian ethnologists received at the hands of some Europeans. Von Leonhardi may not have written in English but he could certainly read it. The correspondence reveals that Mathews supplied the baron with many of his writings, but others he came across independently in his panoramic reading of contemporary anthropology. Von Leonhardi makes a revealing remark when he complains to Mathews that his bookseller can no longer obtain the journal *Science of Man*. Published by the Anthropological Society of Australasia, it was hardly common in Australia. That von Leonhardi could buy it at all is an indication of the ethnological fever then prevalent in Europe. So it is not surprising that von Leonhardi was reported as possessing a 'close to complete anthropological library, including books not readily available in Germany'.[9]

Von Leonhardi was a wealthy aristocrat who resided mainly at his family's country seat in Gross-Karben near Frankfurt, from where these letters were written. A biographical portrait of him, written by the present-day anthropologist Anna Kenny, gives valuable insight to his thinking and background. He received a classic humanist German schooling and for a time studied law at Heidelberg. After a serious bout of illness he abandoned law and turned his attention to natural science and philosophy. In the last decade of his life, anthropology became his abiding interest and he maintained extensive correspondence with many well-known anthropologists in Europe and the British Isles. Kenny emphasises that during this period the anthropological environment of Germany was very different to the Britain scene, dominated as it was by evolutionary thinking. She points out that Germany did not become an imperial power until the last quarter of the nineteenth century, so unlike Britain it had little invested in 'an ideology of racial superiority'.[10] This is enormously significant to understanding the readership Mathews found in Germany and Austria, and the skepticism about the theories of Spencer and Gillen that he shared with both von Leonhardi and Strehlow. As Kenny puts it, '[u]nlike the British anthropological tradition which dominated Australian discourse, German anthropology was based on a humanistic agenda, and as a result it was anti-evolutionistic, as well as anti-racist and anti-colonialist'.[11]

Von Leonhardi had a profound effect upon Pastor Carl Strehlow, missionary at the remote settlement of Hermannsburg in Central Australia. He encouraged him to document language and mythology and arranged for publication of his seven-volume magnum opus, *Die Aranda- und Loritja-Stämme in Zentral-Australien* (1907-20), a work highly esteemed in Germany, although much ignored by the Anglophone world. Even now, it has not been fully translated into English. T. G. H. Strehlow's biographer Barry Hill relates how von Leonhardi urged Strehlow 'to keep on sending his material in the hope that "the spell of the book by Spencer and Gillen will hopefully be broken and destroyed by science"'.[12] Given Mathews' conviction, as he writes to Hartland, that Spencer had done 'all he could to injure me,' it is not surprising that a sympathy grew between them. It is an indication of von Leonhardi's independence of mind that despite his concerns about Spencer and Gillen's work on Central Australia, he upheld their view that the kinship system of the Arrernte people descends patrilineally. Years later, Mathews' arguments for matrilineal descent, advanced so passionately in his letters to Hartland, were robustly dismissed by the younger Strehlow who regarded them as 'utterly worthless misrepresentations of doctored facts'.[13] It is a view now widely accepted.

The Hartland and von Leonhardi letters give two perspectives on Mathews' intransigence about the marriage customs of a part of Australia he had never visited in person. Undoubtedly, his views on this matter were coloured by the shabby treatment he had received from Spencer and his friend Howitt. And almost as strong was Mathews' craving for acceptance in Britain. He urged Hartland to tell him 'what decision the English ethnologists come to regarding my views of the descent of the children in the Central Australian Tribes'. Yet it is doubtful that his opinion could ever have found acceptance in the nation where Spencer and Gillen were high gods of anthropology. The fact that a German ethnologist was prepared to analyse his findings in excruciating detail—a critic informed by Strehlow who had daily contact with Aboriginal people in that very area—did nothing to convince him of his error. His views on patrilineal descent of the Arrernte remained fixed, as can be seen in an article dated 1912 in which Radcliffe-Brown was drawn into the debate.[14] Mathews often preached about the necessity of 'getting among the natives' in person. His stubbornness on this matter is evidence of the soundness of his own advice.

ENDNOTES

[1] Mathews to J. Minnis Hayes, 27 September 1897, Records of the American Philosophical Society.

[2] Diary 1893-1907, R. H. Mathews Papers, National Library of Australia (henceforth NLA) MS 8006/1/2.

[3] Elkin, A. P. 1975, 'R. H. Mathews: His Contribution to Aboriginal Studies: Part I', *Oceania*, vol. 46, no. 1; Elkin, A. P. 1975, 'R. H. Mathews: His Contribution to Aboriginal Studies: Part II', *Oceania*, vol. 46, no. 2; and Elkin, A. P. 1976, 'R. H. Mathews: His Contribution to Aboriginal Studies: Part III', *Oceania*, vol. 46, no. 3.

[4] Hill, Barry 2002, *Broken Song: T. G. H. Strehlow and Aboriginal Possession*, Knopf, Milsons Point, NSW, p. 483.

[5] Dorson, Richard M. 1968, *The British Folklorists: A History*, University of Chicago Press, Chicago, p. 239.

[6] See Hiatt, L. R. 1996, *Arguments about Aborigines: Australia and the Evolution of Social Anthropology*, Cambridge University Press, Cambridge, pp. 109 & 122.

[7] Hartland, E. Sidney 1906, 'Review of *Ethnological Notes on the Aboriginal Tribes of New South Wales and Victoria*', *MAN*, vol. 9, no. 99.

[8] Diary 1893-1907, entry for 17-24 July 1906.

[9] Kenny, Anna 2005, 'A Sketch Portrait: Carl Strehlow's editor Baron Moritz von Leonhardi' in Kenny, Anna and Mitchell, Scott (eds), *Strehlow Research Centre Occasional Paper 4: Collaboration and Language*, SRC, Alice Springs, p. 56.

[10] Ibid, p. 54.

[11] Ibid.

[12] Hill, *Broken Song*, pp. 33-4.

[13] Strehlow, T. G. H. 1999, 'Aranda Regular and Irregular Marriages', *Strehlow Research Centre Occasional Paper 2*, SRC, Alice Springs, p. 41.

[14] RHM 1912, 'Matrilineal Descent in the Arranda and Chingalee Tribes', *MAN*, vol. 12, no. 47.

Letters to E. S. Hartland

R. H. Mathews

From the Edwin Sidney Harland Papers (MS 16889C), collection of the National Library of Wales, Aberystwyth.

'Carcuron'
Hassall Street, Parramatta
New South Wales

February 8th 1907

Dear Mr Hartland

Your kind letter of 16 Sept.r last reached me on 20th October, as well as your reprint. I have been very busy about many things since then and somehow put off writing to you sooner.

I thank you very much for your suggestion that I should publish all my works, adjusted up to date. I have sent the part of my work which comprises N S Wales and Victoria arranged in the order in which I wish to publish it, to my son in England, asking him to interview some publishers, and hope he will succeed. I am telling you this in confidence because I don't want my enemies in Australia to know anything about my movements. I shall write to my son by the same mail as this letter goes by and ask him to communicate with you, and ask your advice. I very much regret that I did not do so before, because you would have known the likely publishing offices to approach.

I saw your name on the Folklore Society's prospectus for 1904 and I presume you are still with them. I posted some folk tales of the N S Wales tribes to them some time back. The Secretary wrote to say he would submit it to the Editorial Committee. Perhaps you would kindly see that my contribution gets a fair 'hearing' as I would like the F. Soc. to publish what I sent. I know scores of similar stories which I could send them.

By this mail I am forwarding you a copy of my 'Eth. Notes & c.'[1] and also a copy of my 'Notes on the Native Tribes of Australia'[2] for your own use. I suppose you saw the copies I sent the Anthrop Inst. of my Ethn Notes Queensland Tribes'[3] and 'Sociology of Some Aus. Tribes'.[4] I asked the Inst. to review them in 'Man' and I suppose they will do so during the next *few years*. The 'American Anthrop[ologist]' reviewed them last September or earlier. By this mail I am sending the Inst. a copy of 'Notes on Some Native Tribes of Aust', and am asking them to review it in 'Man'. They may do so perhaps next year or the year after. But you'll see it reviewed in the 'Am. Anthrop' in 3 months time, about.

I suppose you saw my article in the American Antiquarian, vol. 28.[5] You'll see another in the Jany-Feby issue.[6] You remember the brutal review N W Thomas gave me in 'Nature' of 31st May '06. He was then writing his 'Natives of Australia', and he tried to make as little of my work as possible because he was using Spencer's, Howitt's and [Katherine Langloh] Parker's books as his basis. The motive is very apparent. His book is full of gross errors, some of which could have been avoided if he had consulted my works. For example at p 94 he says 'the heavy stones were brought a considerable distance, with great combined labour'.[7] If he had read my scientific account he would have seen that all the stones were *on the spot*, and were merely rolled into position.

I shall be pleased if you will write me quickly and tell me how my 'Folklore' is getting on at the Society, and any other matters you may choose to refer to. If my son has not already arranged for the publication of my book, you will hear from him as soon as he gets my letter, which goes by the same mail as this. I will enclose a letter for you in my son's letter, so that you will be more fully in possession of the facts.

Very sincerely yours
R. H. Mathews

'Carcuron'
Hassall Street, Parramatta
New South Wales

February 12th 1907

Dear Mr Hartland

I am sending this letter through my son Mr G. M. Mathews, whom I mentioned in my last letter.

He has been endeavouring to place my book for publication. It was submitted to Macmillan & Co, who after keeping it 18 weeks regretted that they could not undertake its publication, although they admit that it 'contains much valuable information'. Judging by the lapse of time, 18 weeks, I think they submitted it to Howitt or Spencer, who it is needless to add would condemn it to make room for their own books.

I am troubling you because you will know exactly how to set about this undertaking, and the prestige of your name will be of very great value. There can be no doubt that my labours should be published. You will remember that you advised me to take the step in your letter of Sep. last but my MS was then in the hands of Macmillan, or else I would have sent it through you.

I am writing to my son by this mail, and he will probably show you my letter, which goes somewhat into detail. I am in a hurry to catch the mail, but my son can tell you anything further.

Yours faithfully,
R H Mathews

Hassall Street, Parramatta

New South Wales

April 9th 1907

Dear Mr Hartland

Referring to previous letters regarding the publication of my work on the Aborigines, I daresay you and my son have been doing your best to place the book on the English market. I should think that every man who is studying the Aborigines of Australia would purchase my book. There is more new material in my book than there is in Howitt's.[8] If you take down Howitt's last volume there is *nothing* really new in it. I think I know as much about the Aborigines as any man in Australia, and I can safely say there is nothing in Howitt's book which has not already been made known either in my pamphlets or his own pamphlets or in the works of other writers. In *my* book there are several chapters which have never been published by anyone but myself, either for the first time or in my previous pamphlets. In Mrs Parker's book there is a good deal which had never been published before, but some of her statements are wild and incorrect. But if you take Howitt's book, chapter by chapter, you will not find anything which you could not find elsewhere. This is absolutely true. At the same time I am glad to have Howitt's book, because it brings together what he has enquired into himself and what he has obtained from others. Then as to Spencer & Gillen, their book, like Mrs Parker's, while reporting some new facts, contains many gross errors, which I need not touch upon.[9]

I am sure it was Spencer who created a prejudice against me in England. He was there in the middle and latter part of 1898 and did all he could to injure me because I was doing work in the Northern Territory. It will be found that my work is quite as accurate as his own. Time will show.

Any mail may bring me a letter from you saying what you recommend me to do. You will have obtained suggestions from some publisher and I will endeavour to carry out what you advise.

I could quite easily make my book larger, but I thought it best to confine it to New South Wales and Victorian Tribes, intending to bring out another work on the Tribes of the other Australian States. I have a large mass of information regarding all the states which has not yet been published anywhere, but it seems to me better to publish a series of smaller books than to publish one large one.

(1) I could send enough mythology of all the Australian states to make a good sized volume, say 200 pages if you advise me to do that. I would, I think, incorporate native songs with them. (2) Then I could publish a separate book on the Australian languages. I have some grammars of all the Australian States, which with corresponding vocabularies would make a volume of say 200 pages.

There does not seem to me to be any occasion for illustrations in any future books on the blacks. Spencer & Gillen have given us enough of that. But I see N W Thomas' book on 'Natives of Australia' has a lot of unnecessary and practically useless illustrations. If that were the *only* book one intended to buy, the illustrations might be necessary, but forming one of many books on Australia, the illustrations are not required. Lang's 'Secret of the Totem' has no pictures, neither has Thomas' 'Organisation & Marriage'. I am quite satisfied for my book to have none, beyond the copies of rock pictures and similar things, which are of course indispensable.

As soon as I get a letter from you I will write again. Of course you know that I would send the publisher a map of NSW and Victoria if he publishes the MS you have charge of with my son.

Yours faithfully
R H Mathews

Hassall Street, Parramatta
New South Wales

July 2nd 1907

Dear Mr Hartland,

My son sent me your letter to him re my book for publication and I beg to thank you very heartily for your advice. I have written to him for the MSS but it will not reach me for a month yet. I shall then go over it and perhaps re-submit it in a different form.

By this mail I am sending W. H. R. Rivers[10] a few sheets of MS on Sociology, with Blood pedigrees of 6 families for 3 generations. I presume you know I must have collected a number of genealogies to enable me to arrive at the conclusion that the two Bloods were found mixed with both cycles (phratries) and the four sections—that is, that the Bloods divisions are quite independent of the other divisions. We cannot expect the natives to give a reason for the Blood divisions any more than they can of the origin of the cycles, sections or totems. We can only report facts as we find them.

I may explain that Dr. Rivers wrote to me, sending me 'separates' of his work in Torres Straits & c and asked me to gather some genealogies. So I have sent him the genealogies I gathered some years ago when I discovered the Blood divisions. I am asking him to get my short article published in 'Man' or 'Folk-Lore' because the Anthrop. Inst. Council will not meet again till November next and I can't wait till then.[11]

I had intended to send the short paper to you, but as Rivers wrote to me I thought it better to enlist his sympathy with my work. I know that you are with me, and I think Thomas is. You have no doubt seen my article in Nature of 9th May and Thomas's remarks thereunder.[12] He has acted quite manly with me and now I shall treat him as a friend. He has also quoted me briefly in his 'Kinship and Marriage'.[13]

May I ask you therefore to cooperate with Dr. Rivers in getting the MS now sent to him published in either 'Man' or 'Folklore' as early as possible, as I wish to show that I am willing to meet the wishes of English ethnologists on all points upon which they may be kind enough to make suggestions upon.

I don't know whether you hold with Spencer & Gillen that descent in Central Australian tribes is through the man. I shall be able to show you that they are quite wrong. But we will say more of this later on.

I have mentioned to Dr. Rivers that I would let you know I had sent the MS to him and that I thought you would co-operate with him in getting it published.

Trusting that I am not intruding too much on your kindness and thanking you for past kindnesses.

I am

Yours faithfully
R. H. Mathews

Hassall Street, Parramatta
New South Wales

August 10, 1907

Dear Mr Hartland

By this mail I am sending you, registered, the MS of an article on 'Sociology of the Arranda and Chingalee Tribes' and am venturing to ask you to 'communicate' it to either *Folk-Lore* or *Man*, whichever of the two you can get to publish it the first.[14] Most of the English Societies have a habit of 'referring' all their papers and such 'references' occupy, say, 6 months. I could say 'yes' or 'no' to such a paper as I am sending you, just in the time it would take me to read it through.

If I can secure *speedy publication* for a few articles such as the one I am now sending you, some of my enemies may see they have come to a wrong conclusion—have been grossly misled. I cannot but regret that several English writers seem to have swallowed the statements of Spencer & Gillen and Howitt about *male descent*. Of course there is such a thing as my being mistaken in my conclusions, but I don't think so, for the following reason. Ever since 1898 the fact has been thrust upon me that Spencer and Howitt looked upon me as 'the opposition candidate' and never lost a chance of doing me an injury. I was thus kept continually 'on my mettle' and took every precaution—double precautions—to keep my statements unassailable. When I found it necessary to amend any of my results I did it immediately, so as not to give my enemies a chance of correcting me. I referred and re-referred the information sent me by old residents of Central Australia back to them for further sifting and inquiry. Half a dozen of my best correspondents were and are located in different parts of the Chingalee, Binbingha, Wombaia and Inchalanchu country peopled with tribes of the 8-section system and they all gave the same results, quite unknown to each other. I also had two excellent men among the tribes of the Victoria river and three more in the Kimberley district of Western Australia where the 8-section system prevails. I was the 'head and front' of the investigation and my men worked and re-worked under my directions. This has been going on for 13 years (since 1894) as shown by my pamphlets. I had the warning continually before me that any mistake of mine would meet with no mercy. When my men differed from S & G I sent them copies of what S & G had said and asked them to try again—to check and re-check.

On the other hand Spencer & Gillen were wallowing in their fancied security, with everybody patting them on the back, until at last they really believed that they knew everything and no one else knew anything. They even succeeded in forcing the same opinion on many of our English ethnologists. On the contrary I was always looking out for something that would either show me I was wrong or that I was right. If I am wrong I want to find it out before anyone else can find it out.

In conclusion, if you can get the MS now sent printed in 'Man' or in 'Folk-Lore' you will help me very much to establish my reputation as one of the reliable Australian workers. Please write at once and tell me what you can do.

With thanks and kind regards

Yours faithfully
R H Mathews

PS. The MS of my book has not yet reached me, but will soon do so, as I asked my son for it a few days after I got your letter to him.

Hassall Street, Parramatta
New South Wales

August 10th, 1908

Dear Mr Hartland,

Your letter of 17th May reached here just at the time I met with a serious driving accident, which broke three of my ribs and a shoulder blade. I am only just able to get about again. I am very thankful for all the items of news you have given me.

I am sending you several 'separata' which will place my views about the marriage laws of Central Australian Tribes more fully before you, and hope you will thoroughly investigate all I have said, in order to test whether my conclusions are sound or not. Mr Strehlow is about publishing a work in which he tells me he is supporting Spencer & Gillen's views as to *male* descent. Mr Strehlow has sent me much MS information, from which I arrive at a diametrically opposite conclusion to his. My conclusions are supported by the reports of several residents of the Finke river and Alice Springs, in the Arranda country.

The Jany-March No. of 'Folk-Lore' has reached our Public Library, containing my article on the Arranda and Chingalee Sociology, but *no separate copies* have yet come to my hands. You will doubtless remember that I forwarded the MS through you, and either you or a friend of yours recommended its publication in 'Folk-Lore'. Possibly the Editor has sent you the 'separata' because of your communicating the MS. In any case will you do me the favour to enquire about the 'separata'. I presume 'Folk-Lore' supplies copies to authors of papers. I hope they will not disappoint me.

Then as regards a short article I sent 'Folk-Lore' on the Tales of the Aborigines I would like you to remind the Secretary or Editor. The paper was accepted for publication more than a year ago. Not only so, but in the same letter the Secretary asked me for further contributions and thanked me for the legends. I cannot understand the delay and will be really grateful if you can expedite the printing of my legends as soon as possible if they are not in type by the time you get this letter.[15] Please write me shortly.

Yours faithfully
R. H. Mathews

P. S.—I am of opinion that Strehlow's phratry names Alarinja and Kwatjarinja are not correct. They are only Father and Son designations like S & G's [Spencer and Gillen's] 'phratries'.

Poor old Strehlow has been out in 'the wilderness' so long that he feels sure that because Schulze, Dr. Stirling of the Horn Exped., and S & G all three agree that there is a *paternal* descent, he thinks it really must be so.

No doubt the blacks told Schulze and all those who have religiously copied him, that descent was through the father—meaning that a man belonged to his father's tribe, inherited his father's country, was taught his father's initiation ceremonies, and was instructed by the men about the totems. If we ask any Kamilaroi, Ngeumba, Wiradjuri & c he will make the same answer as the Arunta man, for the same reason.

Don't pin your faith to Strehlow just because he is *on the spot*.

Hassall Street, Parramatta
New South Wales

August 24, 1908

My dear Mr Hartland

I wrote you a few weeks ago re my papers on descent, which latter I forwarded to you. As soon as you come to a conclusion in regard to my views of the case I shall be greatly obliged if you will write and tell me plainly what you think. Again, if you learn that anyone else has given his conclusion on my reports, please write at once and let me know his views and the work where they are printed. By complying with these requests you will lay me under a lasting obligation, as I am very anxious to know whether my conclusions are approved or not.

Corrigenda

In vol. 41 JR Soc NSW, p 78 and 79.[16] Jack Onze belongs to the section *Kumbo* and *not Ippai*. Same Volume, p. 151, Table B, Paiarola's father was a *Knuraia* and *not* a Pananka.[17]

I forgot to make these corrections in the copies I forwarded to you with my last letter.

Yours faithfully,
R. H. Mathews

Hassall Street, Parramatta
New South Wales

Septr. 27th 1908

My dear Mr Hartland

Referring to my letter of a few weeks back, I am again reminding you that I shall feel grateful if you will let me know *as early as possible*, what decision the English ethnologists come to regarding my views of the descent of the children in the Central Australian Tribes.

My researches and conclusions have been published with sufficient fullness in the 'separata' I sent you recently. Strehlow's report is I presume also published by this time. Spencer & Gillen's conclusions have long been before the public.

I am very anxious to know whether my views have any points of value in them, or whether I am thought by ethnologists to be altogether wrong. If I am entirely in error I do not wish to publish any further particulars until I see the views of my critics and gain enlightenment from them. On the other hand, if any views are upheld by competent authority, it will give me courage to go on in the work I am engaged in.

Kindly, let me know your own criticism. If you have seen Dr Rivers or Dr Haddon and have heard them express any opinion in journals or newspapers, please let me know what they have published.

You see how desirous I am to know what you English authorities think of my labours.

Very sincerely yours
R. H. Mathews

ENDNOTES

[1] Probably RHM 1903-04, 'Ethnological Notes on the Aboriginal Tribes of the Northern Territory', *Queensland Geographical Journal*, vol. 16, 1900-01 or 'Ethnological Notes on the Aboriginal Tribes of Western Australia', *Queensland Geographical Journal*, vol. 19.

[2] Probably RHM 1906, 'Notes on Some Native Tribes of Australia', *Journal and Proceedings of the Royal Society of New South Wales*, vol. 40.

[3] Probably RHM 1904-05, 'Ethnological Notes on the Aboriginal Tribes of Queensland', *Queensland Geographical Journal*, vol. 20.

[4] RHM 1905, 'Sociology of some Australian Tribes', *Journal and Proceedings of the Royal Society of New South Wales*, vol. 39.

[5] RHM 1906, 'The Totemistic System in Australia', *American Antiquarian*, vol. 28.

[6] Ibid.

[7] A reference to the Brewarrina fish traps.

[8] Howitt, A. W. 1996, *The Native Tribes of South-East Australia*, Aboriginal Studies Press, Canberra [1st pub. 1904].

[9] Presumably a reference to Spencer, W. Baldwin and Gillen, F. J. 1968, *The Native Tribes of Central Australia*, Dover, New York [1st pub. 1899]. Spencer and Gillen co-wrote several other books.

[10] William Halse Rivers Rivers (1864-1922), English anthropologist and psychiatrist.

[11] Published as RHM 1908, 'Social Organisation of the Ngeumba Tribe, New South Wales', *MAN*, vol. 8, no. 10.

[12] RHM 1907, 'Ethnological Notes on the Aboriginal Tribes of New South Wales and Victoria [Letter to the Editor]', *Nature*, vol. 76, no. 1958.

[13] Thomas, Northcote W. 1966, *Kinship Organisations and Group Marriage in Australia*, F. W. Cheshire, Melbourne [1st pub. 1906].

[14] Published as RHM 1908, 'The Sociology of the Arranda and Chingalee Tribes (Northern Territory Australia)', *Folk-Lore*, vol. 19.

[15] Probably RHM 1908, 'Folk-Tales of the Aborigines of New South Wales', *Folk-Lore*, vol. 19.

[16] RHM, 'Social Organisation of the Ngeumba Tribe'.

[17] RHM 1907, 'Notes on the Arranda Tribe', *Journal and Proceedings of the Royal Society of New South Wales*, vol. 41.

Letters to R. H. Mathews

Moritz von Leonhardi

From the collection of the Strehlow Research Centre, Alice Springs (RM 1908-1-2; 1908-2-1; 1909-1-1; 1910-1-1). Translated from the German by Christine Winter.

Gross-Karben 9.6.1908
Hessen
Germany

Dear Sir!

Thank you very much for your letter as well as sending some offprints of articles by you. I have instructed the publisher to send you a copy of Strehlow's Aranda Legends on my behalf and will send you the next issues, too. I hope to be able to publish the second booklet in about two months; it will contain Loritja legends and the beliefs of both tribes about totemism and about Churinga.[1] I would be delighted if you closely took note of the publication and helped it to become known in Australia.

I have already read a large number of your many published articles. The ones now sent to me were, however, totally unknown to me. I was very interested particularly in the article: 'Notes on the Aborig. North T. Western Austr. etc.',[2] because of the important information about the natives of Western Australia, still so little known. It turns out more and more that the culture of the Western tribes is very similar to those of Central Australia (Aranda, Loritja, etc); now again with the demonstrations of near identical ideas about the Tjuringa (bull-roarer) associated with each of them; this had already been pointed out by Professor Klaatsch.[3] It is a pity that in this article, as well as in some others of yours, information about new or recently ascertained facts is mostly very brief and does not provide the wording of your correspondents, and for the most part also does not give names and places of residence. With such difficult matters the *ipissima verba* [actual words] of the person reporting often matters a lot. Very interesting also for me were the notes on incarnation and reincarnation of children among the Chingalee. Differing ideas about these matters seem to exist from tribe to tribe; and also within the same tribe. Strehlow has demonstrated this, too, for the Aranda and Loritja. Recently I read an article by you in Folk-Lore and another in Americ. Anthropol[ogist].[4] In both you try to demonstrate that the Aranda had matrilineal descent and not patrilineal descent as reported by Sp. and G. [Spencer and Gillen]. Strehlow arrives at the same result as Sp. and G: patrilineal descent. After examining the material available before me I, however, have to say, that I cannot concede that you are right. You arrange groups in the following way:

A	B
Purula	Pananka
Ngala	Knuraia
Bangata	Kamara
Paltara	Mbitjana

But Strehlow—and here completely in accordance with Sp. and G.—gives the arrangements of groups as follows:

I	II
Purula	Pananka
Kamara	Paltara
Ngala	Knuraia
Mbitjana	Bangata

In the legends (pages 3 and 6) the first phratry[5] is called *Alarinja* and the second Kwatjarinja. The *natives themselves thus arrange like this* and are conscious that these 4 sections belong together and not the other 4. I believe that it is not right to arrange the phratries *differently* to what *the Aranda themselves* do. Only then, when your correspondents state for certain that they have been able to ascertain the arrangements into groups published by you from the natives' own lips, would I perhaps be able to arrive at a different opinion; first of all I would perhaps have to assume—even though this in itself seems improbable to me—that in different parts of the vast Aranda territory groups were differently organised. Strehlow, by the way, discusses the matter in great detail in a later booklet.

In one of your papers in Proc. Amer. Philos. S. Vol. 39 p. 627[6] and ibid Vol. 37 p. 66[7] as well as in Jour. R. Soc. N. S. Wales Vol. 32 p. 250[8] and in Amer. Anthropl. N. S. II. p. 144[9] you briefly mention that during the initiation ceremonies a man was killed and eaten in a ceremonial way. 'I am preparing an article dealing fully with this and similar customs.' Unfortunately I have been unable to find out, nor was I able to ascertain from your bibliography, whether it has happened that you have dealt with this important matter coherently and extensively and by presenting your material in detail?[10] For the fact, if it were really reported soundly, would be of exceptional interest. In the literature known to me I only find in addition to Science of Man, 1897 p. 91, a reference to the matter and the listing of a small paper by a W. A. Squire (Sydney) which, however, has so far remained unobtainable for me; it may perhaps be no longer available even in Australia. The information of a 'sacrifice' of a young girl during Bunya Bunya ceremonies seems to have turned out to be wrong, and would, even if it were true, have nothing to do with the ceremonial killing during initiation ceremonies. Perhaps, however, it is related to the matter reported by Mrs. L. Parker, Euahlayi Tribe pag. 72-73.[11] However there it is only told that disobedient boys were killed and eaten during the Bora; not that this was a regular custom during initiation ceremonies. I would be most obliged if you would be so kind as to tell me if and where you have dealt with this matter. But should you happen not to have got round to carrying out your intention of writing about these matters, I would like to ask you no longer to withhold your material from science.

In Notes Aborig. N. S. Wales you present p. 33 two songs: Dhurramooloon etc.[12]

Are the words not translatable? It would be highly interesting to know the meaning. We are still lacking good texts in the original language with interlinear translation; of course the texts would have to have been recorded with the greatest precision. Such texts, though, would be more pertinent at the moment than grammars and vocabularies, which the scholar in the end—if the texts are only somewhat extensive—could derive from them himself. How much there is still to do on the ethnography of Australia and how soon it will be forever too late!

Most respectfully and humbly Yours
M. von Leonhardi

Gross-Karben 27.9.1908

Dear Mr Mathews!

I have received your letter of the 16th of last month; thank you very much. I have also got the offprints you had sent me which I have read with great interest. I am very sorry about your accident and hope that in the meantime you have been completely restored to heath![13] In regard to the marriage laws I regret not to be able to convert to your point of view, and that for the following reasons:

I. The arranging of the two phratries (cycles) in I. Perula, Kamara, Ngala, Mbitjana and II. Pananka, Paltara, Knuraia, Bangata *comes from the natives themselves*. Thus as long as it has not been demonstrated to me that other natives arrange groups differently I have to assume that Strehlow's information is right, who in this point concurs exactly with Schulze, Gillen and Spencer, and who definitely asserts that *the arrangements of groups was that of the natives themselves*.

II. That this arrangement of groups is that of the natives is in my opinion also evident from the legends from time immemorial. The most curious division into land and water dwellers (which perhaps points north to the Islands of Torres Strait; something similar occurs there) is *part of the legend* as well as the classes, which belong to each division.[14]

III. Your own examples seem to me to speak against matrilineal descent. If the children from the marriage: Paltara *male* = Kamara *female* ... are Knuraia but the children from the marriage: Paltara *male* = Mbitjara *female* are likewise Knuraia, then it seems to me that only the father determines the class of the children irrespective of which woman from which class he has married.[15]

IV. The marriages which you call II, III, and IV seem to me to be clear products of disintegration.[16] One surely has to assume that only Marriage I was original. How could the origin of this strange institution otherwise be imagined, if one does not assume a specific system? Had all or even only some of the presently existing 'irregular' marriages existed together with the 'regular' ones from the beginning, then such an institution would be completely incomprehensible to me. In my opinion the so-called marriage-classes are age levels and originally I was only allowed to marry into the age-level of the other half of the tribe which corresponded with mine. I was therefore never allowed to marry into the levels to which respectively my father and mother or my children and their cousins belonged. When this was no longer practicable as time went by, the presently existing phenomenon of disintegration[17] emerged. I can pass no judgment in regard to the Chingalee as I have no other information about them than yours and that of Spencer. But in my opinion it does not follow necessarily that what is in force with the Aranda also has to be in force with the Ch. [Chingalee] and vice versa. Concerning this tribe perhaps you are right in regard to the arrangement of phratries. My conclusions in III and IV, however, are valid for this tribe, too.

I think it would be very rewarding if you presented your obviously very rich material about this interesting tribe of the Chingalee to us coherently and extensively; it is impossible to gain a good impression on the basis of scattered information and notes.

What you write about 'boy companions' was very interesting for me; but here I would also urgently wish that you would precisely name all tribes, where this occurs and precisely what actually occurs. Your information about this is really a bit too brief and does not go into enough detail. Obviously, among the Aranda such relationships between man and boy do not occur. But it seems that this type of pederasty is prevalent across the board in the north and Western Australia.

I was also very interested in your statement on *how* Spencer and Gillen conducted their research.[18] That such a way of proceeding had to have existed one could only suspect; but it is not scientifically honest of the two gentlemen not to convey the details openly.

In conclusion, could you tell me to whom I have to turn to regularly receive the journal *Science of Man*, published in Sydney? Until 1904 I got it through my bookseller; since then he has tried in vain in London and Sydney to resume it. In the past there was quite often good material in the journal.

Yours very faithfully and humbly
Freiherr v. Leonhardi

The second booklet of Strehlow's research is ready and I will send you a copy in the next days.

Gross-Karben 23.7.1909

Dear Sir!

I still have to thank you for your letter of 15 March. I am delighted about your favourable assessment of the two booklets and the Aranda and Loritja.[19] The 3rd booklet is now in preparation, but will hardly be published before next spring. The preparation required a lot of checking on the spot by Mr Strehlow and studies of the relevant literature by me. We only want to publish work which has been very carefully prepared; there have been more than enough superficial things written and printed, which only cause scientific harm. I will send you the 3rd booklet when it is ready and later also the 4th and 5th booklets. In the latter we will also try to thoroughly present the question of marriage rules, which you have discussed so often; the 4 and 8 sections, and the 'irregular' and 'wrong' marriages. *Very extensive* genealogies are needed for this which are only partially completed. But I can already now say with certainty that your views are *not* supported by the Aranda and Loritja. The arrangement of the 8 sections as given by Spencer and Gillen is *absolutely* right; I particularly draw your attention to the fact that these groupings can be found in legends. How do you want to explain that? There are certainly 'wrong' marriages—the natives themselves call them that—but these marriages were and are simply seen as 'wrong', bad, and were punished in the past. It is fact that among the Aranda, the children always belong to the clan[20] of the father's father, no matter whether a man married the right or a 'wrong' woman. This is also apparent in the short genealogies you cite, which you probably all got from Strehlow. Unfortunately you have made alterations to these genealogies, for example Am. Anth. 1908 p. 90 Tab. D.[21] It should be Arkara male[22] = Tjupuntara female, children are Kamara, and the father of Tjupuntara = Bangata, and so on. You arrive at these arbitrary changes because you erroneously believe that there are not 8 sections in Hermannsburg and surroundings. That is totally false and you actually admit this yourself when you write: 'When we get into the extreme northern limits of the Aranda territory, *say northwest from about the 24th parallel* we find ... 8 intermarrying sections.' For Hermannsburg lies north of the 24th parallel. The northwestern Loritja, too, have 8 sections. This is only briefly to state my point of view more precisely; I regret to have to refer to your counter reasons as inconclusive.

Most respectfully yours
M. v. Leonhardi

Gross-Karben 22 June 1910
Hessen,Germany

Dear Sir!

Thank you for your letter of 16 May this year as well as for sending various offprints. A while ago I sent you an essay by Missionary Siebert about the Dieri from the 'Globus'; I had prepared it for print from information by Siebert.[23] 14 days ago I sent you the III part of Strehlow's work about the Aranda and Loritja. About 2-3 booklets will follow, which I will likewise send you.

In the various articles you sent me I was particularly interested in what you report about 'ceremonial stones'.[24] As far as I know these objects are mentioned in the literature only in the Edge-Partington Album of the Natives of the Pacific Islands III p. 132/4; there they are called 'phallus'—'tribal debt-stones probably phallic'.[25] The shape suggests understanding them as such. What a pity it is that we will now probably never gain certain information about the true nature of the objects.

The genealogy of Inkara published by you in R. Soc. N. S. Wales 42 p. 341[26] I know very well. For you have received this from Strehlow, and it constitutes a small part of the very extensive genealogies of the Aranda which are awaiting publication by me. I am sorry to have to tell you that I still cannot understand your conclusions about maternal descent among the Aranda, and regard your argument as absolutely wrong. It is beyond doubt—and before you do not provide proof to the contrary—also not contested by anybody that an Aranda arranges:

I. Cycle: Purula, Ngala, Kamara, Mbitjara

II Cycle: Pananka, Knuraia, Paltara, Bangata.

It is herein absolutely certain, that eg. a Purula calls all other Purula, and all Ngala, Kamara, and Mbitjara nakarakia, while he calls all Pananka, Knuraia, Paltara, and Bangata etnakarakia. Nakarakia, though, means=we, the fathers and all=our whole family. Etnakarakia=they, their fathers and all=their whole family. This statement really says it all; you would have to remove these facts, if you wanted to be right. As I have written to you before, nearly all of your examples show no matter which woman from which class a man has married, the children always belong to that class which complies with the general rule. Exceptions are only the examples: Paiarde *male*=Ndatjika *female*; Thomas=Katharine; and now Inkara=Ruth. But these are only apparent exceptions. In these cases the men involved have immigrated from the southern territory of the Aranda into the northern and with that a shift into the neighbouring class occurs. Here I can only hint at this and will explicate it more extensively in an essay shortly. When you emphasise that in alternative marriages the child belongs to the class of the mother's mother, then this is right, but what does it prove? For it belongs to that of the father's father, too. And with the marriages which you call, I believe, No. III—this is not and never was the case. E.g.,

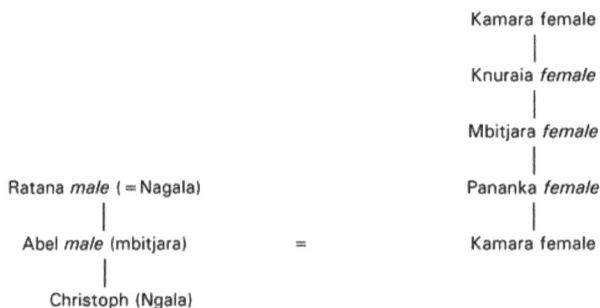

```
                                              Kamara female
                                                   |
                                              Knuraia female
                                                   |
                                              Mbitjara female
                                                   |
     Ratana male ( = Nagala)                  Pananka female
            |                                      |
     Abel male (mbitjara)        =            Kamara female
            |
     Christoph (Ngala)
```

You could then accordingly conclude, for example, patrilineal descent among the Kamilaroi, because

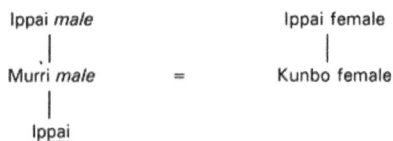

```
   Ippai male              Ippai female
      |                        |
   Murri male     =         Kunbo female
      |
    Ippai
```

But this you will rather not do, will you? I think you really have to give up your theory!

Yours most faithfully and humbly
M. v. Leonhardi

ENDNOTES

[1] A sacred object, now spelled 'tjuringa'.

[2] RHM 1906-07, 'Notes on the Aborigines of the Northern Territory, Western Australia and Queensland', *Queensland Geographical Journal*, vol. 22.

[3] Hermann Klaatsch (1863-1916), German ethnologist who visited Australia.

[4] RHM 1908, 'The Sociology of the Arranda and Chingalee Tribes (Northern Territory Australia)', *Folk-Lore*, vol. 19; and RHM 1908, 'Marriage and Descent in the Arranda Tribe, Central Australia', *American Anthropologist*, vol. 10 (new series),.

[5] Refers to *moiety*.

[6] RHM 1900, 'Phallic Rites and Initiation Ceremonies of the South Australian Aborigines', *Proceedings of the American Philosophical Society*, vol. 39.

[7] RHM 1898, 'Initiation Ceremonies of Australian Tribes', *Proceedings of the American Philosophical Society*, vol. 37.

[8] RHM 1900, 'Marriage and Descent among the Australian Aborigines', *Journal and Proceedings of the Royal Society of New South Wales*, vol. 34.

[9] RHM 1900, 'The Toara Ceremony of the Dippil Tribes of Queensland', *American Anthropologist*, vol. 2 (new series).

[10] Mathews never fulfilled the promise of a detailed discussion of cannibalism.

[11] Parker, K. Langloh 1905, *The Euahlayi Tribe: A study of Aboriginal Life in Australia*, Archibald Constable, London.

[12] RHM 1907, *Notes on the Aborigines of New South Wales*, Government Printer of New South Wales, Sydney.

[13] A riding accident. See Mathews to Hartland 10 August, 1898 (this volume).

[14] 'Class' refers to *sub-section* and 'division' to *moiety*.

[15] The = sign indicates that people of these sections intermarry.

[16] Germ. *Zersetzungsprodukte*.

[17] Germ. *Zersetzungserscheinungen*.

[18] Mathews claimed that Spencer and Gillen artificially prolonged the ceremonies they observed at Alice Springs by supplying large quantities of food. See RHM 1907, 'Notes on the Arranda Tribe', *Journal and Proceedings of the Royal Society of New South Wales*, vol. 41, pp. 157-8.

[19] Strehlow, C. 1907-20, *Die Aranda- und Loritja-Stamme in Zentral-Australien*, Joseph Baer & Co., Frankfurt am Main.

[20] 'Clan' refers here to *sub-section*.

[21] RHM, 'Marriage and Descent in the Arranda Tribe'.

[22] Where we put *male* or *female* Leonhardi used the symbols for male and female, arrow over a circle, and cross under a circle.

[23] Otto Siebert (1871-1957), Lutheran missionary who worked with Diyari people at Killalpaninna.

[24] In 1909 Mathews had published three papers on ceremonial stones: 'Ceremonial Stones used by the Australian Aborigines', *Proceedings of the American Philosophical Society*, vol. 48, 1909; 'Further Notes on Ceremonial Stones, Australia', *Proceedings of the American Philosophical Society*, vol. 48, 1909; and 'Some Australian Magical Stones', *American Antiquarian*, vol. 31, 1909. Further publications followed in 1910-11.

[25] Edge-Partington, J. 1890-8, *An Album of the Weapons, Tools, Ornaments, Articles of Dress, etc. of the Natives of the Pacific Islands*, James Edge-Partington and Charles Heape, London.

[26] RHM 1908, 'Vocabulary of the Ngarrugu Tribe N. S. W.' *Journal and Proceedings of the Royal Society of New South Wales*, vol. 42, 1908.

Letter from R. H. Mathews to Moritz von Leonhardi

From the collection of the R. H. Mathews Papers (MS 1606/1, Item 10), Australian Institute of Aboriginal and Torres Strait Islander Studies, Canberra.

Hassall Street, Parramatta
N. S. Wales

April 21st 1911

My dear von Leonhardi,

By this mail I am sending you, under separate cover, a few new articles written by me since I last had the pleasure of addressing you, which I trust will be found of some interest to you in your valuable ethnological studies.

You were kind enough to send me Mr. Strehlow's work, in 3 parts, all of which reached me safely at different times. I think I wrote thanking for them when they were received. I do not know if you published more of the *same* book after the issue of Part III. If you did publish any further Parts of Mr. Strehlow's researches, may I ask if you will be so kind as to present such to me, so as to make my copies complete.

I intend to get the 3 parts of the work *bound* in one *volume*. Perhaps you have some spare *title pages* used when binding the 3 PartMich may follow it.

I suppose you read in the newspapers about a year ago that Professor A. R. Brown had been appointed to lead an expedition into Western Australia to study the aborigines and the zoology of the country. I have not heard how the work is progressing, but it must be nearly completed by this time.

A Swedish scientific expedition into Western Australia is also doing somewhat similar work to Mr Brown's expedition, but I have not learnt how it is getting on.

I am writing this letter to you on my birthday, 21st April. I am just 70 (seventy) years old today, having been born in 1841 in New South Wales.

Please write to me when you get this letter, stating if the packet of 'separates'[1] has reached you. Also kindly send me any of your own works which you may think proper to give me. Remember the title page to Strehlow's work, if you have one.

Very kind regards and good wishes from yours faithfully,
R. H. Mathews

ENDNOTES

[1] Mathews' term for offprints of articles.

RHM Bibliography

Anthropological publications by R. H. Mathews

Listed in chronological order

* Published in full in this volume.

† Published in part in this volume.

1893: 'Rock Paintings by the Aborigines in Caves on Bulgar Creek, near Singleton', *Journal and Proceedings of the Royal Society of New South Wales*, vol. 27, pp. 353-58.

1894: 'Aboriginal Bora held at Gundabloui in 1894', *Journal and Proceedings of the Royal Society of New South Wales*, vol. 28, pp. 98-129.

1894: 'Aboriginal Rock Paintings and Carvings in New South Wales', *Proceedings of the Royal Society of Victoria*, vol. 7 (new series), pp. 143-56.

1894-95: 'Aboriginal Rock Pictures of Australia', *Proceedings and Transactions of the Queensland Branch of the Royal Geographical Society of Australasia*, vol. 10, pp. 46-70.

1894-95: 'The Kamilaroi Class System of the Australian Aborigines', *Proceedings and Transactions of the Queensland Branch of the Royal Geographical Society of Australasia*, vol. 10, pp. 18-34.

1895: 'Australian Rock Pictures', *American Anthropologist*, vol. 8, pp. 268-78.

1895: 'The Bora, or Initiation Ceremonies of the Kamilaroi Tribe', *Journal of the Anthropological Institute*, vol. 24, 411-27.

1895: 'Rock Paintings and Carvings of the Aborigines of New South Wales', *Report of the Sixth Meeting of the Australasian Association for the Advancement of Science, held at Brisbane, Queensland, January, 1895*, vol. 6, pp. 1-14 (co-written with W. J. Enright).

1895: 'Some Stone Implements used by the Aborigines of New South Wales', *Journal and Proceedings of the Royal Society of New South Wales*, vol. 29, pp. 301-305.

1895-6: 'The Rock Pictures of the Australian Aborigines', *Proceedings and Transactions of the Queensland Branch of the Royal Geographical Society of Australiasia*, vol. 11, pp. 87-105.

1896: 'Additional Remarks Concerning Aboriginal Bora held at Gundabloui in 1894', *Journal and Proceedings of the Royal Society of New South Wales*, vol. 30, pp. 211-13.

1896: 'Australian Class Systems [Part 1]', *American Anthropologist*, vol. 9, pp. 411-16.

1896: 'Australian Ground and Tree Drawings', *American Anthropologist*, vol. 9, pp. 33-49.

1896: 'The Bora of the Kamilaroi Tribes', *Proceedings of the Royal Society of Victoria*, vol. 9 (new series), pp. 137-73.

1896: 'The Bora, or Initiation Ceremonies of the Kamilaroi Tribe (Part II)', *Journal of the Anthropological Institute*, vol. 25, pp. 318-39.

1896: 'The Būnăn Ceremony of New South Wales', *American Anthropologist*, vol. 9, pp. 327-44.

1896: 'The Burbung of the New England tribes, New South Wales', *Proceedings of the Royal Society of Victoria*, vol. 9 (new series), pp. 120-36.

1896: 'The Būrbŭng of the Wiradthuri Tribes', *Journal of the Anthropological Institute*, vol. 25, pp. 295-318.

1896: 'Rock Carving by the Australian Aborigines', *Proceedings of the Royal Society of Queensland*, vol. 12, pp. 97-8.

1896: 'The Rock Paintings and Carvings of the Australian Aborigines', *Journal of the Anthropological Institute*, vol. 25, pp. 145-63.

1896: 'Stone Cooking-Holes and Grooves for Stone-Grinding used by the Australian Aborigines', *Journal of the Anthropological Institute*, vol. 25, pp. 255-9.

1897: 'Aboriginal Customs in North Queensland', *Proceedings of the Royal Society of Queensland*, vol. 13, pp. 33-7.

1897: 'Australian Class Systems [Part 2]', *American Anthropologist*, vol. 10, 345-7.

1897: 'Australian Rock Carvings', *Proceedings of the American Philosophical Society*, vol. 36, pp. 195-208.

1897: 'Bullroarers used by the Australian Aborigines', *Journal of the Anthropological Institute*, vol. 27, pp. 52-60.

1897: 'The Būrbŭng of the Wiradthuri Tribes', *Proceedings of the Royal Society of Victoria*, vol. 10 (new series), pp. 1-12.

1897: 'The Būrbŭng of the Wiradthuri Tribes (Part II)', *Journal of the Anthropological Institute*, vol. 26, pp. 272-85.

1897: 'The Burbung, or Initiation Ceremonies of the Murrumbidgee Tribes', *Journal and Proceedings of the Royal Society of New South Wales*, vol. 31, pp. 111-53.

1897: 'The Keeparra Ceremony of Initiation', *Journal of the Anthropological Institute*, vol. 26, pp. 320-40.

1897: 'Message Sticks used by the Aborigines of Australia', *American Anthropologist*, vol. 10, pp. 288-97.

1897: 'Rock Carvings and Paintings of the Australian Aborigines', *Proceedings of the American Philosophical Society*, vol. 36, pp. 466-78.

1897: 'The Totemic Divisions of Australian Tribes', *Journal and Proceedings of the Royal Society of New South Wales*, vol. 31, pp. 154-76.

1897: 'The Wandarral of the Richmond and Clarence River Tribes', *Proceedings of the Royal Society of Victoria*, vol. 10 (new series) (1), pp. 29-42.

1898: 'Aboriginal Ground and Tree Drawings', *Science of Man*, vol. 1 (new series) (8), pp. 185-7.

1898: 'Aboriginal Initiation Ceremonies', *Science of Man*, vol. 1 (new series) (4 and 9), pp. 79-80, 202-6.

1898: 'Aboriginal Rock Carvings', *Science of Man*, vol. 1 (new series) (2), pp. 34-5.

1898: 'Australian Divisional Systems', *Journal and Proceedings of the Royal Society of New South Wales*, vol. 32, pp. 66-87.

1898: 'Divisions of Australian Tribes', *Proceedings of the American Philosophical Society*, vol. 37, pp. 151-4.

1898: 'Divisions of Queensland Aborigines', *Proceedings of the American Philosophical Society*, vol. 37, pp. 327-36.

†1898: 'Folklore of the Australian Aborigines', *Science of Man*, vol. 1 (new series), pp. 69-70; 91-3; 117-19; 142-3.

*1898: 'Gravures et peintures sur rochers par les Aborigènes d'Australie' (Rock Carvings and Paintings by the Australian Aborigines), *Bulletins et Mémoires de la Société d'Anthropologie de Paris*, vol. 9 (4th series), pp. 425-32.

1898: 'The Group Divisions and Initiation Ceremonies of the Barkunjee Tribes', *Journal and Proceedings of the Royal Society of New South Wales*, vol. 32, pp. 241-55.

1898: 'Initiation Ceremonies of Australian Tribes', *Proceedings of the American Philosophical Society*, vol. 37, pp. 54-73.

1898: 'The Kamilaroi Divisions', *Science of Man*, vol. 1 (new series) (7), 155-8.

1898: 'Message Sticks', *Science of Man*, vol. 1 (new series) (6), pp. 141-2.

1898: 'The Rock Paintings and Carvings of the Australian Aborigines (Part II)', *Journal of the Anthropological Institute*, vol. 27, pp. 532-41.

1898: 'The Victorian Aborigines: Their Initiation Ceremonies and Divisional Systems', *American Anthropologist*, vol. 11, pp. 325-43.

1899: 'Aboriginal Customs in North Queensland', *Science of Man*, vol. 1 (new series) (12), pp. 262-4.

1899: 'Divisions of North Australian Tribes', *Proceedings of the American Philosophical Society*, vol. 38, pp. 75-9.

1899: 'Divisions of Some Aboriginal Tribes, Queensland', *Journal and Proceedings of the Royal Society of New South Wales*, vol. 33, pp. 103-11.

1899: *Folklore of the Australian Aborigines*, Hennessey, Harper and Company, Sydney.

1899: 'Native Tribes of Queensland', *American Anthropologist*, vol. 1 (new series), pp. 595-7.

1899: 'Rock Art', *Proceedings and Transactions of the Queensland Branch of the Royal Geographical Society of Australasia*, vol. 14, pp. 9-11.

1899-1900: 'The Walloonggurra Ceremony', *Proceedings and Transactions of the Queensland Branch of the Royal Geographical Society of Australasia*, vol. 15, pp. 67-74.

1900: 'The Burbung of the Wiradthuri Tribes', *Proceedings of the Royal Society of Queensland*, vol. 16, pp. 35-8.

1900: 'Divisions of Some West Australian Tribes', *American Anthropologist*, vol. 2 (new series), pp. 185-7.

1900: 'Divisions of the South Australian Aborigines', *Proceedings of the American Philosophical Society*, vol. 39, pp. 78-93.

1900: 'Marriage and Descent among the Australian Aborigines', *Journal and Proceedings of the Royal Society of New South Wales*, vol. 34, pp. 120-35.

1900: 'Native Tribes of Western Australia', *Proceedings of the American Philosophical Society*, vol. 39, pp. 123-5.

1900: 'The Organisation, Language and Initiation Ceremonies of the Aborigines of the South-East Coast of N. S. Wales', *Journal and Proceedings of the Royal Society of New South Wales*, vol. 34, pp. 262-81 (co-written with M. M. Everitt).

1900: 'The Origin, Organization and Ceremonies of the Australian Aborigines', *Proceedings of the American Philosophical Society*, vol. 39, pp. 556-78.

1900: 'Phallic Rites and Initiation Ceremonies of the South Australian Aborigines', *Proceedings of the American Philosophical Society*, vol. 39, pp. 622-38.

1900: 'The Toara Ceremony of the Dippil Tribes of Queensland', *American Anthropologist*, vol. 2 (new series), pp. 139-44.

1900: 'The Wombya Organization of the Australian Aborigines', *American Anthropologist*, vol. 2 (new series), pp. 494-501.

1900-01: 'Ethnological Notes on the Aboriginal Tribes of the Northern Territory', *Queensland Geographical Journal*, vol. 16, pp. 69-90.

1900-01: 'The Murrawin Ceremony', *Queensland Geographical Journal*, vol. 16, pp. 35-41.

1901: 'Aboriginal Rock Pictures in Queensland', *Proceedings of the American Philosophical Society*, vol. 40, pp. 57-8.

1901: 'The Gundungurra Language', *Proceedings of the American Philosophical Society*, vol. 40, pp. 140-8.

1901: 'Initiation Ceremonies of the Wiradjuri Tribes', *American Anthropologist*, vol. 3 (new series), pp. 337-41.

1901: 'Organisation sociale des tribus aborigènes de l'Australie', *Bulletins et Mémoires de la Société d'Anthropologie de Paris*, vol. 2 (5th series) (4), pp. 415-9.

1901: 'Pictorial Art Among the Australian Aborigines', *Journal of the Transactions of the Victoria Institute*, vol. 33, pp. 291-310.

1901: 'Rock-Holes used by the Aborigines for Warming Water', *Journal and Proceedings of the Royal Society of New South Wales*, vol. 35, pp. 213-6.

1901: 'Some Aboriginal Tribes of Western Australia', *Journal and Proceedings of the Royal Society of New South Wales*, vol. 35, pp. 217-22.

1901: *Thurrawal Grammar: Part I*, self-published, Parramatta.

1901: 'The Thurrawal Language', *Journal and Proceedings of the Royal Society of New South Wales*, vol. 35, pp. 127-60.

1901-02: 'The Thoorga Language', *Queensland Geographical Journal*, vol. 17, pp. 49-73.

1902: 'The Aboriginal Languages of Victoria', *Journal and Proceedings of the Royal Society of New South Wales*, vol. 36, pp. 71-106.

1902: 'Languages of some Native Tribes of Queensland, New South Wales and Victoria', *Journal and Proceedings of the Royal Society of New South Wales*, vol. 36, pp. 135-90.

*1902: 'Les Indigènes d'Australie' (The Natives of Australia), *L'Anthropologie*, vol. 13, pp. 233-40.

1902: 'The Thoorga and other Australian Languages', *American Antiquarian*, vol. 24, pp. 101-6.

1902-03: 'The Murawarri and other Australian Languages', *Queensland Geographical Journal*, vol. 18, pp. 52-68.

1903: 'The Aboriginal Fisheries at Brewarrina', *Journal and Proceedings of the Royal Society of New South Wales*, vol. 37, pp. 146-56.

1903: 'Das Kumbainggeri, eine Eingeborenensprache von Neu-Süd-Wales', *Mitteilungen der Anthropologischen Gesellschaft*, vol. 33, pp. 321-8.

1903: 'Language of the Bungandity Tribe, South Australia', *Journal and Proceedings of the Royal Society of New South Wales*, vol. 37, pp. 59-74.

1903: 'Languages of the Kamilaroi and Other Aboriginal Tribes of New South Wales', *Journal of the Anthropological Institute*, vol. 33, pp. 259-83.

1903: 'Languages of the New England Aborigines, New South Wales', *Proceedings of the American Philosophical Society*, vol. 42, pp. 249-63.

*1903: 'Le langage Wailwan' (The Wailwan Language), *Bulletins et Mémoires de la Société d'Anthropologie de Paris*, vol. 4 (5th series) (1), pp. 69-81.

1903: 'Native Languages of Victoria', *American Anthropologist*, vol. 5 (new series), pp. 380-2.

1903: 'Notes on Some Native Dialects of Victoria', *Journal and Proceedings of the Royal Society of New South Wales*, vol. 37, pp. 243-53.

1903: 'Some Aboriginal Languages of Queensland and Victoria', *Proceedings of the American Philosophical Society*, vol. 42, pp. 179-88.

1903-04: 'Ethnological Notes on the Aboriginal Tribes of Western Australia', *Queensland Geographical Journal*, vol. 19, pp. 45-72.

*1904: 'Die Mŭltyerra-Initiationszeremonie' (The Mŭltyerra Initiation Ceremony), *Mitteilungen der Anthropologischen Gesellschaft*, vol. 34, pp. 77-83.

1904: 'Die Sprache des Tyeddyuwurru-Stammes der Eingebornen von Victoria', *Mitteilungen der Anthropologischen Gesellschaft*, vol. 34, pp. 71-6.

1904: 'Ethnological Notes on the Aboriginal Tribes of New South Wales and Victoria', *Journal and Proceedings of the Royal Society of New South Wales*, vol. 38, pp. 203-381.

*1904: 'Langage des Kurnu, tribu d'Indigènes de la Nouvelle Galles du Sud' (Language of the Kurnu Tribe, New South Wales), *Bulletins et Mémoires de la Société d'Anthropologie de Paris*, vol. 5 (5th series) (2), pp. 132-8.

1904: 'Language of the Wuddyawurru tribe, Victoria', *Zeitschrift für Ethnologie*, vol. 36, pp. 729-34.

1904: 'Language, Organization and Initiation Ceremonies of the Kogai Tribes, Queensland', *Zeitschrift für Ethnologie*, vol. 36, pp. 28-38.

1904: 'The Native Tribes of Victoria: Their Languages and Customs', *Proceedings of the American Philosophical Society*, vol. 43, pp. 54-70.

1904: 'The Wiradyuri and other Languages of New South Wales', *Journal of the Anthropological Institute*, vol. 34, pp. 284-305.

1904-05: 'Ethnological Notes on the Aboriginal Tribes of Queensland', *Queensland Geographical Journal*, vol. 20, pp. 49-75.

1905: *Ethnological Notes on the Aboriginal Tribes of New South Wales and Victoria*, F.W. White General Printer, Sydney.

1905: 'Social Organization of the Chingalee Tribe, Northern Australia', *American Anthropologist*, vol. 7 (new series), pp. 301-4.

1905: 'Sociology of some Australian Tribes', *Journal and Proceedings of the Royal Society of New South Wales*, vol. 39, pp. 104-23.

1905: 'Sociology of the Aborigines of Western Australia', *Proceedings of the American Philosophical Society*, vol. 44, pp. 32-5.

1905: 'Some Initiation Ceremonies of the Aborigines of Victoria', *Zeitschrift für Ethnologie*, vol. 37, pp. 872-9.

1906: 'Australian Tribes—Their Formation and Government', *Zeitschrift für Ethnologie*, vol. 38, pp. 939-46 (published in English).

*1906: 'Bemerkungen über die Eingebornen Australiens' (Remarks on the Natives of Australia), *Mitteilungen der Anthropologischen Gesellschaft*, vol. 36, 167-73.

1906: 'Notes on Some Native Tribes of Australia', *Journal and Proceedings of the Royal Society of New South Wales*, vol. 40, pp. 95-129.

*1906: 'Organisation sociale de quelques tribus australiennes' (Social Organisation of some Australian Tribes), *Bulletins et Mémoires de la Société d'Anthropologie de Paris*, vol. 7 (5th series) (3), pp. 164-74.

1906: 'Sociology of Aboriginal Tribes in Australia', *American Antiquarian*, vol. 28, pp. 81-8.

1906: 'The Totemistic System in Australia', *American Antiquarian*, vol. 28, 140-7.

1906-07: 'Initiation Ceremonies of the Murawarri and Other Aboriginal Tribes of Queensland', *Queensland Geographical Journal*, vol. 22, pp. 64-73.

1906-07: 'Notes on the Aborigines of the Northern Territory, Western Australia and Queensland', *Queensland Geographical Journal*, vol. 22, pp. 74-86.

*1907: 'A Giant in a Cave—An Australian Legend', *American Antiquarian*, vol. 29, pp. 29-31 (unsigned but attributed to Mathews).

1907: 'Aboriginal Navigation and other Notes', *Journal and Proceedings of the Royal Society of New South Wales*, vol. 41, pp. 211-5.

1907: 'The Arran'da Language, Central Australia', *Proceedings of the American Philosophical Society*, vol. 46, pp. 322-39.

*1907: 'Beiträge zur Ethnographie der Australier' (Contributions to the Ethnography of the Australians), *Mitteilungen der Anthropologischen Gesellschaft*, vol. 27, pp. 18-38.

1907: 'Ethnological Notes on the Aboriginal Tribes of New South Wales and Victoria' [Letter to the Editor], *Nature*, vol. 76 (1958), pp. 31-2.

1907: 'Folklore of some Aboriginal Tribes of Victoria', *American Antiquarian*, vol. 29, pp. 44-8.

1907: 'Language of the Birdhawal Tribe in Gippsland, Victoria', *Proceedings of the American Philosophical Society*, vol. 46, pp. 346-59.

1907: 'Languages of some Tribes of Western Australia', *Proceedings of the American Philosophical Society*, vol. 46, pp. 361-8.

1907: 'Literature relating to Australian Aborigines' [Letter to the Editor], *Nature*, vol. 77 (1987), p. 81.

1907: 'Note on the Social Organisation of the Turrubul and adjacent Tribes', *MAN*, vol. 7 (97), pp. 166-8.

1907: 'Notes on some Aboriginal Tribes', *Journal and Proceedings of the Royal Society of New South Wales*, vol. 41, pp. 67-87.

1907: *Notes on the Aborigines of New South Wales*, Government Printer of New South Wales, Sydney.

1907: 'Notes on the Arranda Tribe', *Journal and Proceedings of the Royal Society of New South Wales*, vol. 41, pp. 146-64.

1907: 'Notes on the Australian Aborigines', *American Antiquarian*, vol. 29, pp. 149-52.

1907: 'Sociologie de la tribu des Chingalee du territoire septentrional', *Bulletins et Mémoires de la Société d'Anthropologie de Paris*, vol. 8 (5th Series) (5-6), pp. 529-36.

1907-08: 'Aboriginal Navigation', *Queensland Geographical Journal*, vol. 23, pp. 66-81.

1908: 'Descendance par la lignée maternelle dans la tribu des Binbingha du territoire septentrional', *Bulletins et Mémoires de la Société d'Anthropologie de Paris*, vol. 9 (5th series) (6), pp. 786-9.

1908: 'Folk-Tales of the Aborigines of New South Wales', *Folk-Lore*, vol. 19, pp. 224-27, 303-8.

*1908: 'Initiationszeremonie des Birdhawal-Stammes' (Initiation Ceremony of the Birdhawal Tribe), *Mitteilungen der Anthropologischen Gesellschaft*, vol. 38, pp. 17-24.

1908: 'Marriage and Descent in the Arranda Tribe, Central Australia', *American Anthropologist*, vol. 10 (new series), pp. 88-102.

1908: 'Matrilineal Descent, Northern Territory', *MAN*, vol. 8 (83), pp. 150-2.

1908: 'Matrilineale Deszendenz beim Wombaia-Stamme, Zentralaustralien', *Mitteilungen der Anthropologischen Gesellschaft in Wien*, vol. 38, pp. 321-3.

1908: 'Social Organisation of the Ngeumba Tribe, New South Wales', *MAN*, vol. 8 (10), pp. 24-6.

1908: 'The Sociology of the Arranda and Chingalee Tribes (Northern Territory Australia)', *Folk-Lore*, vol. 19, pp. 99-103.

1908: 'Sociology of the Chingalee tribe, Northern Australia', *American Anthropologist*, vol. 10 (new series), pp. 281-5.

*1908: 'Some Mythology of the Gundungurra Tribe, New South Wales', *Zeitschrift für Ethnologie*, vol. 40, pp. 203-6 (published in English).

1908: 'Some Native Languages of Western Australia: Part I', *American Antiquarian*, vol. 30, pp. 28-31.

1908: 'Vocabulary of the Ngarrugu Tribe N. S. W.', *Journal and Proceedings of the Royal Society of New South Wales*, vol. 42, pp. 335-42.

1908: 'Zur australischen Deszendenzlehre', *Mitteilungen der Anthropologischen Gesellschaft*, vol. 38, pp. 182-7.

1909: 'Aboriginal Navigation in Australia', *American Antiquarian*, vol. 31, 23-7.

*1909: 'Australian Folk-Tales', *Folk-Lore*, vol. 20, pp. 485-7.

1909: 'Ceremonial Stones used by the Australian Aborigines', *Proceedings of the American Philosophical Society*, vol. 48, pp. 1-7.

1909: 'The Dhudhuroa Language of Victoria', *American Anthropologist*, vol. 11 (new series), pp. 278-84.

1909: 'Folklore Notes from Western Australia', *Folk-Lore*, vol. 20, pp. 340-2.

1909: 'Further Notes on Ceremonial Stones, Australia', *Proceedings of the American Philosophical Society*, vol. 48, pp. 460-2.

1909: 'The Kumbainggeri, Turrubul, Kaiabara, and Mycoolon Tribes, Australia', *Science*, vol. 30 (778), pp. 759-60.

1909: 'Sociology of some Australian Tribes', *American Antiquarian*, vol. 31, pp. 206-13.

1909: 'Some Australian Magical Stones', *American Antiquarian*, vol. 31, pp. 205-6.

1909: 'Some Burial Customs of the Australian Aborigines', *Proceedings of the American Philosophical Society*, vol. 48, pp. 313-8.

1909: *Some Peculiar Burial Customs of the Australian Aborigines: Paper read before the Third Australasian Catholic Congress, Sydney, September, 1909*, William Brooks, Sydney.

1909: 'The Wallaroo and the Willy-Wagtail: A Queensland Folk-Tale', *Folk-Lore*, vol. 20, pp. 214-6.

1909-10: 'Initiation Ceremonies of some Queensland Tribes', *Queensland Geographical Journal*, vol. 25, pp. 103-18.

1909-10: 'Notes on Some Tribes of Western Australia', *Queensland Geographical Journal*, vol. 25, pp. 119-36.

*1910: 'Die Bundandaba-Zeremonie in Queensland' (The Bundandaba Ceremony of Initiation in Queensland), *Mitteilungen der Anthropologischen Gesellschaft*, vol. 40, pp. 44-7.

1910: 'Does Exogamy Exist in Australian Tribes?' *Revue d'Ethnographie et de Sociologie*, vol. 5, pp. 1-2 (published in English).

1910: 'Further Notes on Burial Customs, Australia', *Proceedings of the American Philosophical Society*, vol. 49, pp. 297-306.

1910: 'Language and Sociology of the Kumbaingerri Tribe, New South Wales', *Report of the Twelfth Meeting of the Australasian Association for the Advancement of Science, held at Brisbane, 1909*, J. Shirley (ed.), Brisbane, Published by the Association, vol. 12, pp. 485-93.

*1910: 'Relevé de quelques dessins gravés ou peints sur rochers par les indigènes de la Nouvelle Galles du Sud (Australie)' (Plan of some Drawings painted or carved on Rock by the Natives of New South Wales, Australia), *Bulletins et Mémoires de la Société d'Anthropologie de Paris*, vol. 11, pp. 531-5.

1910: 'Some Articles used in Burial and other Rites by the Australian Aborigines', *Queensland Geographical Journal*, vol. 24, pp. 63-72.

1910: 'Some Rock Engravings of the Aborigines of New South Wales', *Journal and Proceedings of the Royal Society of New South Wales*, vol. 44, pp. 401-5.

1910: 'Some Rock Pictures and Ceremonial Stones of the Australian Aborigines', *Report of the Twelfth Meeting of the Australasian Association for the Advancement of Science, held at Brisbane, 1909*, vol. 12, pp. 493-8.

1911: 'Matrilineal Descent in the Kaiabara Tribe, Queensland', *MAN*, vol. 11 (66), pp. 100-3.

1911: 'Some Curious Stones used by the Aborigines', *Journal and Proceedings of the Royal Society of New South Wales*, vol. 45, pp. 359-65.

1912: 'Matrilineal Descent in the Arranda and Chingalee Tribes', *MAN*, vol. 12 (47), pp. 93-6.

1912: 'Notes on some published Statements with regard to the Australian Aborigines', *Report of the Thirteenth Meeting of the Australasian Association for the Advancement of Science, held at Sydney, 1911*, vol. 13, pp. 449-53.

1912: 'Some Mourning Customs of the Australian Aborigines', *Report of the Thirteenth Meeting of the Australasian Association for the Advancement of Science, held at Sydney, 1911*, vol. 13, pp. 445-9.

1916-18: 'Initiation Ceremony of the Birdhawal Tribe', *Queensland Geographical Journal*, vol. 32-33, pp. 89-97.

1917: 'Description of Two Bora Grounds of the Kamilaroi Tribe', *Journal and Proceedings of the Royal Society of New South Wales*, vol. 51, pp. 423-30.

www.ingramcontent.com/pod-product-compliance
Lightning Source LLC
Chambersburg PA
CBHW041119280326
41928CB00061B/3389